AutoCAD® Release 14 For Dummies®

COMPUTER BOOK SERIES FROM IDG

W9-ALW-909

Ten Top Release 14 Features (Plus Two)

Feature	Benefit	Alert
AutoCAD uses less memory	More room in RAM for drawings	Too much RAM is never enough
Realtime pan and zoom	Move more easily around AutoCAD drawings	Got a fast enough machine?
Web integration	Launch a browser from AutoCAD; link from a drawing to a Web URL	Is the Web ready for production use?
AutoSnap for aligning objects	Easier to connect to "interesting" points	Can still be hard to find desired points in complex drawings
Windows user interface conformity	Finally, AutoCAD works like your other programs!	Macintosh and UNIX users are left behind
Command line scrolling and editing	Makes the command line even more powerful	No problem, all plus
Smaller hatches and solid fills	Hatching works better and faster	Remember to include those custom PAT files with your drawing!
All the documentation is online	Easier to find what you need	Full set of printed documents costs extra
Integrated Preferences dialog box	Easier to set up and modify AutoCAD	The sheer number of options can be bewildering
Better text editing and TrueType fonts	Easier to use and manage good-looking text in your drawings	Don't forget to get the geometry right before you document it!
Layer and object control from toolbars	Make object's layer current, change layer settings from toolbar	This one's all good
Release 13 features	If you're upgrading from Release 12, you get these, too	Associative hatches move with their boundaries, drawing previews in File Open dialog boxes; multiline text editing in AutoCAD; spell checker; tool tips that describe icons; true ellipses and splines

New Icons

Icon	Tool Tip	Purpose
	Print preview	On-screen preview of drawing printout
	Match properties	"Borrow" properties from one object and assign to another
	Launch browser	Launch a Web browser from within AutoCAD
	Tracking	Identify points of interest by extending objects
	Distance	Measure the distance and angle between selected points
	Pan realtime	Interactive drag-and-pan in drawing window
	Zoom realtime	Interactive drag-and-zoom in drawing window
OSNAP	OSNAP	Running object snap can be turned on and off from status bar

...For Dummies: #1 Computer Book Series for Beginners

AutoCAD® Release 14 For Dummies®

Cheat Sheet

Top Release 14 Dialog Boxes

Command	Dialog Box Name	Purpose
ddCHprop	Change object properties	Change the color, layer, linetype, and thickness of an object
Ddim	Dimension Styles	Set options for dimensioning
ddInsert	Insert	Insert a block
DDLMODES or LAyer	Layer Control	Create, set options for layers; use Object Properties toolbar instead for most functions
ddMOdify	Modify <object type>	Set options such as color, layer, linetype, thickness for objects; additional options depend on the type of object selected
ddOSnap or OSNAP	Running Object Snap	Turn object snaps on and off; in Release 14, manages AutoSnap as well
DDRmodes	Drawing Aids	Set modes for current drawing such as Blips, Groups; control Snap and Grid.
ddVPoint	Viewpoint Presets	Change the viewing angle; best used for 3-D objects
ddUNits	Units Control!	Manage and change unit settings

Ten Top Commands

Command	Key Options	Purpose
OPEN	Preview	Find and open drawing files
QSAVE	If not named: "Save As" dialog box	Save currently open file to current name, no options
U	None	Undo last step of steps
Zoom	Dynamic	Zoom in or out; Dynamic option pans, too
Pan	Displacement	Pan left, right, up, down; draw line to indicate direction and distance
Line/PLine	From point/To point	Draw line segments as separate objects/ single object
Move	Press Enter for second point to specify a relative displacement	Move objects in your drawing
COpy	Enter **m** for multiple copies	Copy objects in your drawing
Erase	Uses all object selection methods	Get rid of stuff in your drawing
Stretch	What gets stretched	Alters the size of the lines in an object; practice this one!

...For Dummies: #1 Computer Book Series for Beginners

AUTOCAD® RELEASE 14 FOR DUMMIES®

by Bud Smith

IDG Books Worldwide, Inc.
An International Data Group Company

Foster City, CA ♦ Chicago, IL ♦ Indianapolis, IN ♦ Southlake, TX

AutoCAD® Release 14 For Dummies®

Published by
IDG Books Worldwide, Inc.
An International Data Group Company
919 E. Hillsdale Blvd.
Suite 400
Foster City, CA 94404
www.idgbooks.com (IDG Books Worldwide Web site)
www.dummies.com (Dummies Press Web site)

Library of Congress Catalog Card No.: 97-73305

ISBN: 0-7645-0104-6

Printed in the United States of America

10 9 8 7 6 5 4 3 2

1O/QU/RR/ZX/IN

Distributed in the United States by IDG Books Worldwide, Inc.

Distributed by Macmillan Canada for Canada; by Transworld Publishers Limited in the United Kingdom; by IDG Norge Books for Norway; by IDG Sweden Books for Sweden; by Woodslane Pty. Ltd. for Australia; by Woodslane Enterprises Ltd. for New Zealand; by Longman Singapore Publishers Ltd. for Singapore, Malaysia, Thailand, and Indonesia; by Simron Pty. Ltd. for South Africa; by Toppan Company Ltd. for Japan; by Distribuidora Cuspide for Argentina; by Livraria Cultura for Brazil; by Ediciencia S.A. for Ecuador; by Addison-Wesley Publishing Company for Korea; by Ediciones ZETA S.C.R. Ltda. for Peru; by WS Computer Publishing Corporation, Inc., for the Philippines; by Unalis Corporation for Taiwan; by Contemporanea de Ediciones for Venezuela; by Computer Book & Magazine Store for Puerto Rico; by Express Computer Distributors for the Caribbean and West Indies. Authorized Sales Agent: Anthony Rudkin Associates for the Middle East and North Africa.

For general information on IDG Books Worldwide's books in the U.S., please call our Consumer Customer Service department at 800-762-2974. For reseller information, including discounts and premium sales, please call our Reseller Customer Service department at 800-434-3422.

For information on where to purchase IDG Books Worldwide's books outside the U.S., please contact our International Sales department at 415-655-3200 or fax 415-655-3295.

For information on foreign language translations, please contact our Foreign & Subsidiary Rights department at 415-655-3021 or fax 415-655-3281.

For sales inquiries and special prices for bulk quantities, please contact our Sales department at 415-655-3200 or write to the address above.

For information on using IDG Books Worldwide's books in the classroom or for ordering examination copies, please contact our Educational Sales department at 800-434-2086 or fax 817-251-8174.

For press review copies, author interviews, or other publicity information, please contact our Public Relations department at 415-655-3000 or fax 415-655-3299.

For authorization to photocopy items for corporate, personal, or educational use, please contact Copyright Clearance Center, 222 Rosewood Drive, Danvers, MA 01923, or fax 508-750-4470.

About the Author

Bud Smith started with computers as a data entry clerk in 1981. He has since worked as a computer programmer, technical writer, computer journalist, and product marketing manager. He is quite at home around computers — even those loaded with programs as complex as AutoCAD. *AutoCAD Release 14 For Dummies* is his third book about AutoCAD and his tenth book about computing topics in general.

ABOUT IDG BOOKS WORLDWIDE

Welcome to the world of IDG Books Worldwide.

IDG Books Worldwide, Inc., is a subsidiary of International Data Group, the world's largest publisher of computer-related information and the leading global provider of information services on information technology. IDG was founded more than 25 years ago and now employs more than 8,500 people worldwide. IDG publishes more than 275 computer publications in over 75 countries (see listing below). More than 60 million people read one or more IDG publications each month.

Launched in 1990, IDG Books Worldwide is today the #1 publisher of best-selling computer books in the United States. We are proud to have received eight awards from the Computer Press Association in recognition of editorial excellence and three from *Computer Currents'* First Annual Readers' Choice Awards. Our best-selling *...For Dummies*® series has more than 30 million copies in print with translations in 30 languages. IDG Books Worldwide, through a joint venture with IDG's Hi-Tech Beijing, became the first U.S. publisher to publish a computer book in the People's Republic of China. In record time, IDG Books Worldwide has become the first choice for millions of readers around the world who want to learn how to better manage their businesses.

Our mission is simple: Every one of our books is designed to bring extra value and skill-building instructions to the reader. Our books are written by experts who understand and care about our readers. The knowledge base of our editorial staff comes from years of experience in publishing, education, and journalism — experience we use to produce books for the '90s. In short, we care about books, so we attract the best people. We devote special attention to details such as audience, interior design, use of icons, and illustrations. And because we use an efficient process of authoring, editing, and desktop publishing our books electronically, we can spend more time ensuring superior content and spend less time on the technicalities of making books.

You can count on our commitment to deliver high-quality books at competitive prices on topics you want to read about. At IDG Books Worldwide, we continue in the IDG tradition of delivering quality for more than 25 years. You'll find no better book on a subject than one from IDG Books Worldwide.

John J. Kilcullen
John Kilcullen
CEO
IDG Books Worldwide, Inc.

Steven Berkowitz
Steven Berkowitz
President and Publisher
IDG Books Worldwide, Inc.

Eighth Annual Computer Press Awards ≥1992

Ninth Annual Computer Press Awards ≥1993

Tenth Annual Computer Press Awards ≥1994

Eleventh Annual Computer Press Awards ≥1995

Dedication

This book is for my loving wife, Jacyn, and for the kids, James and Veronica. It's been said that it takes a whole village to raise a child. It also takes a whole family to write a book, and rarely more so than on this one. Thanks, you guys.

Acknowledgments

The staff at Dummies Press has helped create something uncommon: a highly approachable and easy to follow book about AutoCAD. As Project Editor, Jennifer Ehrlich has been both patient and persistent. Christy Meloy Beck copyedited my sometimes tortured prose and introduced a degree of consistency and correctness that I couldn't have achieved on my own. Mike Kelly signed me to the original contract and oversaw the whole process with his usual calm and good humor.

This book also benefitted greatly from the efforts of my coauthor on a previous AutoCAD book, and technical editor on this one, Mark Middlebrook of Daedalus Consulting. Mark's thorough review of this book in progress has improved it greatly, unfortunately at Mark's expense, since he put in many more hours on this than what the standard technical reviewing fee covers. Luckily, in doing so he learned about a few nooks and crannies of Release 14 that he might not have looked as hard at otherwise.

Publisher's Acknowledgments

We're proud of this book; please register your comments through our IDG Books Worldwide Online Registration Form located at `http://my2cents.dummies.com`.

Some of the people who helped bring this book to market include the following:

Acquisitions, Development, and Editorial

Project Editor: Jennifer Ehrlich

Acquisitions Editor: Michael Kelly

Product Development Director: Mary Bednarek

Senior Copy Editor: Christine Meloy Beck

Technical Editor: Mark Middlebrook

Editorial Manager: Leah P. Cameron

Editorial Assistants: Chris H. Collins, Darren Meiss

Production

Project Coordinator: Valery Bourke

Layout and Graphics: Elizabeth Cárdenas-Nelson, Todd Klemme, Maridee V. Ennis, Anna Rohrer, M. Anne Sipahimalani, Brent Savage, Michael A. Sullivan

Proofreaders: Renee Kelty, Kelli Botta, Christine Berman, Rachel Garvey, Nancy Price, Robert Springer

Indexer: Sharon Hilgenberg

Special Help

Stephanie Koutek, Proof Editor;
Dwight Ramsey, Reprint Editor;
Diana R. Conover, Associate Editor/Online

General and Administrative

IDG Books Worldwide, Inc.: John Kilcullen, CEO; Steven Berkowitz, President and Publisher

IDG Books Technology Publishing: Brenda McLaughlin, Senior Vice President and Group Publisher

Dummies Technology Press and Dummies Editorial: Diane Graves Steele, Vice President and Associate Publisher; Mary Bednarek, Acquisitions and Product Development Director; Kristin A. Cocks, Editorial Director

Dummies Trade Press: Kathleen A. Welton, Vice President and Publisher; Kevin Thornton, Acquisitions Manager

IDG Books Production for Dummies Press: Beth Jenkins, Production Director; Cindy L. Phipps, Manager of Project Coordination, Production Proofreading, and Indexing; Kathie S. Schutte, Supervisor of Page Layout; Shelley Lea, Supervisor of Graphics and Design; Debbie J. Gates, Production Systems Specialist; Robert Springer, Supervisor of Proofreading; Debbie Stailey, Special Projects Coordinator; Tony Augsburger, Supervisor of Reprints and Bluelines; Leslie Popplewell, Media Archive Coordinator

Dummies Packaging and Book Design: Patti Crane, Packaging Specialist; Lance Kayser, Packaging Assistant; Kavish + Kavish, Cover Design

◆

The publisher would like to give special thanks to Patrick J. McGovern, without whom this book would not have been possible.

◆

Contents at a Glance

Cartoons at a Glance

By Rich Tennant

page 307

page 195

page 117

page 9

page 251

page 291

Fax: 508-546-7747 • E-mail: the5wave@tiac.net

Table of Contents

Introduction

AutoCAD is kind of an amazing thing. It was dreamed up at a time when most people thought that personal computers weren't all that big a deal, when even someone who liked PCs would hardly dream of pushing them to do something as hard as CAD (which can stand for Computer-Aided Design, Computer-Aided Drafting, or both, depending on whom you talk to). But AutoCAD, to the surprise of many, was a hit from its first day, and it has grown to define a whole new way of creating architectural, mechanical, geographical, and other kinds of drawings.

In its evolution, however, AutoCAD has also grown more complex and somewhat difficult to use. The newest version, AutoCAD Release 14, takes important steps toward fixing this problem. And this book helps bridge the gap that still remains between AutoCAD and the rest of the world of PC software. This book doesn't tell you how to become an AutoCAD maven your first time out, but it does show you where some of the bones are buried from AutoCAD's difficult-to-use past — and, more important, how to step around those bones. With this book, you have an excellent chance of creating an attractive, usable, and printable drawing on your first or second try without putting a T-square through your computer screen in frustration.

About This Book

This book is not designed to be read straight through, from cover to cover. It's designed as a reference book so that you can dip in and out of it as you run into new topics. Look for the part that contains the information you want, narrow your search down to a specific chapter, find out what you need to know, and then get back to work. This book is also not designed to be completely comprehensive. Thousands of pages of documentation are required to describe completely how to use AutoCAD, and the resulting proliferation of weighty manuals and third-party books just leaves many people confused. With this book, you're able to get right to work.

How to Use This Book

AutoCAD is bound to leave you wondering what's going on at some point. If you're new to the program, the first time you click an icon and the only response is that a prompt shows up on a command line, you may wonder whether something's wrong with your computer. Slightly more experienced users are likely to trip up on the intricate relationship between setup, drawing, and printing. And sometimes even experts may stumble over the details of paper space or making things work well in 3D.

Use the table of contents and the index in this book to find the topic that stumps you. Go to that section and read up on the topic. Usually, you find a set of steps, a picture, or a description of how to do the task that's troubling you — and often, you find all three. (How's that for service?) Use that section to get yourself back on track and then close the book and go on.

What's Not in This Book

Unlike many other ...*For Dummies* books, this one does tell you to consult the manuals sometimes. AutoCAD is just too big and complicated for a single book to attempt to describe it completely (though some 1,000-page-plus tomes on AutoCAD do try). The manual set is so big that Autodesk doesn't even print all of it; in Release 14, several of the manuals are included only in online help, and you have to pay extra for printed versions.

Make no mistake about it: AutoCAD is a beast, a huge program/environment that is an entire world of computing unto itself. So occasionally, this book points you off to the manuals for more detailed or advanced information.

This book is also carefully restricted as to which versions of AutoCAD it covers. This book doesn't talk about the less-capable, lower-cost sibling of AutoCAD, AutoCAD LT, for example, except for some general discussion in Chapter 1.

Among the many releases of AutoCAD, this book focuses on Release 14, the newest and easiest-to-use version of the program. This book tells new users how to become productive quickly with Release 14; it tells current users who are upgrading from Release 12 or Release 13 what's new and how to take advantage of those new features. This book doesn't give a great deal of coverage to higher-end features such as customization, add-on programs that make new features available, and other complicated areas.

Please Don't Read This!

Sprinkled through the book are icons labeled *Technical Stuff.* These icons alert you to discussions of minute detail that are unlikely to concern you unless you're a confirmed AutoCAD techno-nerd. As you slowly advance to expert status, however, you may find yourself going back through the book to read all that technical stuff. (At that point, you may also want to ask your boss for a vacation, because you just may be working a little too hard!)

Who Are — and Aren't — You?

AutoCAD has a large, loyal, and dedicated group of long-time users. This book may not meet the needs of all these long-time members of the AutoCAD faithful. This book is probably not for you if

- ✔ You were using AutoCAD when it still had Versions instead of Releases.

- ✔ You wrote the benchmarks that Autodesk used to test Release 14's performance while it was being developed.

- ✔ You have lectured at Autodesk University.

- ✔ You founded Autodesk University.

- ✔ You read all those 1,000-page-plus technical tomes about AutoCAD for pleasure.

- ✔ You sent suggestions for changes in Release 14 to the AutoCAD Wish List and had them incorporated in the new Release.

- ✔ After your suggestion was incorporated into the program, you sent e-mail to Autodesk explaining how they did it wrong.

If you don't fall into any of these categories, well, this is definitely the book for you.

However, you do need to have some idea of how to use your computer system before tackling AutoCAD — and this book. You need to have a working computer system on which to run AutoCAD and be able to connect it to a monitor, printer, and network, as well as the World Wide Web. If not, pick up *PCs For Dummies,* 4th Edition, by Dan Gookin (from IDG Books Worldwide, Inc.).

You also need to know how to use either Windows 95 or Windows NT to copy and delete files, create a subdirectory (the DOS word for it) or folder (the official Windows term), and find a file. You need to know how to use a mouse to select (highlight) or to choose (activate) commands, how to close a window, and how to minimize and maximize windows. If not, run — don't walk — to your nearest bookstore and get IDG Books' *Windows 95 For Dummies,* 2nd Edition, by Andy Rathbone, or *Windows NT 4 For Dummies* by Andy Rathbone and Sharon Crawford, and try to master some basics before you start with AutoCAD. (At least have those books handy as you start using this book.)

How This Book Is Organized

This book is really well-organized. Well, at least it's organized. Well, okay, I drew some circles on the floor, threw scraps of paper with different ideas and topics written on them toward the circles, and organized the book by which scrap landed in which circle.

Seriously, the organization of this book into Parts is one of the most important, uh, *parts* of this book. You really can get to know AutoCAD one piece at a time, and each Part represents a group of closely related topics. The order of Parts also says something about priority; yes, you have my permission to ignore the stuff in later Parts until you've mastered most of the stuff in the early ones. This kind of building-block approach can be especially valuable in a program as complex as AutoCAD.

The book breaks down into the following parts:

Part I: AutoCAD 101

Need to know your way around the AutoCAD screen? Why does AutoCAD even exist anyway? What's different in Release 14 versus Release 13? versus Release 12? Is everything so slooow because it's supposed to be slow, or do I have too wimpy a machine to truly use this wonder of modern-day computing? And why am I doing this stuff in the first place?

Part I answers all these questions — and more. This Part also includes what may seem like a great deal of excruciating detail about setting up your drawing. But what's even more excruciating is to do your setup work incorrectly and then have the printer laugh at you as you attempt to print the final version of the drawings due the next day at 9 a.m. (And let me tell you, a Hewlett-Packard pen plotter can click its pen advance mechanism in a rhythm eerily reminiscent of an evil chuckle.) Read this stuff.

Part II: Let There Be Lines

This Part contains "real" AutoCAD — drawing two-dimensional lines, circles, rectangles, and so on, all of which become a CAD drawing that represents a real-world design (if you're both lucky and good). After you get these lines and circles, also known as *geometry,* down and find out about the new AutoSnap feature in Release 14, you'll undoubtedly want to know how to edit and view your drawing. Or someone else's drawing. Or something. This Part has you covered.

Part III: Make Your Drawing Beautiful

AutoCAD has more ways to gussy up a drawing than you could ever think of. And maybe more than you need. Text, dimensions, and hatch patterns all contribute to the appearance of your drawings. This Part helps you find your way through the maze of possibilities to a good solution and then tells you how to get the drawing off your screen, out through a plotter, and onto paper where it belongs. It also tells you how to take advantage of the new capability in AutoCAD to print your drawing to the World Wide Web.

Part IV: Having It Your Way

All right, I admit it: This Part is less than perfectly organized. The main relationship between paper space, blocks, and external references to data, Release 14's newfound ability to include scanned images, and 3D is that they're all things you can probably wait to investigate until after you've mastered the basics of making AutoCAD work. They're also powerful features that would be nearly inconceivable in old-style, pencil-and-paper design and drafting. Dip in and out of this Part to experiment and do even more neat things with AutoCAD.

Part V: The Part of Tens

Everyone loves lists, unless it's the overdue list at the local library. This Part contains pointers to AutoCAD resources and some details on how to use the World Wide Web with AutoCAD. Are these things tightly related or loosely related to AutoCAD? You be the judge.

Part VI: Appendixes

Yes, this book has appendixes, and we'd prefer that you not have them taken out! The appendixes here give you some tips on correctly installing AutoCAD Release 14, detailed tables relating paper sizes to drawing scales to AutoCAD settings, and a glossary of AutoCAD terms.

Icons Used in This Book

Icons, once confined to computer screens, have escaped and are now running amok in the pages of this book. (Yeah, I know that icons started out in print in the first place, but computer people stole them fair and square. Now we writers are getting even.) These icons are like the ones in AutoCAD Release 14, except that they're fewer, simpler, easier on the eyes, and used more consistently. (Who, me, an attitude problem?) The icons used in this book are as follows:

This icon tells you that a pointed insight lies ahead that can save you time and trouble as you use AutoCAD. For example, maybe learning how to type with your nose would help increase your speed in entering commands and moving the mouse at the same time. (And maybe not . . .)

The Technical Stuff icon points out places where you may find more data than information. Unless you're really ready to find out more about AutoCAD — much more — steer clear of these paragraphs.

This icon tells you how to stay out of trouble when living a little close to the edge. Failure to heed its message may have disastrous consequences for you, your drawing, your computer — and maybe even all three.

Remember when Spock put his hand over McCoy's face and implanted a suggestion in his brain that later saved Spock's life? This icon is like that. Helpful reminders of things you already know but that may not be right at the tip of your brain . . . or whatever.

This icon tells you how to do things from the keyboard instead of by using menus, toolbars, or whatever. The keyboard stuff is usually harder to remember, but quicker to use.

This icon points to new stuff in AutoCAD Release 14. It's mostly designed for those of you who know AutoCAD pretty well already and just want to find out what's new in this release, but other people may find this stuff interesting, too.

Sometimes I feel the urge to point you to some good information on the Information Superhighway, and this icon lets you know that it's time to grab your wet suit — you're going surfin'!

A Few Conventions — Just in Case

You probably can figure out for yourself all the information I'm about to impart in this section, but just in case you want to save that brain power for AutoCAD, here it is in print.

Text you type into the program at the command line, in a dialog box, text box, and so on appears in **boldface type**. Examples of AutoCAD commands and prompts appear in a `special typeface`, as does any other text in the book that echoes a message, a word, or one or more lines of text that actually appear on-screen. (Longer segments also have a shaded background.)

Sidebars also are set off in their own typeface, with a fancy head all their own, and are surrounded by a shaded box, much like this:

This is a sidebar head

And this is how the text in a sidebar appears. Neat, huh? Well, different at least. Hey, two-column text can be pretty nifty all on its own, even without peripheral AutoCAD material to occupy its space! What? You don't buy that? Oh, well, back to our main event then.

Regarding menus and menu items or commands, if you're told to open a menu or choose a command, you can use any number of methods to do so — pressing a shortcut key combination on the keyboard, clicking an icon, or clicking the menu or command name with the mouse, highlighting the name by moving over it with the cursor arrow keys, and then pressing Enter — whatever way you're most comfortable with. Sometimes I tell you to do it a certain way, because that's how I, as the AutoCAD authority du jour, think it's done best. But if you know what I'm talking about, feel free to do it your way instead. (And if it doesn't work, of course, you didn't hear this from me.)

Anytime you see a menu name or command name with an underlined letter, such as Eile, it means that the underlined letter is the Windows shortcut key for that menu name or command. Hold down the Alt key and press the first underlined key to select the menu. Then, continue to hold down the Alt key and press the second underlined key to select the command. (You can let up on the Alt key after you select the menu if you'd like, then press the command's shortcut key to access it. But don't press the Alt key down a second time, or Windows will select a different menu instead of the command you want.) Oh, and often in this book you see phrases such as "choose Eile⇨Save As from the menu bar." The funny little arrow (⇨) separates the main menu name from the specific command on that menu. In this example, you would open the File menu and choose the Save As command. Again, the underlined letters are the *hot keys* — keys you can press in combination with the Alt key to open menus and activate commands.

AutoCAD has an interesting convention for command-line shortcuts: the shortcut letters appear in capital letters, while the rest of the command appears in lowercase. So when you see a sentence like "enter **DimLInear** for a linear dimension," it means "for a linear dimension, enter **DIMLINEAR**, or **DLI** for short, at the command line." Because you will be seeing this convention used continuously in AutoCAD, I used it in this book as well.

Well, that covers the basics. The details — ah, those are yet to come. And believe me when I tell you with the utmost sincerity that you have much to look forward to . . . (Cue lightning, thunder, and a low moan from the nether regions of your computer.)

Where to Go from Here

If you've read this Introduction, you're probably at least a little bit like me: You like to read. (People who don't like to read usually skip this front matter stuff and scurry to the index to get to exactly, and only, the part they need at that moment.) So take a few more minutes to page through and look for interesting stuff. And pick up a pen and some stick-on notes; the icons and headings in this book are only a start. Personalize your book by circling vital tips, drawing a smiley face if you like a joke, even X-ing out stuff that you disagree with. (And I've hidden plenty of my own opinions in this book, so get those Xs ready.)

Part I
AutoCAD 101

In this part . . .

AutoCAD is more than just another application program; it's a complete environment for design and drafting. So if you're new to AutoCAD, you need to know several things to get off to a good start. These key facts are described in this part of the book.

If you're an experienced AutoCAD user, you may be most interested in the high points of the new release and a quick look at how to get productive on it fast. All that information is here, too. (*Tip:* Look for the Release 14 icons for highlights of the new version.)

Chapter 1

Introducing AutoCAD Release 14

In This Chapter

▶ Why AutoCAD?

▶ Why Release 14?

▶ Windows and Release 14

▶ AutoCAD Release 14 and the novice user

▶ AutoCAD Release 14 and the experienced user

AutoCAD isn't just another software program. It's actually a demanding, separate drawing environment that engages in a sometimes friendly, sometimes antagonistic relationship not only with you, the user, but also with the hardware on which it runs and with the other software programs on your computer.

On a good day with AutoCAD, you may agree that it's a wonderful tool — one of the more important extensions of the human intellect yet to be committed to software. On a bad day, you may be tempted to think of it as the world's largest computer virus, and you may start looking for ways to terminate it with extreme prejudice. With Release 14, you're likely to have more good days than bad.

In recent years, Autodesk has reduced the number of versions of AutoCAD that it continues to upgrade to two: AutoCAD Release 14 for Windows 95 and Windows NT, and AutoCAD LT for Windows 95. The colloquial names for these products are "Release 14," or "R14," and "LT." These two products continue to be improved and upgraded to new versions. Other versions of AutoCAD for UNIX and Macintosh are stuck on earlier releases — Release 12 for Macintosh, Release 13 for UNIX. Autodesk may release minor updates to fix bugs, but these products are basically like a fly with its feet stuck in amber: not dead yet, but not going anywhere either.

So Autodesk has committed the future of AutoCAD — and by extension, the future of the company — to Windows. Understanding something about the history of AutoCAD, the best and worst of Release 14, and some of the highs and lows of Windows helps you get a good start with AutoCAD overall (if you're new to it) and Release 14 in particular. (This way, if you're cursing at Release 14, you can at least know exactly what part of the program and its overall environment to curse at.)

Why AutoCAD?

AutoCAD may seem like a basic fact of life — like gravity or the tendency of the phone to ring as soon as you step into the shower. And AutoCAD has, indeed, been around a long time: since 1982, at the beginning of the PC revolution. It was the very first product of Autodesk, a company founded with a commitment to giving programmers fun things to do. Autodesk actually planned four products for introduction, but AutoCAD was such an instant hit that it quickly became the mainstay of the fledgling company.

AutoCAD was the first product in its category, microcomputer-based CADD, or Computer-Aided Design and Drafting (now usually referred to as simply *CAD*). AutoCAD has stayed so popular that using it for any CAD work you're doing may seem a foregone conclusion. But before you spend nearly 400 pages trying to make AutoCAD do your bidding, take a brief look at the purpose of AutoCAD and the reasons for its current success.

AutoCAD is, first and foremost, a program to create printed drawings. The drawings you create with AutoCAD must adhere to standards established long ago for blueprints and other very specific types of drawings that have long been drawn by hand and that, in many cases, are still hand-drawn. The up-front investment to use AutoCAD is certainly more expensive than the investment needed to use pencil and paper, and the learning curve is much longer, too; you have to learn to use a computer as well as learn AutoCAD. So why bother?

The key reasons for using AutoCAD over pencil and paper are

  ✔ **Exactitude:** When AutoCAD is properly set up (something I discuss extensively in Chapter 4), creating lines, circles, and other shapes of the exactly correct dimensions is much easier with AutoCAD than on paper.

  ✔ **Modifiability:** Drawings are much easier to modify on the computer screen than on paper. (Though both traditional and computer-aided drafters are often far too reluctant to consider the possible speed advantages of just giving up on a drawing that's really out of whack and starting over from scratch!)

Figure 1-1 shows a simple drawing on the AutoCAD Release 14 screen.

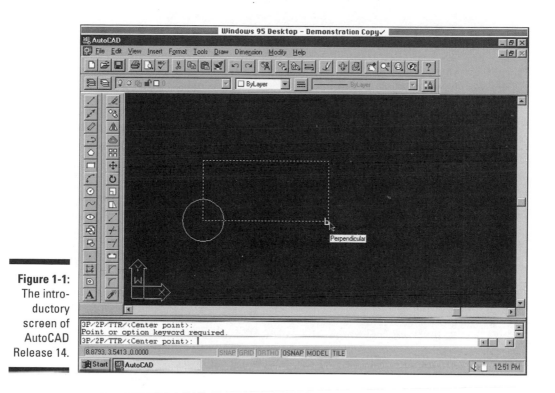

Figure 1-1:
The intro-
ductory
screen of
AutoCAD
Release 14.

Now that I've established the advantages of computer-aided drafting over pencil and paper for much of the design and drafting work that people want to do, why choose AutoCAD over the competition? Well, AutoCAD is just the starting point of a whole industry of software and hardware products designed to work with AutoCAD. Autodesk has helped this process along immensely by designing a whole series of programming interfaces to AutoCAD that other companies have used to extend the application. (Some of these products are winners, some are dogs, but the point is that Autodesk keeps hacking away at extensibility.) Every new programming interface generates new books, new training courses, new add-ons, and ideas for even more new stuff. As a result, when you compare "whole products" — not just the core program, such as AutoCAD, but all the add-ons, extensions, training courses, books, and so on — AutoCAD doesn't really have much competition.

With Release 14, AutoCAD has greatly improved the ease with which you can create exact drawings and then modify those drawings. For example, Release 14 makes drawing lines that connect at interesting points, like the end of a line or the corner of a rectangle, much easier; the program high-lights such points on the display as you draw and actually attracts the cursor to those points. Autodesk has also reduced some of the disadvan-tages that using a computer program can have as compared to working on paper: slow performance, bugs, and crashes.

AutoCAD as a Platform

Various versions of AutoCAD run on different computer hardware/software "platforms" such as UNIX, the Macintosh, and Windows. A *platform,* as the name implies, is a foundation on which other products build. It has a set of core software and/or hardware elements; third-party developers and users provide the missing pieces to create complete solutions based on the platform.

By this definition, AutoCAD itself is a platform; other companies and even customers have built an almost unimaginable array of hardware and software extensions and add-ons to solve various needs. And millions of people use one version or another of AutoCAD. These people form a labor and service pool that anyone using AutoCAD can draw from to help complete projects and to get service and support. Conversely, after you master AutoCAD, you become employable within a large and growing worldwide community of AutoCAD users.

 For Release 14, AutoCAD has decided to drop support for any computing platforms besides Windows 95 and Windows NT (referred to together as *32-bit Windows*) so that the AutoCAD CAD platform can be more tightly coupled with the 32-bit Windows platform. The effects of this decision are described in more detail later in this chapter.

Windows and Release 14

The story of AutoCAD Release 14 is very much the story of AutoCAD moving lock, stock, and barrel to the 32-bit Windows platform, meaning Windows 95 and Windows NT. After years of work to make AutoCAD work well cross-platform, Autodesk has finally put all its eggs in the Windows basket. For most AutoCAD users, the effects of this change are good.

Why Windows?

Like the Macintosh before it, Windows offers users many benefits over DOS. Compared to the infamous DOS C> prompt, a graphical environment is much easier to pick up and use. Users have much less to memorize and can spend more time doing their work and less time thinking about how to do it.

AutoCAD LT

It may seem odd that one of AutoCAD's biggest competitors is the LT, or "light," version of AutoCAD, a product made by Autodesk. But the situation isn't so odd if you know a little bit about the history of AutoCAD LT.

AutoCAD LT started life as a recommendation by John Walker, the key person and personality in the early history of Autodesk. Walker recommended the creation of an "AutoCAD Lite" to capture the entry-level two-dimensional drafting market. A couple of years later, Autodesk created AutoSketch, a product that became quite successful in Europe. But in the U.S., the most successful product for entry-level CAD was Generic CADD from Generic Software. Autodesk first bought Generic CADD, then developed AutoCAD LT, dropping Generic CADD a few years later.

If you're interested in a true insider's view of the early history of Autodesk, read John Walker's book, *The Autodesk File*, available in a free, updated form online at

http://www.fourmilab.ch/
    autofile/www/autofile.html

AutoCAD LT for Windows is a "light" (or "lite," depending on your preference) version of AutoCAD for Windows. With a street price of less than $500 — compared to $3,000 or so for "full" AutoCAD Release 14 — and lower hardware requirements, LT is, in many ways, a real bargain. LT is also the only CAD program costing less than $3,000 that offers full native support for the DWG — short for "drawing" — file format used by regular AutoCAD to store drawings. It lacks most of the AutoCAD programming interfaces, so there are very few third-party applications available for it.

For a detailed comparison of Autodesk CAD products, see the CAD Products Comparison Chart on the Autodesk Web site at

http://www.autodesk.com/
    products/autocad/compari.htm

People who create hardware device drivers and application programs also benefit — the graphical environment provides standard ways for hardware devices and application programs to communicate with the computer and the user, making more innovation possible. So the last ten years of PC history have largely been consumed with the move from DOS to Windows.

Seeing these changes in progress, Autodesk made a strong strategic commitment to Windows. By the early 1990s, the company was planning its future releases around the idea of making a complete move to Windows NT, running on Pentium systems, within five years.

The move of PC users from DOS to Windows that AutoCAD wanted to be part of has been slow and painful, but it is nearly complete; all new PCs come with Windows, and few new programs are available for DOS. Only two areas of the software world have resisted the move to Windows: games, many of which still come as DOS programs, and AutoCAD.

Commands versus objects in AutoCAD

In the early 1980s, when AutoCAD was first introduced, the problem of how to work with graphical images on a personal computer was being worked on by many different people and companies. The two approaches used then are still in use today: the command-based approach and the object-based approach.

In the command-based approach, the user enters a command, usually by typing it, and then enters some parameters, usually by typing them. This approach is fast, because any computer can easily process text strings such as commands. However, the user has to know the commands and what parameters to use with each command. System and program settings are also managed by commands and parameters, meaning that the user has to remember even more. The DOS and UNIX command lines are examples of a command-based approach.

In accordance with the computers used at the time, AutoCAD started out as a command-driven program. Initially, the user would enter the command, such as RECTANGLE, and then enter parameters, such as the corners of the rectangle to draw. Later, as the graphics capabilities of small computers advanced, the user would still enter a command such as DRAW, but then he or she could either enter the parameters or click on the screen ("pick") to indicate the rectangle's corners.

The object-based approach is different. The user deals with an onscreen representation of whatever the final product will be: a text document, a drawing, or what have you. To make a change, the user clicks on an object or area of the screen to select it and then selects a command or performs some kind of manipulation or data entry to operate on the object or area of the screen. Dialog boxes are used to manage system and program settings. The object-based approach demands a more powerful computer that can display and quickly update onscreen representations of real-world objects. The Macintosh and Windows are examples of an object-based approach.

As AutoCAD becomes more and more tightly integrated with Windows, it is moving more and more to an object-based approach. However, AutoCAD continues to support the command line as well, and a few operations are still only available via the command line. Though the command line is very efficient, it also makes AutoCAD, as a whole, hard to master, because you have to switch frequently between two very different approaches to use it well. Until you have enough experience with AutoCAD to "switch gears" between these approaches without thinking, expect to run into some problems remembering exactly how to get things done.

This resistance is not a coincidence, and game players and AutoCAD users are not reactionary or slow. Until recently, graphics performance for CAD and games was a lot slower in Windows than in DOS, and game players and AutoCAD users share a nearly absolute commitment to fast display speed. That commitment makes sense: Game players can't fully enjoy a game that is slow to display changes, and AutoCAD users can't be fully productive when using a computer that is slow to display changes. That's why game players and AutoCAD users are also prone to buy the fastest, most powerful machines.

With Release 13, Autodesk attempted to move the bulk of its users to Windows — and failed. Though Release 13 was buggy and lacking in compelling features, the main problem was that it was slower than Release 12 for DOS. The initial slow acceptance that this problem caused was exacerbated by AutoCAD application developers and leading figures in the AutoCAD community, who sent out signals to either go slow or not move at all. All these factors made Release 13 more of a boondoggle than a benefit for Autodesk and AutoCAD users.

The other problem with Release 13 was the greater hardware requirements demanded by Windows. Most users didn't want to buy a Pentium computer, 32MB of RAM, and a large hard disk just to run a new software release. (Keep in mind that, two years ago, the Pentium chip was brand-new and very expensive; RAM prices were heading up, not down; and a 170MB hard disk was still a monster, not a throwaway.) Users who did buy such beefed-up systems wanted to run the DOS version anyway in order to get the full performance benefit from their new computers.

So the biggest challenge for Release 14 is to make the move to Windows palatable for AutoCAD users. One thing that has helped in the years since Release 13 was introduced has been the fantastic growth of the World Wide Web; you need Windows to run any decent Web browser, and AutoCAD users have been caught up in the Web just like everyone else. This momentum has led many of them to upgrade to Windows and find out how to use it while still running AutoCAD in DOS. The continuing improvement in systems has also helped, with yesterday's monster high-end system now available for around $1,499. (And those $1,499 CompUSA specials all come with Windows preinstalled!) You can even get a machine that is almost robust enough to run AutoCAD — just add a few more megabytes of RAM — for under $1,000! If the AutoCAD world is ever to be ready to move up to Windows, Release 14 is Autodesk's best chance so far to help it do so.

Windows and the look of AutoCAD

The move to 32-bit Windows brings a number of advantages to Release 14, but the most noticeable difference is in the AutoCAD look and feel. Autodesk has moved so completely to a Microsoft-based approach that it now uses Microsoft Foundation Classes, code that Microsoft provides for use by applications that want to be fully Windows-compliant. (The Autodesk of years past would have snorted with disgust at the prospect of using code from Microsoft.)

Windows 95 or NT?

As I mention earlier in this chapter, Autodesk once thought that Microsoft Windows NT would be the operating system of choice by now — not only for AutoCAD, but for any serious computer user. But things haven't worked out that way, and even Microsoft has revised its strategy; Windows 95 and its upcoming follow-up, commonly referred to as *Windows 98,* are expected to be the most widely used PC operating systems through the end of the decade. For the next few years, Windows NT is expected to be used mainly in heavily networked corporate environments and by the most demanding power users.

But wait! Because most AutoCAD users are "demanding power users," you may resemble that remark. And you may be hearing that NT is a "real operating system," that Windows 95 is a "toy," and on and on.

So, should you upgrade to NT? Well, no. Here's why not:

- **More $:** A system running NT requires at least 8MB more RAM than a system running Windows 95 — RAM you could be using for your programs and drawings. NT also takes up more hard disk space and costs more to buy.

- **Device support:** Windows NT doesn't support as many devices as Windows 95, including many devices attached to portable computers, such as PCMCIA cards. Because AutoCAD benefits from unusual devices such as drawing tablets and plotters, no AutoCAD user wants to take on problems in getting device support.

- **Application support:** Windows NT doesn't support as many applications as Windows 95 (including most games).

- **Missing features in applications:** The main advantages of Windows NT have to do with multithreading, multitasking, and multiprocessor support, all great things — and all things that your applications have to be rewritten to take advantage of.

- **Not yet the standard:** Windows NT is not yet the standard. It's harder to get device drivers, support, books, magazine articles, and all the other little helpers that make using a computer easier.

Now, you may not have a choice. Your company may decide to go to NT and sweep you along in the change. No problem; they're taking on the additional expense and hassles, so go along for the ride. Or you may be a true power user who can't wait for the latest and greatest; I wish you well. But if you aren't under the grip of some external or internal compulsion, wait.

As you may guess, AutoCAD has not yet been upgraded to take full advantage of Windows NT. Why take on NT's current negatives when you aren't going to get the full benefits? So my opinion is, wait until you can get an upcoming, revved-up version of AutoCAD that supports multiple processors. Then buy a multiprocessor machine — which will, almost by definition, be running Windows NT — and hold onto your hat.

For an exhaustive discussion of the NT versus Windows 95 decision by the inimitable David Cohn of *CADENCE*, with a detailed decision tree and other contributions by Peter Sheerin and Roopinder Tara, see

```
http://www.cadence-mag.com/1997/
    feb/Windows.html
```

But enough politics; how does this approach affect you? The experience of using AutoCAD Release 14 is subtly different from Release 13 for Windows and miles different from the still-popular Release 12 for DOS. AutoCAD Release 14 looks very much like a Microsoft Office program, with identical buttons, pull-down menus, and even tool tips for the dozens of icons in the program. Although you occasionally see a DOS-style text screen and the DOS-like command line is still very much present, most of the experience of using AutoCAD is quite Windows-like.

The AutoCAD Help system is based on the Windows Help system, with content from Autodesk. Because the "plumbing" for Help is both free to Autodesk and familiar to many users, the company could concentrate on the content and on doing creative work beyond the basic Help system. So AutoCAD Release 14 features far more computer-based tutorial and reference information than most products, plus the respectable beginnings of an online component available on the World Wide Web.

The new Windows-like appearance of Release 14 even extends to the workings, not just the look, of the program's dialog boxes. Not only are the ugly DOS dialog boxes of earlier versions of AutoCAD gone, but Release 14 also uses cool new features such as column sorting. Figure 1-2 shows the AutoCAD Release 14 Layer & Linetype Properties dialog box. In part A, new layers have just been created; they're listed in the order of creation. In part B, the user has clicked on the Name column header twice: One click sorts the layers into descending (Z through A) alphabetical order; clicking a second time sorts them into ascending (A through Z) alphabetical order.

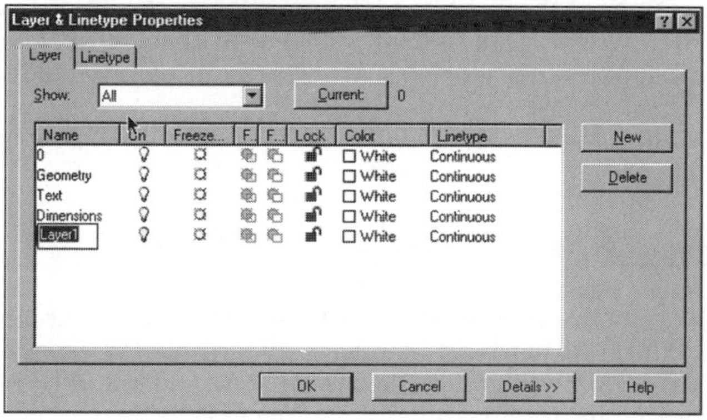

Figure 1-2A:
A Windows
dialog box
displays
layers.

2 clicks to sort in ascending alphabetical order

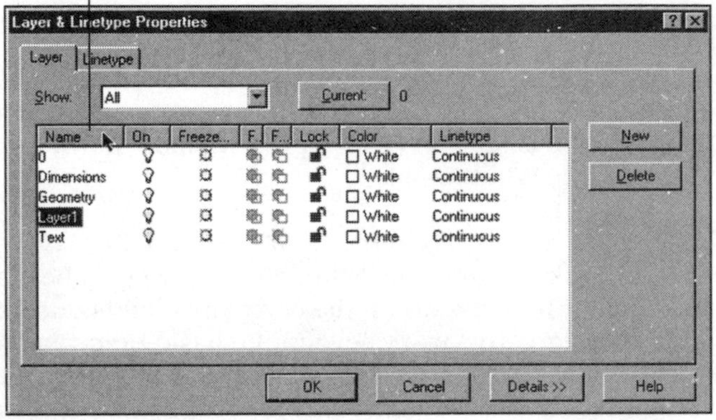

Figure 1-2B:
Clicking on
a column
header
sorts the
layers.

Release 14 and You

AutoCAD and the market of products around it have grown and progressed to the point that most of the features users need can be found either in AutoCAD or in its array of add-ons and extensions. The biggest problem now is that most AutoCAD users run a DOS version, Release 12 for DOS or earlier, and would prefer an otherwise equivalent version that runs on Windows. So what is mostly needed from Release 14 is a fast, stable Windows version of AutoCAD that runs on a reasonable hardware configuration. Also needed are compatibility with existing add-on applications, followed immediately by upgraded versions of the most important add-on applications that take advantage of new features in the program and the new file format. Of course, a few new capabilities to make AutoCAD more feature-rich would be nice, too.

Take a look at how AutoCAD Release 14 stacks up on these basic requirements.

Windows compliance — 95 and NT

The best thing about AutoCAD Release 14 is that it's a true 32-bit Windows application. Autodesk has redesigned and, where needed, rewritten AutoCAD to run very well under 32-bit Windows (and not to run on any other platform). This new Windows compliance shows up in the following ways:

✔ **Look and feel:** AutoCAD Release 14 looks and acts much like a Microsoft Office application. Floating toolbars, Explorer-style dialog boxes, help through the Windows Help system, and other features all adhere very closely to 32-bit Windows standards.

✔ **Multitasking:** If you're coming from DOS, the next thing you notice — and this is big — is the capability to do several things at once. You can run other applications and multiple AutoCAD sessions all at the same time. (Those of us with plenty of Macintosh or Windows experience can't imagine working any other way.) This difference is a huge productivity and ease-of-use win.

✔ **Optimization:** As a 32-bit application optimized for Windows, AutoCAD runs faster, is more stable, and is better integrated with other programs than before. For the vast majority of AutoCAD users who are also Windows users, this change is a big improvement.

✔ **ActiveX Automation:** AutoCAD now partly supports ActiveX Automation, and Autodesk is said to be working on a faster version so AutoCAD can be much more fully customized via Visual Basic. With this change, everyone from individual users to in-house programmers in your organization to third-party application developers to Autodesk itself will be able to extend and improve AutoCAD much more easily. You will be able to write the Visual Basic code yourself or pick and choose from all the new tools that will be written by others.

If you're coming to AutoCAD Release 14 from DOS, the first thing you'll be tempted to do is surf the Web during redraws, plots, or any other break in your AutoCAD work. Be careful; Web browsers are among the less stable Windows applications, especially when you're surfing Web sites with plenty of Java, ActiveX controls, multimedia files, and other goodies. Always save your open AutoCAD files before switching to other programs, especially Web browsers.

Ease of use

Windows and its programs are much easier to use than DOS and *its* programs. The consistent, attractive interface just makes everything work better. So if you're a new user, you'll be happier with AutoCAD Release 14 than you would have been with any previous version (which may not be saying much; AutoCAD is both a complicated program and one that works in unusual ways, so you have a long learning curve ahead of you regardless).

AutoCAD Release 14 is easier for novices than previous releases, which will help AutoCAD maintain its market leadership and make it possible, if not easy, for occasional users to get something done in AutoCAD. But other CAD programs, including AutoCAD LT, are easier. Ease of use in Release 14 is improved but still not a strong plus for AutoCAD, whether you're starting fresh or upgrading.

Experienced AutoCAD users who are considering upgrading should be aware of one important caveat: The hardest interface imaginable becomes the easiest when you know it inside and out. When your fingers are completely trained to do things one way, anything different is harder. Though Autodesk has tried hard to retain command-line compatibility, enough changes have been made in all parts of the program that experienced users will flounder for a while before retraining themselves.

Speed thrills?

For AutoCAD users, speed thrills. In fact, most AutoCAD users can't afford to take any step backward in speed. Although I leave detailed benchmark testing to the experts, it seems that AutoCAD Release 14 is faster than AutoCAD Release 12 for DOS and is much faster than AutoCAD Release 13 for either DOS or Windows. On their Web site, *CADALYST* magazine shows a benchmark comparison of testing on the beta. Keep in mind that this chart shows "out of the box" speed; third-party drivers should speed the performance of AutoCAD even more. For once, speed is not a reason to hold back on an AutoCAD upgrade. To see the most up-to-date results for yourself, visit the *CADALYST* Web site at

```
http://www.cadonline.com
```

AutoCAD achieves much of its performance improvement by using a drawing pathway, or *graphics pipeline,* based on a technology called HEIDI. HEIDI is based on HOOPS, a graphics technology acquired by Autodesk about five years ago amid much — drumroll, please — "hoops"-la. (Insert rimshot.) HEIDI has already been used in the Autodesk 3DMAX product and the WHIP! AutoCAD display driver. HEIDI replaces the former approach, which generated large refresh lists in memory. You can program to HEIDI interfaces to create applications that work within AutoCAD or stand-alone applications. If you're not a programmer, you still benefit from the fact that AutoCAD and new third-party applications use this faster graphics technology.

System requirements: reasonable for today

AutoCAD Release 14 doesn't meet the tough test of running on the same minimum configuration as AutoCAD Release 12 for DOS. However, it does meet the more reasonable test of running well on a mainstream, or slightly better than mainstream, machine of today, just as Release 12 for DOS ran well on a slightly better than mainstream machine of its time. Release 14 requires a Pentium machine — faster is better — with 32MB of RAM and about 100 megabytes of free hard disk space. An 800 x 600 screen with 256 colors is recommended, although a larger screen with an add-in graphics card and graphics acceleration software to speed up Windows and AutoCAD and more colors works better.

AutoCAD Release 14 actually uses less memory than Release 13 for Windows; about 4MB more RAM is free after the program is loaded. Because R14 only loads certain modules, such as the code needed for solid modeling, when you access a command that needs them, startup time decreases, and RAM is freed when you're doing non-mechanical work.

More stability for less liability

Possibly the most important attribute of a demanding computer program like AutoCAD is stability. If the program crashes frequently, fails to save files correctly, can't run add-on applications consistently, or has other problems, it's far more trouble than it's worth.

Autodesk has made a huge effort to make AutoCAD Release 14 stable, with the low-water mark set by early versions of Release 13 firmly in mind. The company has helped itself by targeting only 32-bit Windows, which is inherently more stable than 16-bit Windows and is a clear target as compared to the multiplatform AutoCAD releases of the past. That concentration still leaves a great many hardware system, peripheral, networking, and software configurations to try to test. The alpha and beta tests for AutoCAD Release 14 have been very large and have been conducted very openly, with Autodesk clearly putting first priority on getting sufficient customer feedback before shipping. The shipping version has gotten a lot of praise for its stability.

Having said all that, however, the main concern for you is how stable AutoCAD Release 14 is running on your computer, using your peripherals and networking setup, with your add-on applications, multitasking with your other DOS, 16-bit Windows, and 32-bit Windows applications. Before upgrading, check some of the information sources in Chapter 22 to get a sense of the AutoCAD community's opinion as to the stability of Release 14. Then ask coworkers, fellow user group members, and anyone you can track down who has a computer system and software configuration similar to yours. Assure yourself that Release 14 is likely to run safely on your system before upgrading.

Windows 95 is inherently less stable than Windows NT because, for compatibility's sake, it gives applications and device drivers more freedom to do things that can, in some circumstances, be dangerous to system stability. You can help yourself by not running 16-bit Windows applications and old device drivers. Upgrade relentlessly to Windows 95 versions of all your software, and stay on the lookout for the latest and greatest hardware drivers.

Application compatibility: under test

Along with stability testing, Autodesk has tested Release 14 for compatibility with tens of thousands of AutoLISP and other add-on applications. This backward compatibility is good for getting started, but make sure that your major add-in applications are upgraded to Release 14 before you upgrade. Taking this precaution does the most to ensure that your overall system is as stable and fully functional as possible — and also gives you someone to pin the rap on if problems develop.

DWG file compatibility improved

One of the main bugaboos of upgrading to a new AutoCAD release is the fact that the file format keeps changing. Autodesk can argue that it needs to do make these modifications to support new features, but in every release for the last five years? That's a bit much. However, Release 14 does have a nice new feature in which multiple versions of an AutoCAD drawing entity can be stored in the file. So, if you save a Release 14 file as a Release 13 drawing, AutoCAD saves any new entity types in both Release 13- and Release 14-compatible formats. The Release 13 user sees a Release 13-compatible version of each entity; when you bring the drawing back to Release 14, you can access the Release 14-specific entities again.

This multiple-version-saving stuff is okay for limited use, but don't make it your normal routine. If you do, you put work into creating geometry that you and your colleagues can't fully share. If you're sharing drawings with others who are on Release 12 or other earlier releases, don't use features that produce R14-specific file elements (which means that you have to remember to avoid those features). Better yet, wait to upgrade until most of the "pod" of people that you share drawings with can upgrade with you.

What's the bad news?

Although Release 14 is a strong release, all is not rosy. I've mentioned several of the major concerns: a relatively small number of truly new features in AutoCAD itself; greater system requirements than for the still-popular DOS version of Release 12; the need to wait until one's add-on applications are upgraded to Release 14; and the general hassle anyone experiences in changing anything.

RELEASE 14

14

So what's really new in Release 14?

Here's a quick list, in the order that they appear in this book, of some of the key lower-level features that affect your daily work in AutoCAD Release 14:

- Integrated Preferences dialog box includes configuration options. See Chapter 3.

- New templates and wizards for drawing setup. (You may need extra help with this one.) See Chapter 4.

- Recall and editing of previously typed commands on the command line. (Yes, the command line is still there, and it works better than ever!) See Chapter 5.

- Lightweight polylines, a new, flexible linetype. See Chapter 6.

- Better management of running object snaps. See Chapter 7.

- AutoSnap for improved snap functionality and snap point selection. See Chapter 7.

- Many fewer REGENs and redraws. See Chapter 8.

- Much better text editing and more fonts. See Chapter 9.

- Smaller hatch files. See Chapter 11.

- True solid fills. See Chapter 11.

- Direct plotting to network print queues; no AUTOSPOOL. See Chapter 12.

- Fewer REGENs make real-time pan and zoom in paper space possible, so paper space is much more usable. See Chapter 13.

- Built-in support for raster images such as scanned blueprints and maps. See Chapter 14.

- Clipping of XREFs to save memory. See Chapter 14.

- Much better 3D rendering. See Chapter 15.

- Web publishing of drawings and Web drawing access (but no built-in VRML support). See Chapter 17.

All of these new Release 14 features are covered in detail in the rest of this book. Anything that's new to Release 14 has a Release 14 icon, like the one at the top of this sidebar, next to it.

Some other quirks will bother many people, too. I haven't mentioned the new drawing setup wizards yet because, at least at this writing, they're not worth mentioning. They don't ask key setup questions or work all that well. Plot Preview is improved in Release 14, but it could be better: It doesn't distinguish between lines of different weights, so you still have to plot to really "see" your drawing. And Release 14 has problems, inherited from Release 13, with multilines and stacked fractions. (***Tip:*** Don't stack your fractions.)

In addition, some key features are missing. On the ease-of-use front, AutoCAD isn't completely redone, just made-over. It isn't a truly simple program to use, and probably never will be; if it were, it would have to lose some of the power-user features, such as the command line, that experienced users know and love. A less-excusable omission is the lack of multiprocessor support. AutoCAD users are speed freaks; this one feature, whenever it arrives, will do more to increase the satisfaction of AutoCAD users (and sellers of high-end multiprocessor PCs) than any other. For now, multiprocessor support is sorely missed.

Another missed opportunity awaits in the 3D area. First, AutoCAD Release 14 still lacks the capability to save as Virtual Reality Modeling Language (VRML), an exciting 3D standard for the Web. Instead, Autodesk relies on its WHIP! plug-in and proprietary DWG file format for use on the Web. Although the AutoCAD cognoscenti may install WHIP!, many ordinary people are reluctant to install plug-ins, especially those that aren't among the top few (Shockwave, RealAudio, and QuickTime come to mind).

Yet again in the 3D world, the whole 3D arena has a clear need for new ideas in terms of user-interface conventions and overall capabilities. If Autodesk were to successfully tackle this problem within AutoCAD, it could bring as much excitement to the 3D world as AutoCAD brought to the 2D drafting world over a decade ago.

So what does Windows get me?

In addition to the new features that are specific to Release 14, users of Release 12 for DOS get, for the first time, many new features that were either introduced in Release 13 or that are inherent in any Windows program:

✔ Toolbars and toolboxes. See especially Chapter 2.

✔ Windows dialog boxes, Windows tutorials, Windows help. See especially Chapter 3.

✔ Aerial view built into AutoCAD. See Chapter 8.

✔ New dimensioning features. See Chapter 10.

✔ Built-in solid modeling support. See Chapter 15.

✔ Cut and paste.

✔ Multiple Windows applications open at once.

✔ And best of all: multiple AutoCAD sessions open at once.

Should you upgrade, and if so, when?

So if you haven't already bought AutoCAD Release 14, either as an upgrade or as a new package, should you do so? And if the package is sitting on your shelf, is now the time to fire it up and start getting to know it?

There's no one right answer for everyone. Instead, consider a couple of do's and don'ts:

✔ **Don't move in mid-project.** If you're in a deadline situation, don't upgrade. Finish your work and then set aside a few days to install the new software, experiment with it, and test it to ensure that you can have a fully usable configuration with it.

✔ **Do consider a new computer.** Starting out with a new Windows system gives you the opportunity to start with a known, working configuration and then create your new environment a piece at a time, with minimum confusion. If you buy from a computer vendor who's reputable in the CAD market — especially from a dealer who will install and stand behind AutoCAD Release 14 — you're even better off.

✔ **Don't upgrade without an escape hatch.** Back up before you start, and keep in mind how to get back to square one if things don't work out. Give yourself sufficient time to do the upgrade and experiment with it so that you can go back to your old setup if needed.

✔ **Do move to AutoCAD Release 14 when the time is right.** Check with AutoCAD experts and your colleagues. If they're making the move, and Release 14 looks good for your system and software configuration, set aside time now to do the upgrade.

Chapter 2
Le Tour de AutoCAD Release 14

*W*ith Release 14, AutoCAD finally moves both feet into the world of Windows. If you're a new user or an experienced user who prefers Windows, that migration is nothing but good news. But if you're an experienced user coming from DOS, it means that you lose the comfortable simplicity of the DOS command prompt.

For anyone used to the conventions of the Macintosh and Windows, AutoCAD before Release 14 has been a truly weird program. The look of the AutoCAD for DOS screen and of features such as dialog boxes has been ugly, worse than any other major program still available today. The Windows version of Release 13 fell short of other Windows programs in several ways as well.

In Release 14, most of that weirdness is gone. AutoCAD is an attractive, modern Windows program. The command line is still an odd feature, very un-Windows-like, but at least it has been made more powerful and flexible in this release. Those of you who are used to that DOS interface that I just called ugly can find some comfort in the command line.

You may notice other holdovers as well. In configuring AutoCAD, you occasionally run into DOS-like text screens. Except for CompuServe, the favorite online service of AutoCAD users, few modern programs have anything like these screens. The side-screen menu (described later in this chapter), if you turn it on, is another anachronism. The black background of the drawing window is unusual, too, though appropriate for AutoCAD. (And you can easily change the background if you want to. I suggest that you change it to the color of the paper you're plotting to. See Chapter 3 for details.) Still, with Release 14, AutoCAD has irrevocably made the leap to Windows, which means that this tour is easier and more fun than it would otherwise be.

Like the rest of the book, this chapter is written for someone who has used other Windows programs but has never used AutoCAD before, and also includes pointers and insights for experienced users who are upgrading. If you're new to AutoCAD or new to the Windows version, read this chapter carefully — while running AutoCAD if you can. Try things that are new or seem like they may be confusing. An hour invested in poking around now can greatly improve your productivity later. And for more in-depth information if you're upgrading from DOS or from Windows 3.1, check out *Windows 95 For Dummies* by Andy Rathbone (published by IDG Books Worldwide, Inc.).

If you're experienced with Windows versions of AutoCAD, especially Release 13 for Windows, most of this chapter is old hat for you. Just scan through it and read the parts marked with the Release 14 icon, which indicates something truly new.

Getting AutoCAD installed

One of the most interesting things about past releases of AutoCAD has been getting it installed correctly. In Release 14, this situation has improved considerably. The AutoCAD installation process is easier, is much better integrated with the Windows environment, and is well-documented in the AutoCAD Release 14 Installation Guide that comes with the product. It describes the installation process including network installations, hardware locks, the Preferences dialog, and user profiles, a new feature in Release 14 that allows you to customize your AutoCAD setup for multiple users.

This book assumes that you have AutoCAD installed and running already. If you are having trouble, the Installation Guide is your first resource. Appendix A includes installation tips, including a pointer to the excellent Release 14 Upgrade Guide, available on the World Wide Web. If you need this guide, written by two prominent AutoCAD dealers and our own Mark Middlebrook, the technical editor of this book, you can find it at:

```
http://www.mcneel.com/
    whatsnew.html
```

Winning with Windows

Finding your way around AutoCAD Release 14 can be an odd experience. You recognize from other Windows applications much of the appearance and workings of the program, such as its toolbars and pull-down menus, which you use for entering commands or changing system settings. But other aspects of the program's appearance — and some of the ways in which you work with it — are quite different from nearly any other program.

You can, in many cases, tell the program what to do in at least three ways — the menu bar, the command line, or keyboard shortcuts — none of which is necessarily the best method to use for every task. The experience is much like that of having to act as several different characters in a play; you're likely to forget your lines (whichever "you" you are at the time!) at least every now and then.

To get started with AutoCAD Release 14, focus on using the menus at the top of the screen. These menus enable you to access most of the program's functions and are the easiest to remember of the three methods of issuing commands. You can safely delay committing to memory the other, faster ways of making AutoCAD do your bidding until after you master these handy little menus.

The menus are significantly different in Release 14 than in previous releases, even the otherwise similar-looking Release 13 for Windows. If you're upgrading from an earlier version of AutoCAD, take some time to tour the menus and see where things are. Playing around with the program helps you figure out where to find the commands that you need quickly without too much distraction from your actual work.

The extensive Help system in AutoCAD is another saving grace; expect to spend a great deal of time using it, especially if you don't like referring to printed manuals. Because the AutoCAD Help system is based on Microsoft's widely used Help engine (vrooommm!), you may already know how to use it. If not, what you discover in mastering the AutoCAD Release 14 Help system can help you get more out of the Help systems of other Windows programs.

Try looking up something in the Help system for AutoCAD Release 14. Then try looking up something in the Help system for Microsoft Windows 95 or NT. You can see that the interface is nearly identical.

Honey, I changed the screen!

The on-screen appearance of AutoCAD is often different for different users' AutoCAD setups. AutoCAD Release 14, even more than previous versions, is very easy to *configure* — that is, to modify, change, add to, rebuild, or whatever you want to do to it. (Hey! Maybe you too can be an AutoCAD guru, if only you configure it out! Sorry — again.)

The screen shots and descriptions in this chapter refer to the *default* version of AutoCAD — that is, the way the screen looks if you haven't changed anything about your AutoCAD setup and haven't added any third-party programs that change its appearance. If you have installed the Bonus tools, you will have an additional Bonus menu and an Internet toolbar. These additions, which are useful but not officially supported by AutoCAD, are briefly described in Chapter 16 and Chapter 17.

If someone has already changed your configuration or added a third-party program to your setup, your screen may look somewhat different from the ones depicted in the figures in this chapter (and in others). But most of what's written herein still applies, and by reading this chapter, you should be able to figure out what's different about your setup — and why.

The Magnificent Seven

The starting screen for AutoCAD Release 14 has seven parts, as shown in Figure 2-1. The screen displays all the elements found in other modern Windows programs, plus a few more. Make no mistake about it — this screen is busy! It's simply bursting with activity — and that's even before you start using it!

But don't worry; for now, you can just ignore that pesky command line and most of those enigmatic icons. (Later, they become key to your productivity.) The most important elements you need to get started are the *title bar* and *menu bar* at the top of the screen, the *status bar* at the bottom, and the *Create New Drawing dialog box* and the *drawing area* in the middle. The icons on the *toolbars* and the *command line* are accelerators that help you do your work faster after you master the basics. All the pieces of the screen make sense — really they do! — and this chapter gets you well on your way to understanding exactly what they all do.

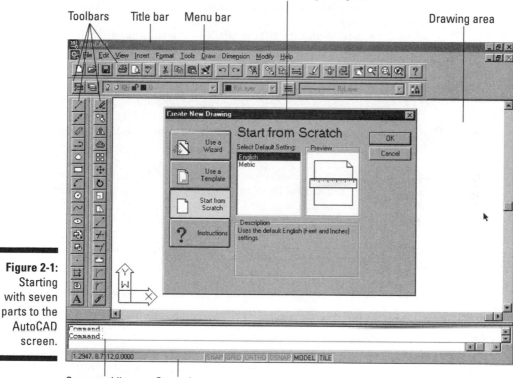

Create New Drawing dialog box

Toolbars   Title bar   Menu bar

Drawing area

Figure 2-1:
Starting
with seven
parts to the
AutoCAD
screen.

Command line   Status bar

The title bar — where everybody knows your (drawing's) name

Okay, so this is where you go to order a royal coat of arms on the rocks, right? No, nothing so esoteric, I'm afraid. The *title bar* is simply the little bar across the top of the screen that shows you the name of the drawing you're currently working on. Here's where one of the wonders of Windows comes up: If your system has sufficient memory, you can keep several drawings open at once, each in its own AutoCAD session with its own title bar visible on-screen.

You can also use a Windows 95 capability to *minimize* your AutoCAD session — that is, reduce its on-screen appearance to a button in the Windows 95 taskbar — by clicking the little button with a flat line in the upper-right corner of the screen. This button is loads of fun; you can have a very complex AutoCAD drawing open and then clear it from your screen with a single mouse click. Or you can use the button next to the minimize button, the one with a rectangle across it, to *maximize* the AutoCAD window so that it fills the screen — another great trick for multitasking with other programs. Be careful about clicking the X in the title bar, though; it shuts down AutoCAD entirely.

Bellying up to the menu bar

The *menu bar* contains the names of all the primary menus in your version of AutoCAD.

The AutoCAD Release 14 menu bar looks just like the menu bars in other Windows 95 programs. Like the AutoCAD title bar, the menu bar also contains minimize, maximize, and close buttons. Minimizing the *program title bar* reduces the whole program to a button in the taskbar; minimizing a *drawing* simply reduces it to a small, floating menu bar in the AutoCAD window. You can't have multiple drawings minimized in the AutoCAD window, so this capability doesn't really do you any good.

Don't click the X, or close, button when you actually want to minimize the overall window.

The way to have multiple AutoCAD drawings open is to have multiple AutoCAD sessions running at once. AutoCAD is designed to reuse memory in such a way that only the first session takes up a whole bunch of memory; each additional session takes up much less.

Figure 2-2 shows the menu bar for AutoCAD Release 14 with the Draw menu open. If you spend a few minutes in AutoCAD Release 14 touring the menus, opening dialog boxes, and so on, you quickly notice that Release 14 makes considerable use of dialog boxes. You find more information about using these dialog boxes in the section "Dancing with dialog boxes," later in this chapter.

Getting creative in the Create New Drawing dialog box

The *Create New Drawing dialog box,* shown in Figure 2-3, is the first thing you see when you start a new drawing in AutoCAD. The dialog box appears when you start AutoCAD by double-clicking on it or when you start AutoCAD and then choose File⇨New. (When you start AutoCAD by double-clicking a drawing or when you choose File⇨Open, the Create New Drawing dialog box doesn't appear.)

Hot-wiring the menu bar

Some standard tips and tricks for Windows are especially useful in AutoCAD. Possibly the biggest single example of a generic tip that works well for AutoCAD Release 14 is the use of keyboard shortcuts for menu choices. To fly around the menus, just press and hold the Alt key and then press the letters on your keyboard that correspond to the underlined letters on the menu bar and in the menu choices. To save your drawing, for example, press and hold the Alt key, press F for File, and then press S for Save. If all you glean from this book is to press Alt+F,S to save and to do so frequently, you've learned more than all too many other users.

As I mention in the Introduction, I give the shortcut keys in this book whenever I mention an AutoCAD or Windows menu name and command name. The names are given in the right order for you to enter them from the keyboard. For example, to open a new drawing by using the File menu's New command, hold down the Alt key and then choose File⇨New. The Create New Drawing dialog box appears.

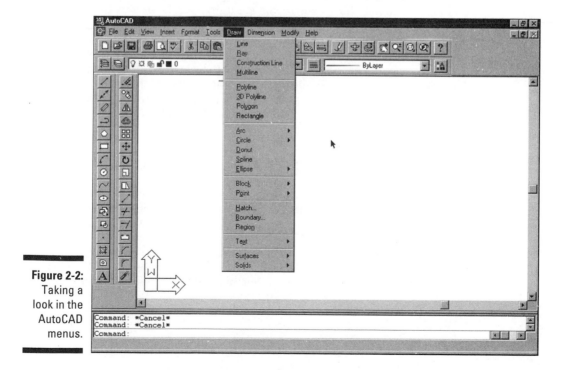

Figure 2-2:
Taking a look in the AutoCAD menus.

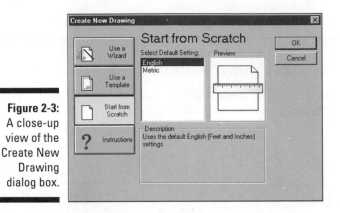

Figure 2-3:
A close-up
view of the
Create New
Drawing
dialog box.

The Create New Drawing dialog box's purpose is to help you create a new drawing that works the way you want — that is, a drawing that fits on the page, with text in proportion to the drawing, and that easily scales to larger or smaller paper. In earlier releases of AutoCAD, you had to do a bunch of separate setup steps before starting, or odds were good that your drawing wouldn't fit well on the paper, that text would be out of proportion to the rest of the drawing and to the paper, and more. With the Create New Drawing dialog box, you can use a Microsoft Office-style wizard to step through the drawing setup process, use an existing drawing as a template (the recommended option), or start from scratch.

Starting from scratch seems simplest because you don't have to make any other choices before starting to draw. However, if you choose this option, it's easy to end up with a drawing that doesn't print well and is hard to fix. The wizards may seem like the next best choice, but at this writing, they don't work all that well. The easiest way is to use a template that is already set up like the end result that you want. For more details, see Chapter 5.

Drawing on the drawing area

Although the AutoCAD *drawing area* seems to just sit there, it's actually the program's most important and valuable piece of on-screen real estate. The drawing area is where the images you create in AutoCAD take shape. And the drawing area can actively help you do your work. If you enter the correct configuration settings to set the screen up the way you want, as described in Chapter 3, the drawing area can almost magically take on the dimensions and other characteristics you need to help you create the exact drawing you want.

Two important configuration settings help determine the drawing area's effectiveness:

- ✔ **Limits:** The first of these settings is the *limits* of the drawing you're working on. To draw a football stadium, for example, the limits may be set at about 500 units (yards or meters) in the horizontal direction and 300 units (yards or meters) in the vertical direction. After you set these limits, the drawing area acts as a 500- by 300-unit grid into which you can place objects. (Footballs, hot dog vendors, and rabid fans excepted, of course.) Figure 2-4 shows a drawing in the drawing area.

- ✔ **Snap setting:** The second important setting for the drawing area is the *snap* setting, which causes the mouse pointer to gravitate to certain points on-screen. If you're working on your football stadium and set the snap setting to ten units, for example, you can easily draw end lines and sidelines that fall on 10-yard intervals. To draw in the seating area, however, you may want to set snap to a finer setting, such as one unit, or turn off snap altogether so that you can start your line anywhere you want. No matter what changes you make, the point is to make the drawing area help you do your work.

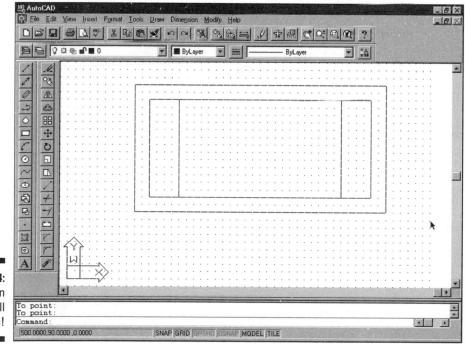

Figure 2-4: Canadian football rules!

As you can see, you can make the drawing area work absolute wonders for your drawings — but only if you set up AutoCAD correctly in the first place. If you don't configure these settings correctly, however, the drawing area can become really, really mad at you and may even fight back — with potentially devastating results to your drawings. Wrong settings can, for example, turn perfectly acceptable on-screen text into microscopic — and unreadable — ant tracks on paper. But don't freak out just yet: Valuable setup information awaits your discovery in Chapters 4 and 5 of this book.

The drawing area appears essentially the same in all versions of AutoCAD. (Well, what do you expect from a big blank area in the middle of the screen?) Skip ahead to Figure 2-7, which shows the drawing area in AutoCAD Release 14 with a drawing already created inside it.

Looking for Mr. Status Bar

The *status bar,* at the very bottom of the screen, tells you several important bits of information about the drawing you're working on, some of which may not make sense at first glance. These elements include the current *coordinates* of the mouse cursor; whether *snap, grid,* and *ortho* modes are on or off; whether running object snaps are on or off; whether you're in *model space* or *paper space;* and whether *tile* mode is on. (What all of these things mean are explained briefly in the next few paragraphs and in depth as you go through the book.) Figure 2-5 pinpoints these areas of the status bar. If you're new to the program, these areas bear some explanation. The following list does just that:

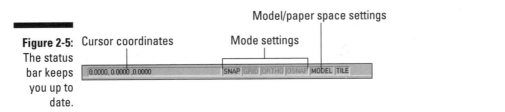

Figure 2-5: The status bar keeps you up to date.

Coordinates of the cursor: Model/paper space settings — Mode settings — Cursor coordinates

`0.0000, 0.0000 ,0.0000`   `SNAP` `GRID` `ORTHO` `OSNAP` `MODEL` `TILE`

✔ **Coordinates of the cursor:** The current *cursor coordinates* are extremely important in CAD (computer-aided design, as you may recall) because they actually relate the drawing to the real-world object or scene the drawing represents. In a CAD drawing of a soft drink can, for example, the top of the can should be about 5 inches, or 12.5 centimeters, from the bottom of the can. After you set up AutoCAD correctly for your drawing, the cursor coordinates on the status bar reflect the real-life dimensions of the object or scene you're working on. You can customize the number of digits displayed for the coordinates.

If you're new to AutoCAD, try rolling the cursor around the drawing area to watch the cursor coordinates update. (After that, you can go out and watch the grass grow for even more excitement!)

If the coordinates in the lower left-hand corner of the screen are grayed out, double-click them until they appear in dark lettering that updates when you move the cursor.

✔ **Snap, Grid, and Ortho modes:** As described in Chapter 3, you can bring order to the AutoCAD drawing area by telling it to *snap* the cursor to certain regularly spaced "hot spots," enabling you to more easily draw objects a fixed distance apart; by making the drawing area display a *grid* of dots to align objects with; and by setting *Ortho* mode, which makes drawing straight horizontal and vertical lines easy. The snap, grid, and ortho buttons appear on the status bar in dark text if the mode is on, in gray text if the mode is off.

✔ **Running Object Snap mode:** A *running object snap* is a setting that causes the cursor to snap to specific locations on objects that you've drawn, such as corners and centers of shapes. This feature is nice to have turned on sometimes and a real pain to have on at other times. (For example, if you're trying to click a point near but not on a corner, and AutoCAD keeps snapping to the corner, you're going to get frustrated.) In Release 14, you can easily set the features you want to snap to and then turn the whole set on or off with a single click, as explained in Chapter 7. This capability makes using running object snaps much more practical.

✔ **Model/Paper Space and Tile modes:** Briefly, *model space* is where you create and modify objects; *paper space* enables you to arrange elements in your drawing for printout. Stick with model space until you master it; then learn paper space to create multiple views on objects you've drawn. Tile mode is a system variable that controls model space and paper space; you turn Tile mode off to turn paper space on. (This seemingly backward setup is necessary for compatibility with previous releases of AutoCAD that didn't know anything about paper space.) See Chapter 13 for fuller descriptions — in excruciating detail — of these settings.

✔ **Time:** Unlike previous versions of AutoCAD, the status bar no longer shows you the time, because the Windows 95 taskbar does that instead. (Of course, if you've hidden the taskbar to get more drawing space, you're out of time!)

Better living with power toolbars

The most important elements in making AutoCAD Release 14 do your bidding quickly are the various *toolbars* that enable you to enter commands quickly and control how you draw, what you draw, and maybe even whether you're quick on the draw. The following sections describe how to use tool-bars in the default setup that's standard for AutoCAD, how to move the toolbars, and how to customize the toolbars.

Toolbars exist to hold icons, so they're also called *icon menus* (not the menu of 3-D surfaces in Release 12) or *icon toolbars*. Even if you use Release 12 for DOS, you may have toolbars already as a third-party add-on to AutoCAD. The toolbars in Release 14 are standardized and well-integrated into the program, two significant advantages.

All the AutoCAD Release 14 toolbars provide *tool tips,* an indispensable feature that identifies each icon by its function . . . if you lean on it a bit. Simply hold the mouse pointer over an icon — no need to click it — and, like magic, the name of the icon appears in a little yellow box below the icon. The tool tip feature incorporates yet another component that can be easy to miss: A longer description of the icon's function appears in the status bar, at the very bottom of the screen. If the identifying name and the description at the bottom of the screen aren't enough to tell you what the icon does, you can always bring in a little "out-of-town muscle" — in other words, look it up in the Help system, which is described in the section "Fun with F1," later in this chapter.

Figure 2-6 shows the tool tip, tool description, and help for the Undo icon on the standard toolbar. The tool tip identifies the icon, and the tool descrip-tion in the status bar gives a longer explanation of the icon's function. If AutoCAD were to suddenly talk when you were stuck and say, "Icon help!," it wouldn't be exaggerating much!

Use the AutoCAD Release 14 menus as your first stop in getting to know the program. Then begin clicking icons for the functions you use most, and, finally, move on to the command line equivalents for the fastest power use.

Setting the standard in toolbars

AutoCAD ships with toolbars in a default setup:

- ✔ Standard toolbar on top, just below the menu bar.
- ✔ Object Properties toolbar beneath the Standard toolbar.
- ✔ Draw toolbar (vertical) on the far left edge of the screen.
- ✔ Modify toolbar vertically aligned just inside the Draw toolbar.

The picture of the AutoCAD screen in Figure 2-1 at the start of this chapter shows the default toolbar setup. Use this figure for reference in case you change your toolbar setup and want to go back to the original!

Tool tip   Help for the tool

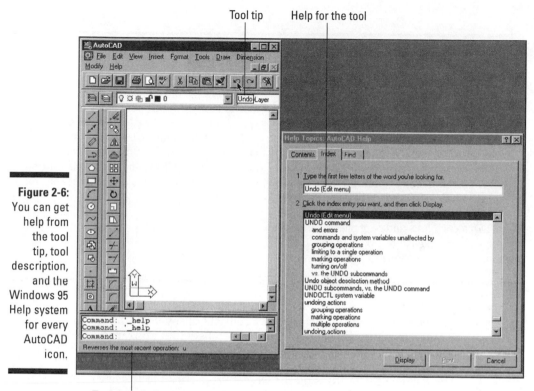

Figure 2-6:
You can get
help from
the tool
tip, tool
description,
and the
Windows 95
Help system
for every
AutoCAD
icon.

Tool description

The toolbar setup in Release 14 is subtly different from earlier releases: In Release 14, all toolbars are initially *docked* (that means snuggled up against the edge of the screen, with part of the border around the toolbar removed to save space). In the previous release, the Standard and Object Properties toolbars at the top were docked, but the Draw and Modify toolbars on the side were floating. The new approach looks better but makes it easy to miss the fact that the toolbars have names and that they can be moved around and even modified.

The Standard toolbar helps you quickly access a number of file management, drawing management, and view functions. Using the Standard toolbar enables you to change which drawing you're working on by clicking the Save and Open icons, fix a mistake by clicking the Undo or Redo icon, and move around in your drawing by clicking the Pan, Zoom In, and Zoom Out icons. You can even go to the World Wide Web with the Launch Browser icon.

Looking at layers

In AutoCAD, a drawing consists of one or more *layers.* Layers are similar to those clear sheets of mylar (not plastic, *The Graduate* notwithstanding) that you place on top of one another to build up a complete drawing. (You may remember something like this from a textbook about human anatomy, with the skeleton on one sheet, the muscles on the next sheet that you laid over the skeleton, and so on until you built up a complete picture of the human body. That is, if your mom didn't remove some of the more grown-up sections.)

Layers are the most important organizational tool for your drawing, and knowing which layer you're currently working in is vitally important. The Object Properties bar lists the layer name after several icons that tell you things about the current layer. The initial layer in a drawing that hasn't yet had layers added to it is named *0* (zero).

The Object Properties bar actually consists of several different elements lumped together. By using the drop-down lists that appear on the Object Properties bar, you can change the current layer and modify its characteristics, change your drawing's colors, and change the linetype used to draw objects. You can use the buttons on the Object Properties bar to view or change the properties that relate to text and to different objects in your drawing. Although all these capabilities are highly desirable, the ways in which their functions differ can be highly confusing. The capability to change layers quickly, however, is well worth the price of admission by itself. (See the sidebar "Looking at layers" for a somewhat technical description of AutoCAD layers.)

The Draw toolbar roughly matches the functions available in the AutoCAD Draw menu. The Draw toolbar may be the one you use most when starting a new drawing; it pulls together frequently used drawing functions into a single place. It gives you quick access to several kinds of lines, basic shapes, hatching, and text. If a drawing function that you use frequently isn't already on the Draw toolbar, consider adding it by using the customization capability described later in this chapter.

Like the Draw toolbar, the Modify toolbar is patterned after its namesake menu, in this case the Modify menu. This setup is different than in Release 13, which introduced toolbars but had less correspondence between the toolbars and the menus. In use, the Modify toolbar is the kissing cousin of the Draw toolbar and may be the toolbar you use most frequently when you edit an existing drawing. The Erase icon is right at the top, followed by different options for creating new geometry from existing parts of the drawing and for adjusting lines and shapes that you have already added to the drawing. As with the Draw toolbar, consider customizing the Modify toolbar if a modification function that you use frequently isn't there.

The default toolbar setup is intended to expose as many of the frequently used commands in AutoCAD as possible in a convenient and easy-to-access yet unobtrusive format. Although you can move and even customize the toolbars, you may not want to; part of the value of the toolbars is that you become accustomed to clicking key icons quickly and without conscious effort. If you move the toolbars around, your "muscle memory" of where your most-used icons are must be retrained each time.

Try moving each of the toolbars around and then moving each back to where it started. I found the toolbars pretty easy to move, with the exception of the command line, which can float as well (good), but is harder than the others to get back into place (bad).

The icons in the default setup of the Release 14 toolbars reflect some of the new and changed functions in AutoCAD. For example, new features that have been given icons in the Standard toolbar are the Match Properties icon, which makes setting object properties consistently much easier, and Launch Browser, which quickly launches your favorite World Wide Web browser. In the Draw toolbar, the Hatch and MTEXT (for Multiline Text) icons are not new but represent significantly different functions.

Toolbars on the move

You can easily move the toolbars around the screen — just grab a corner and drag. As you drag the toolbar, it changes shape to reflect how it would appear if you were to let it go right then and there — a nice feature, but one that takes a little getting used to.

Actually, moving toolbars around may be a little easier in concept than in practice. Toolbars don't really have easy-to-grab borders, as do windows and dialog boxes — just little strips around the edges that you can grab with the mouse if you try hard. You may need a little practice to find just the right spot on the edge to click and drag.

You can move toolbars into either a *docked* or a *floating* position. When you move a toolbar right up against any edge of the drawing area, it docks; the toolbar seems to become part of the border that AutoCAD puts around the drawing, and the drawing area gets redrawn to exclude the area where the docked toolbar is. All the toolbars are docked in the AutoCAD default startup configuration, so if you weren't reading this paragraph, you might think that the toolbars are stuck in place.

AutoCAD also allows *floating toolbars* — toolbars that "float" over the program window. A floating toolbar is any toolbar not pushed up into a docked position against the edge of the screen. Instead of disappearing behind whatever window you clicked most recently, it continues to be visible, or to "float" in front of the drawing area. For me personally, floating toolbars and dialog boxes are more of a pain than a pleasure; they constantly get in the way as I try to draw or pan and zoom around a drawing. But if you like this sort of thing, AutoCAD is more than ready to accommodate you. Figure 2-7 shows the AutoCAD window with the toolbars rearranged and the Draw and Modify toolbars floating, as they were in Release 13.

Knowing a couple of tricks about floating toolbars is useful: When a toolbar floats, a title appears on it, which makes it take up a little more screen space. And some toolbars dock well only in certain places; for example, the Standard toolbar is too long to dock well on the sides of the AutoCAD window, and the Object Properties toolbar's pull-down menus only work if the toolbar is kept horizontal; you can't dock it vertically on the left or right edge of the AutoCAD windows and still use the menus. Here are a few tips:

✔ Undo doesn't work for moved toolbars. Make sure that you take a moment to notice where a toolbar is before you grab it in case you want to move it back to where it started.

✔ Hold down the Control key while floating a toolbar to keep it from docking.

✔ Drag the bottom edge of a toolbar to change its layout — for instance, from a horizontal strip to a vertical one.

✔ The Windows 95 toolbars are draggable and droppable, too. Try resizing the taskbar (the one at the bottom of the screen with the Start menu in it). Then try moving it to different locations on the screen. This drag-and-drop capability is just one of the ways in which AutoCAD Release 14 is consistent with Windows 95.

Toolbars to the nth degree

Though most people are likely to take the four toolbars in the default setup as a given, 17 toolbars are actually available in AutoCAD, and turning each of them on and off is pretty easy. Choose View⇨Toolbars. The Toolbars dialog box appears (see Figure 2-8). With the Toolbars dialog box, you can turn toolbars on and off, select from among named groups of turned-on toolbars, change the button size, and toggle tool tips on and off.

No one set of toolbars is right for everyone, so start out by just using the default set. As you become more expert, experiment with all the toolbars until you know which ones work for you. Basically, the more time you spend using a given type of AutoCAD function, the more good it may do you to have the corresponding toolbar turned on while you work.

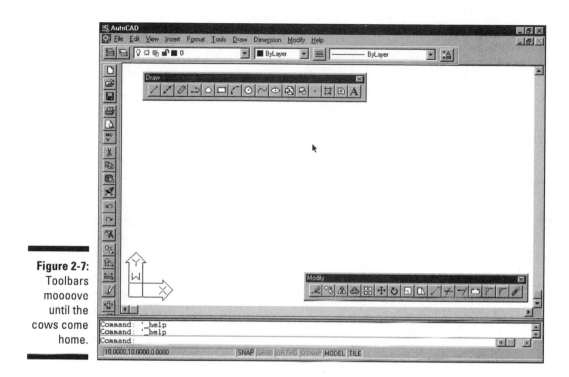

Figure 2-7:
Toolbars
moooove
until the
cows come
home.

The AutoCAD screen gets pretty crowded when you start turning on toolbars. Consider getting a fast video card that supports high resolutions and a big monitor to display results on. (If you display at high resolution on a medium-sized monitor, everything is small; you can get eyestrain trying to find details and read text.)

To make text appear larger on your screen, right-click on the desktop; a menu appears. Choose Properties. Within the dialog box that appears, choose the Settings tab and then change Font size from Small Fonts to Large Fonts. Text will appear larger.

Custom toolbars

The (nearly) final frontier of setting up the AutoCAD toolbars to meet your needs is the capability to customize them. I'm not going to describe this procedure in detail; I'm just telling you that it can be done. If you want to modify the toolbars so that they have just the icons you want on them, click the Customize button in the Toolbars dialog box. You can move icons among toolbars until you have the configuration just the way you want it.

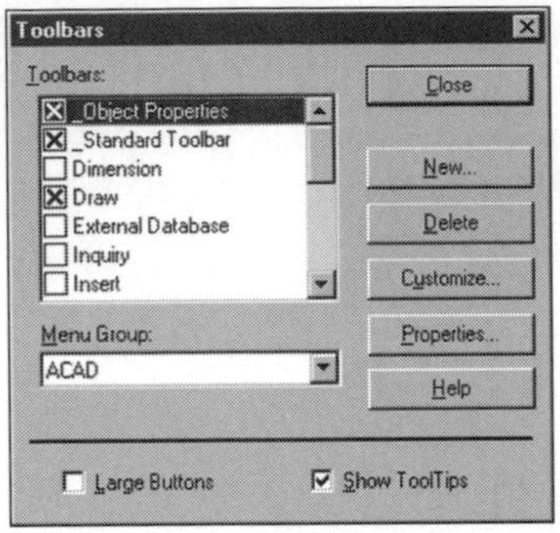

Figure 2-8:
The
Toolbars
dialog box
lets you
turn on and
drop in
toolbars.

Do try to get to a stable state for your AutoCAD display window so that your subconscious can start taking over icon clicking without troubling your overburdened conscious mind.

The actual final frontier is that the icon population, like everything else in AutoCAD, is extensible. You can create custom icons and assign them to any function you want. This capability is covered in the AutoCAD documentation. Even if you never go to this extreme yourself, you may well find yourself getting new toolbars with custom icons as part of add-on applications that you buy for AutoCAD.

Who are we and why are we here? Like many other capabilities in AutoCAD, being able to customize icons can help make you forget what your purpose is. Are you using AutoCAD to do design and drafting or some other kind of real work, or has AutoCAD become an end in itself? Don't get so caught up in the fine points of AutoCAD customization that the amount of time you spend outweighs any possible benefits.

Commanding the command line

The *command line* is a unique feature of AutoCAD and is probably the hardest for new users to get used to. Windows users who thought that they had escaped the dreaded DOS command line may be especially surprised to find a command line still lurking smack dab at the heart of AutoCAD. Yet the command line is actually a very handy tool for increasing speed and productivity in AutoCAD. Figure 2-9 shows the command line as it appears after you first open AutoCAD, which is skulking away down at the bottom of the screen, hoping you don't notice it below that big, open drawing area.

If you have an 800 x 600 screen or larger and like to use the command line, I suggest that you make the command line taller. If you have the Windows 95 taskbar hidden, you can make the command line six lines instead of its normal three without obscuring any of the icons in the default toolbar set.

To make the command line bigger, just rest the mouse over the top edge of the command line; it turns into a vertical two-headed arrow. Click down the mouse button and hold, and then drag the top edge of the command line upward.

Figure 2-9:
The
AutoCAD
Release 14
command
line.

```
Command:
Command: _toolbar
Command:
```

If you don't like to use the command line, you can minimize it. Just drag the top edge of the command line window downward until it's down to a single line.

What is it? Why is it here?

The command line dates back to a long-ago time in the mists of computer history, when computer screens that used graphics were still relatively new. CAD users used just one main, text-only screen for communicating with the program; a second, graphics-only screen showed the results of the commands they entered. The fairly recent adoption of graphical screens, *graphical user interfaces* (or *GUIs*), and direct manipulation of on-screen elements by using a mouse has relegated the AutoCAD command line to the status of a lost relic from the "good ol' days" of computerdom. Yet even today, the command line, when mastered, can have a strongly positive effect on productivity.

The command line is especially challenging if your main experience in using PCs is with Windows rather than DOS. (DOS users actually have a rare advantage here.) The difference between the AutoCAD command line and the hated DOS command line that most Windows users try to avoid is that the AutoCAD command line need not be your main vehicle for interacting with AutoCAD. You can instead use the menu bar and icons to find and enter most of your commands, and use the command line primarily as an accelerator to quickly enter those commands you use most.

By using the command line, you can quickly instruct AutoCAD to perform functions via your keyboard that otherwise require opening several menus and navigating your way through one or more dialog boxes. And, unfortunately, you must use the command line to carry out some functions that you can't perform in any other way. (Drat!) If you treat it as a productivity tool and an adjunct to the menus whenever possible, however, the command line actually helps you more than it frustrates you. (Well, most of you, anyway.)

Using the command line

AutoCAD actually makes finding out how to use the command line fairly easy. After you choose a command from the menus, for example, AutoCAD echoes that command on the command line, preceding the command with an underscore character: _DDRMODES, for example, is how the AutoCAD command line displays the command to open the Drawing Aids dialog box.

Watch the command line as you use the menus and dialog boxes and memorize those commands that you use most — or write 'em down if you're a card-carrying member of the MTV generation (short attention span and all that, you know. . . .). Then enter the command directly from the command line whenever you need to use that function swiftly.

In Release 14, along with making the strongest possible commitment to Windows 95, Autodesk has actually improved the command line. You can now use the arrow keys to move up in the list of commands that you have previously entered; each time you press the up-arrow key, another previously entered command appears. When the command you want is in your sights, edit it if needed and then press Return to execute it (so to speak). This function, similar to the DOSKEY program that helps users manage DOS commands, should further improve command-line productivity.

You can bring up a text window with command line contents in it. (You can also panic really inexperienced AutoCAD users by pulling this trick on their screens when they're not looking!) Just press F2 at any time and a large text window will appear, as shown in Figure 2-10; press F2 again and it will vanish. (The "magic key" used to be F1, but Autodesk finally yielded to Microsoft's insistence that F1 means "help.")

Unlike in DOS versions of AutoCAD, you can scroll up and down in the text window through all the commands you've entered during your entire current session — not just the last several that are all the DOS-crowd can access this way. Just press F2 again to return the command line to its previous size and position.

When you scroll up to choose a previous command from the AutoCAD command line, only commands that you typed are available, not commands that you generated by making menu choices or changing settings in a dialog box. And when you do press Return to choose a command, you then must press the down-arrow key if you want to get back to the bottom of the "stack" of commands; in DOSKEY and some similar utilities, you drop back to the bottom of the stack as soon as you enter a command.

The way AutoCAD handles the command stack is the same as the way Windows NT does it, so if you ever upgrade to Windows NT, you'll know what to do.

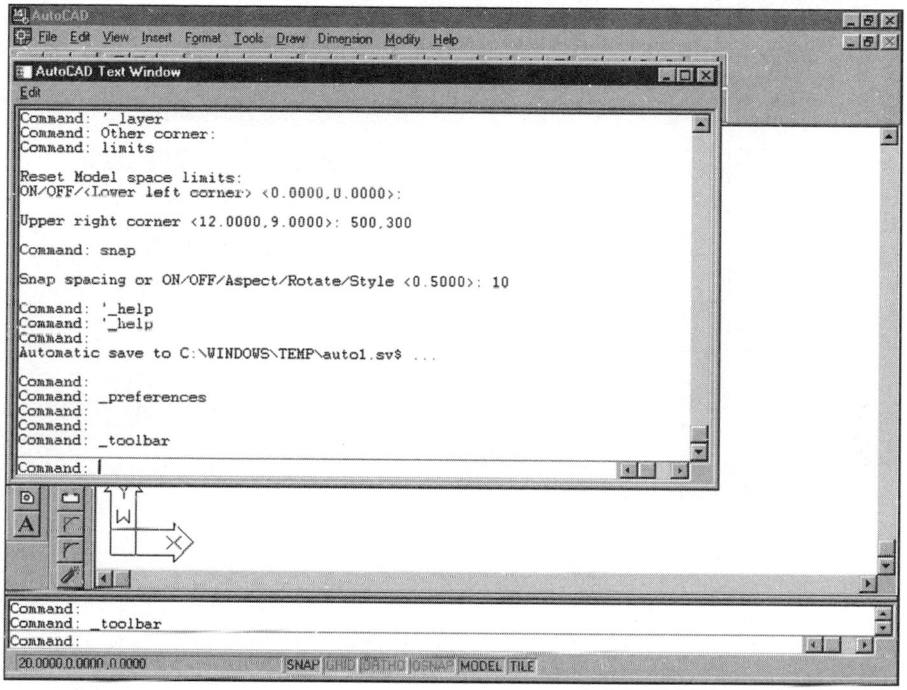

Figure 2-10:
The
command
line that ate
Detroit.

A Bright Light and a Dim Bulb

One of the biggest difficulties in using AutoCAD is the tradeoff between ease-of-use features, such as toolbars, and the ever-present need for more screen space. Two optional AutoCAD features take up a great deal of screen space but differ radically in the value they offer you. One of these screen hogs is not strictly necessary but is highly useful; the other is clumsy and hard to use, but it's a real necessity for running some older programs.

Taking the aerial view

The *aerial view* is a feature idea borrowed from third-party utilities and included as a built-in feature of AutoCAD Release 14. The aerial view is flexible and powerful — but, unfortunately, like a toolbar, it takes up valuable space in the drawing area. And, like a floating toolbar, it floats on top of everything; if you open a dialog box, the aerial view (which is also sort of like a dialog box) pops up right on top of it — plop! But the aerial view is truly indispensable when you're first investigating the Pan and Zoom features and otherwise navigating your way into and out of complicated drawings. Figure 2-11 shows the Aerial View window.

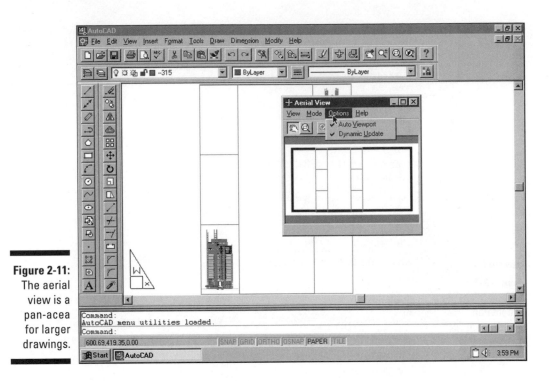

Figure 2-11:
The aerial
view is a
pan-acea
for larger
drawings.

The aerial view hasn't changed much in Release 14, but the need for it is reduced. Release 14 supports a real-time pan and zoom feature that provides instant feedback and may, in many cases, be more convenient than the aerial view. But for large drawings — whether large in extent or just in drawing complexity and file size — real-time pan and zoom may not be enough. Having the aerial view in your bag of tricks to use with big drawings is a real plus.

Because aerial view takes up so much screen space, you'll probably want to turn it on and off frequently. The button with the airplane-shaped icon about two-thirds of the way across the Standard toolbar turns aerial view on and off; just click the button to make the Aerial View dialog box appear and disappear. Or from the command line, enter DSVIEWER to make the Aerial View come and go.

Snapping to the side-screen menu

Figure 2-12 shows the *side-screen menu,* or *screen menu* for short. The side-screen menu has largely served its purpose and is on the way out. It will undoubtedly hang on for a while, however, because many people are used to it and because so many third-party programs place their options in this menu.

KEYBOARD

Menus versus the command line

Some experienced AutoCAD users — especially those who are long-time DOS users — think that menus, icons, and so on are for wimps. New users, on the other hand, may want to get rid of that seemingly annoying command line altogether. But each feature actually has a useful purpose all its own.

For starting out in AutoCAD and for parts of the program that you use occasionally (for some people, that's the whole darn program), menus and other parts of the graphical user interface are great. You can just mouse around on-screen until you locate the exact command, icon, or dialog box you need.

To get fully up to speed in AutoCAD, however, you really do need to use the keyboard to enter your most common commands. (Unless, of course, your typing speed makes a dead tortoise look swift in comparison.) So a good tactic is to memorize any commands you use frequently that aren't represented by an icon in the toolbars displayed on-screen and then use the command line to enter them without navigating your way through the menus.

The side-screen menu is used extensively by programs written in the special AutoCAD program language, AutoLISP, and by *digitizers,* which are drawing tablets that you use to control AutoCAD as well as for drawing. Digitizers tend to incorporate drivers that use side-screen menus to control the program. A healthy debate continues between those who love and hate digitizers, but for most users, they're on the way out, too. (Digitizers are great for tracing paper drawings and for freehand sketching, but as a way to drive AutoCAD itself, they're not worth the trouble to buy, hook up, learn, and use.)

RELEASE 14

14

With Release 14's new support for scanned objects (such as old paper drawings and freehand sketches), the need to trace the outlines by hand to bring them into AutoCAD may fade fast.

WARNING!

The AutoCAD dialog boxes, Help files, and documentation refer to the side-screen menu as the "screen menu." This name is kind of dumb, because all the AutoCAD menus are on the screen; so just think "side-screen menu" and you'll have no problems.

If you do need the side-screen menu, it's always available. Just choose Tools⇨Preferences to see the Preferences dialog box. Click the Display tab and then click in the top line of the Drawing window parameters area to turn on the Display AutoCAD screen menu in drawing window option. (If you like ancient history, you may be interested to know that the initial choices on the screen menu are the same as the menu choices from an AutoCAD release many years back. If you're *really* interested in ancient history, you're probably running that release right now!)

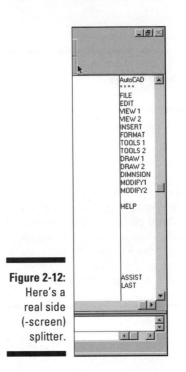

AutoCAD
* * * *
FILE
EDIT
VIEW 1
VIEW 2
INSERT
FORMAT
TOOLS 1
TOOLS 2
DRAW 1
DRAW 2
DIMNSION
MODIFY1
MODIFY2

HELP

ASSIST
LAST

Figure 2-12:
Here's a
real side
(-screen)
splitter.

What Really Makes AutoCAD Tick?

In reading about and using AutoCAD, you encounter two topics frequently: *system variables,* which are very old, and *dialog boxes,* which in their current, highly usable forms are relatively new. System variables and dialog boxes are closely related, because they both affect the settings that control the way AutoCAD works. Understanding them and how they work together can dramatically speed your ascent to proficiency in AutoCAD.

Setting system variables

System variables are settings that AutoCAD checks before it decides how to do something. If you set the system variable SAVETIME to 10, for example, AutoCAD automatically saves your file every ten minutes; if you set SAVETIME to 60, the time between saves is one hour. Hundreds of system variables control the operations of AutoCAD.

Of these hundreds of system variables in AutoCAD, more than 40 system variables control dimensioning alone. (*Dimensioning* is AutoCAD's automatic generation of labels that show the distance between two points. Different professions have very different standards for how dimensions on their drawings should look. Using dimensions is described in detail in Chapter 12.)

To change the name of a system variable, just type its name at the AutoCAD command prompt. The capability to change a system variable directly is very powerful, and knowing the names and appropriate range of settings for the system variables that you use regularly is worth the time and effort. But expecting you to remember literally hundreds of variables, how they work, and how they interact with one another is just too much — even for all you "power users" out there. This is where dialog boxes come in.

To see all the system variables in AutoCAD as shown in Figure 2-13, type **SETvar ?** at the AutoCAD command prompt.

Sometimes, watching AutoCAD work as you use it is like having X-ray vision into the workings of the program. Even as you use a modern-looking program with menus, dialog boxes, and icons, you can watch AutoCAD turn your mouse clicks into typed commands and system variable settings on the AutoCAD command line. At startup, you can even watch the program load its menus file and then display the menus. Watching AutoCAD work can be hours of fun if you're kind of strange and don't have any real work to do. But, more seriously, every one of the operations you see represents another area where third-party developers can — and most likely will — customize the look, feel, and function of AutoCAD.

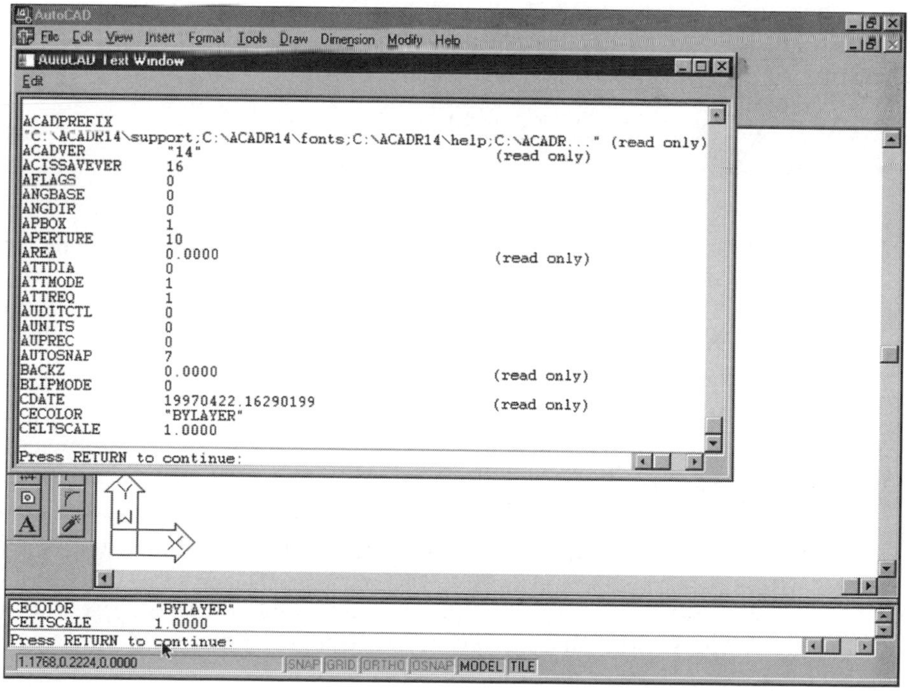

Figure 2-13:
The first few dozen system variables in AutoCAD.

```
ACADPREFIX
"C:\ACADR14\support;C:\ACADR14\fonts;C:\ACADR14\help;C:\ACADR..." (read only)
ACADVER        "14"                                (read only)
ACISSAVEVER    16
AFLAGS         0
ANGBASE        0
ANGDIR         0
APBOX          1
APERTURE       10
AREA           0.0000                              (read only)
ATTDIA         0
ATTMODE        1
ATTREQ         1
AUDITCTL       0
AUNITS         0
AUPREC         0
AUTOSNAP       7
BACKZ          0.0000                              (read only)
BLIPMODE       0
CDATE          19970422.16290199                   (read only)
CECOLOR        "BYLAYER"
CELTSCALE      1.0000
Press RETURN to continue:
```

```
CECOLOR        "BYLAYER"
CELTSCALE      1.0000
Press RETURN to continue:
```

Dancing with dialog boxes

The AutoCAD dialog boxes are an easy way to control collections of related system variables, much like a dashboard controls a car's functions. By using dialog boxes, you can handle all the related settings that may otherwise be confusing if you changed them directly through system variables.

The best single example of the power inherent in using dialog boxes to set system variables can be demonstrated through the set of dialog boxes that enable you to manage dimensions. Because you can specify so many differ-ent elements about each dimension, AutoCAD enables you to create *dimen-sion styles,* which are named groups of dimension settings that you can choose from a pull-down list. The Dimension Styles dialog box, as shown in Figure 2-14, controls dimension styles.

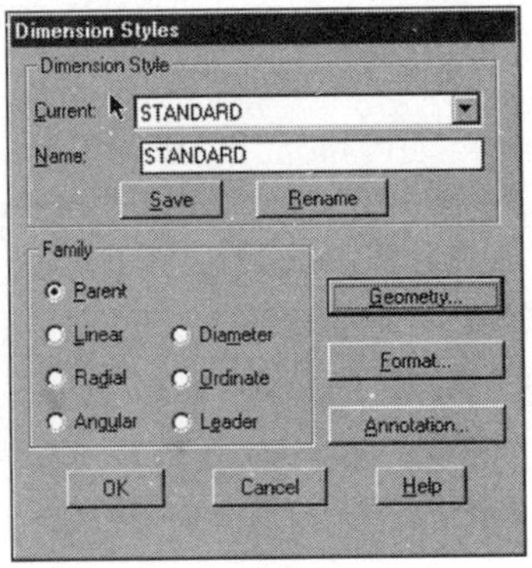

Figure 2-14: Setting your dimensions with style(s).

To access this dialog box, choose Format⇨Dimension Style or type **Ddim** on the command line and press Enter. Each of the options on the right side of the Dimension Styles dialog box — Geometry, Format, and Annotation — opens another dialog box, each of which in turn controls several more system variables.

Fun with F1

AutoCAD Release 14 features a powerful Help system, shown in Figure 2-15, based on the Windows Help system. The Release 14 Help includes a search-able database of topics, information on how to use Help, a quick tour of AutoCAD, and an overview of what's new in Release 14.

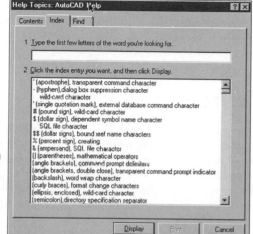

Figure 2-15:
Your
AutoCAD
SOS.

AutoCAD Release 14 includes a full documentation set, accessible through the Help system. Click the Index tab in Help to see the documents available, which include a tutorial, an ActiveX guide, and a guide to the AutoCAD Release 14 bonus tools.

Release 14 even goes beyond the bounds of the AutoCAD program and Windows 95 to give you help. You can install a CD-ROM called *AutoCAD Learning Assistance* that now comes with AutoCAD. You choose AutoCAD Learning Assistance from the AutoCAD Release 14 Help menu, but it actually runs as a separate program. Also available from the Help menu is a Connect to Internet option. It links you to an Autodesk Web site with frequently updated help information about AutoCAD Release 14. For more information on both options, keep reading.

Help yourself?

You can even annotate Help and put bookmarks in it. (No, don't go trying to shove a paper bookmark into your screen; these are electronic bookmarks.) Bookmarks are probably worthwhile only if you make a real project out of creating them and then distribute the resulting bulked-up Help file to all the other AutoCAD users in your organization. Then, of course, you must be prepared to redo them — that's the bookmarks, not the other AutoCAD users! — the next time you get a good idea about what should be bookmarked. Check out the Bookmark entry in the AutoCAD Help system if you really want (and think you need) instructions on how to use bookmarks; because most of you are unlikely to use bookmarks in the normal course of human events, they're not covered any further in this book.

AutoCAD Help, accessed through the F1 key or Help⇨AutoCAD Help Topics, is context-sensitive: If you access it in the middle of executing a command, Help for that specific command appears first. (You can then navigate to anyplace else in the Help system.)

Extra-sensitive Help

No, *extra-sensitive Help* isn't some kind of new, improved psychotherapy. It's just another term for *context-sensitive Help,* which is probably the most useful kind of Help in AutoCAD Release 14. You access context-sensitive Help in AutoCAD in two ways: by pressing F1 or by clicking the Help button in a dialog box. And if you're in the middle of entering a command, you can access Help by pressing the F1 key. Help then appears for that command.

If you've used Release 13 for Windows, the Help system in Release 14 isn't much of a shock to you; it's very much like Release 13, with just a few changes in buttons and the "look" of individual Help panels. (Plus, as one would hope, some updated content!) But if you've never used a Windows version of AutoCAD before, you're in for a treat. The Help system is a major asset of Windows versions of AutoCAD.

If you simply hold the mouse cursor over the Circle icon in the Draw floating toolbar and then press F1, for example, the Help screen titled Contents appears. But if you click the Circle icon, a command appears on the command line. If you press F1 to choose Help at this point, a specific Help screen for the CIRCLE command appears. Figure 2-16 shows AutoCAD Help for the CIRCLE command.

Figure 2-16: Get Help going around in circles.

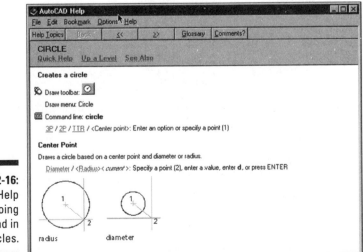

It's not unreasonable to think that, if AutoCAD knows enough to put up the tool tip for CIRCLE when the cursor is over the Circle icon, it should know enough to get Help for circles if you press F1 at that point. But no luck; maybe next release!

F1 doesn't work when you have a dialog box open, either, but you can access Help for dialog boxes by pressing the Help button in a dialog box. This Help feature is otherwise identical to Help for other parts of AutoCAD.

Help runs as a separate task in AutoCAD. Any time you use Help in Release 14, you can keep Help open in the background and return directly to the main AutoCAD screen by pressing the Alt+Tab key combination to cycle through your currently running tasks.

A typical Help screen contains several live areas, which enable you to move around in the Help system, as well as dead areas, which just kinda lie there and contain information. (If the latter start to decompose a bit, don't worry; no one can smell anything in cyberspace anyway!) The live areas of the Help screen include the following elements (refer to Figure 2-17 for a look at some of them):

✔ **Menu bar:** Each Help window has its own menu bar that you can use to control Help in general. The most important function here is probably the Print Topic option on the File menu.

✔ **Toolbar:** If you were most recently in the Display tab, Help even has its own toolbar for use in navigating through the Help system by using the following buttons:

- The *Help Topics* button opens a window that enables you to type in an entry or select the entry from a scrolling list. You can then click the Display button in the Search window to move to a secondary topic.

- The *Back* button returns you to previously viewed Help screens visited during the current session. Back is something you're likely to use often, because it keeps you from feeling lost in the Help system.

- The << button takes you to the topic just before the current topic in some kind of logical or alphabetical order which I can't quite figure out.

- The >> button takes you to the topic just after the current topic in the same unknown order as for the << button.

- The *Glossary* button displays a glossary of AutoCAD terms.

✔ **Live icons:** Some of the icons in the Help screens are considered *live* — that is, they do something. (Unlike some of the winners in the last election!) Holding the mouse pointer over one of these icons turns the pointer into a hand with a raised index finger (a rude gesture in some cultures), indicating that something happens after you click the mouse button at that point:

- Clicking the *Quick Help* label in the upper area of the Help screen gives you a quick update as to how the buttons in the Help toolbar work.

- Clicking the *Up a Level* label next to Quick Help moves you up a level in the Contents hierarchy.

- Clicking the *See Also* label next to Up a Level opens a pop-up window containing a list of topics related to the currently selected item.

✔ **Solid green underlined text:** Text underlined in solid green is linked to other topics related to the one described in the current Help screen. Clicking this text opens a new window that gives you additional information.

✔ **Dotted green underlined text:** Text underlined in a dotted green line opens a pop-up box containing a definition of the underlined term.

Indexing your way to better Help

You can access the same Help screens a couple of other ways. Pressing F1 whenever you're not in the middle of any specific command or choosing Help⇨AutoCAD Help topics opens the Help Topics dialog box with the Index tab selected. This tab enables you to find help for AutoCAD menu items, for commands, or for system variables, as shown in Figure 2-17. This feature is pretty useful, and just clicking around in it is a good way to get familiar with some basics of AutoCAD.

Finding happiness in Help

Clicking the Find tab within Help opens a dialog box containing a long, scrolling list of topics. Unfortunately, this dialog box contains literally hundreds of topics, and finding the one you need can be very difficult unless you already know the command name, menu name, or system variable name you want. (The first time you use this dialog box, you have to tell AutoCAD how to set it up. I recommend that you choose Maximize Search Capabilities rather than Minimize Database Size, because if you need help, you really need it.)

If you harbor only the vaguest idea of the topic you seek — say, different ways to output your drawing file — you can expect to spend a great deal of time clicking around in the Find tab of the AutoCAD Help dialog box. As you discover more details about how AutoCAD works, however, the Find option becomes more valuable to you.

The mechanics of using the Find tab also can be a little difficult to master. To locate the topic you want in the scrolling list of Search items, you must *scroll,* or drag, the button in the scroll bar up and down, up and down. . . . Merely typing the first few letters of a potential search item doesn't jump you down to that topic on the list, as doing so does in some programs. Then, if you simply click an item in the list, nothing happens; you must double-click it to get anywhere. What's more, after you finally double-click an item, you don't even get immediate Help for it; instead, a list of topics related to the double-clicked item appears in a separate scroll box lower on the Find tab. (Aarrgh!)

Unfortunately, only one item often appears in this second box, and moving the mouse down to double-click yet again seems like extra work for so little reward. This complaint is really just a minor quibble, however, and you'll probably get used to the process much more quickly than I did. After you double-click the item in this separate area, the Help you need quickly appears in a regular AutoCAD Help screen. (At last!) Figure 2-17 shows a Find search already in progress.

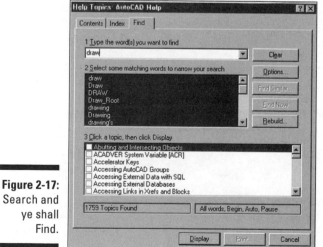

Figure 2-17:
Search and
ye shall
Find.

What's new

If you're an experienced AutoCAD user, What's New is an especially valuable Help menu option. Just choose Help⇨What's New to access a presentation-style display of all the new features and commands in Release 14. Click a topic to find out about new features relating to that topic. To exit, click the red button in the lower-left corner.

Taking the Quick Tour

The Release 14 Quick Tour feature of AutoCAD Help also is pretty useful for becoming familiar with new as well as long-standing features of the program. You can access the Quick Tour by choosing Help⇨Quick Tour. Then select from two major topics: Introducing AutoCAD Release 14 or Drawing with AutoCAD.

Each Quick Tour topic screen automatically shows you how a new feature or part of the interface works. The quick tour doesn't cover all possible AutoCAD topics (what does?), but it's a good tool for getting to know the functions it does describe. Figure 2-18 shows a Quick Tour screen that explains the Object Properties toolbar. Exit by clicking the red button in the lower-left corner. (If you don't notice this, you might be stuck in the "Quick" Tour for quite a while!)

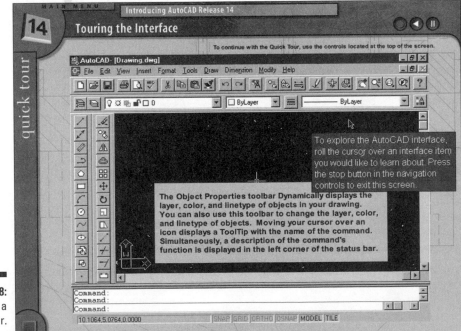

Figure 2-18:
Getting a
toolbar tour.

Discovering AutoCAD with the tutorial

The AutoCAD Learning Assistance tutorial is intended to be a bigger deal than either of the two features described in the preceding sections. To access it, choose Help⇨Learning Assistance. Then set aside some time to go through the whole tutorial (it's pretty self-explanatory). Unless you already know AutoCAD well, this tutorial is a worthwhile investment of your time.

And if that's not enough help . . .

The Help system in AutoCAD Release 14 also contains the entire Release 14 documentation set online. That's thousands of pages of manuals, all readable and searchable while you run AutoCAD. Don't read the manuals online for long, however; use the online version for searching and jumping around. If you really need to read big sections, grab the printed versions. By reading from paper instead of from a glowing, flickering screen, your eyes are much less likely to feel like hard-boiled eggs halfway through a section. (Better yet, start by grabbing this book!)

The Help system, like AutoCAD itself, can be kind of intimidating. If you use it on an as-needed basis to search for specific topics you're wondering about, you'll get comfortable with it without getting lost in it.

Chapter 3

Taking Control of AutoCAD

• •

• •

You can customize a ton of features in AutoCAD, but you absolutely must configure a few AutoCAD settings correctly before you can even start doing productive work. Even working through examples is hard unless you have a few of the program's configuration options set up correctly. So use this chapter to fix up AutoCAD and make it look sharp and act cool — just the way you want it to.

AutoCAD was one of the first PC graphics programs available, so its developers had to make some best guesses in deciding how things should work in the program. They tried hard, but in several cases, they guessed wrong. Starting with Release 12, and continuing to a greater degree with Releases 13 and 14, AutoCAD opened the door for you to configure many aspects of the program to the point that it can now work like a standard Windows program. Many, but, alas, not all. So . . . follow the instructions in the remainder of this chapter to make AutoCAD work as it should. Kinda. Maybe. (Fingers crossed.)

How to Make AutoCAD Work with You

If you're experienced in working with a graphical user environment such as Windows, Macintosh, or even a typical DOS drawing program, using the mouse has probably become second nature to you. You simply click a command, an object, or almost anything else on-screen to *select* (or highlight) it; you can then click something else to select that item instead. To select two items, click the first, press and hold the Shift (Mac) or Ctrl (Windows) key, and then click the second. (Ditto for the third, fourth, and so on.)

It's not my (de)fault

Your copy of AutoCAD is currently set up as it is for many reasons. Autodesk can change the default settings created at installation for different versions of AutoCAD and for different releases. The AutoCAD dealer, CAD manager, or other person who set up your system may have changed some things around. A third-party program you're using also may change certain default settings. Finally, if you or anyone else has used your version of AutoCAD at all, it's more than likely that a few settings have changed.

This book tells you how to modify the default AutoCAD settings that come with Release 14.

If some of the settings are already set correctly on your system because someone already reconfigured your program to the correct settings, that's one less thing for you to worry about.

More important than "what" to do, this book tells you "why" to do it — what the settings mean, so that you can understand when they should be set different ways. After you understand these settings and what they control — no mean feat, because AutoCAD is one of the most configurable programs around — you can always change them again if you need to.

But not in AutoCAD! AutoCAD works exactly the opposite of every major operating environment or graphics program known to man, woman, child, or computer nerd. But never fear! This chapter helps you fix whatever you can and work around what you can't. Left to its own devices, AutoCAD can seem to be working against you. But with some effort, you can get AutoCAD on your side and get to work.

If you're an experienced AutoCAD command-line user, you may want to do the opposite of what this chapter says. No problem; just read the descriptions of each setting, and then set it the way that works for you. If you share a machine with others who are less battle-hardened, though, be sure to let them know how to change the settings back to a more Windows-like approach.

Making AutoCAD work like other programs

Using a graphical interface such as Windows can be likened to driving a car: After you know how to do it, you don't think about the details any longer. But to make AutoCAD work right, you must explicitly specify to the program certain details that may, to you, seem obvious. (Ah, but not to AutoCAD! At least not until you set them. . . .) You must, therefore, correctly configure the following settings, called *selection settings,* to make AutoCAD work more intuitively. (This section describes what the settings are; how to set them is described on following pages.) The settings you need to know about are:

✔ **Noun/Verb Selection:** AutoCAD's long-time, built-in mode of interaction calls for you to enter a command and then choose the objects to which the command applies. In Windows, you normally select objects first and then specify the command. AutoCAD calls the Windows method Noun/Verb Selection.

Release 14, like Release 13, has Noun/Verb selection turned on by default. People who are used to the Macintosh and Windows mode of operation usually find this setting most comfortable. If you're an experienced AutoCAD command-line user, you may want to turn Noun/Verb selection off.

Some advanced AutoCAD commands do not work on objects that you've already selected, even if Noun/Verb Selection is turned on. These commands ignore your current selection after you enter the command and ask you to make a new selection.

✔ **Use Shift to Add:** In other programs, clicking different items changes the current selection; you must press and hold the Shift or Ctrl key to add additional items to the selection. AutoCAD, on the other hand, adds items to the current selection when you click each subsequent item; if you hold Shift to click a second item, that item is actually deselected and removed from the current selection set. (Hmmm. Maybe the programmer working on this feature got the Shift scared out of him? Naaaaahhhh.) This crazy feature, of course, drives non-AutoCAD veterans nuts! To make the Shift key work as it does in Windows, turn on the Use Shift to Add option.

✔ **Press and Drag:** To create a selection window in AutoCAD, you click one place in the drawing area, let go of the mouse button, and then click again somewhere else. In doing so, you establish the two corners of the selection window; this procedure is called "picking" the corners of the window. But in Windows, you click on the spot where you want one corner, hold down the mouse button, and drag to the other corner. To enable this click-drag-release style of windowing that the rest of the world is used to, turn on the Press and Drag option.

✔ **Implied Windowing:** With the Implied Windowing option on, AutoCAD enables you to use selection windows in two different ways: If you drag from left to right, everything inside the window is selected; if you drag from right to left, everything inside and crossing — that is, partly in and partly out of — the window is selected. This feature takes practice to use effectively but is well worth the trouble. On the other hand, if you don't turn this feature on — well, believe me, you don't want to know what it takes to establish a selection window if you leave this option turned off. So leave this feature on.

Why is AutoCAD so weird?

As is true of so many other questionable practices in computing, the odd style of AutoCAD user interaction is an attempt to maintain *backward compatibility* — the same commands and working style — with earlier versions of the program. Or in other words: "Gee, we did a really bad job of interface design in the previous 17 versions; better not change anything now, or our users may be upset."

In its defense, the AutoCAD default mode of operation is fast, and it works well after you get used to it. But anytime you work in another program or even on the Windows desktop, you get un-used to it. So unless you work almost exclusively in AutoCAD, or unless you're willing to "mode switch" seamlessly between AutoCAD on the one hand and everything else on the other, you want AutoCAD to work the same way as other programs.

✔ **Object Grouping:** Although the Object Grouping selection setting is not a "fix-it" item, as are the previous four settings, it's a neat new feature, so be sure to enable Object Grouping. In Release 13, AutoCAD added the capability to create named groups of objects and select them by typing in the name (if you're upgrading to Release 14 from a previous release, this feature is new to you). You can lump together all the executives' desks in a building, for example, and name them Executive Desks. (Then, if you're paid late for the drawing, you can specify that all objects in the Executive Desks group be made out of particle board. Heh, heh, heh. . . .)

Hands-on: Making AutoCAD Release 14 work like Windows 95

If you want to make AutoCAD work like Windows instead of driving you nuts, you need to change a few settings. To set the selection settings from the AutoCAD Object Selection Settings dialog box, follow these easy steps:

1. **Choose Tools⇨Selection. (Or type** ddSElect **on the command line and press Enter.)**

    The Object Selection Settings dialog box appears (see Figure 3-1).

    Releases 13 and 14 use the word *object* to refer to a single, selectable element in the drawing; previous releases used the word *entity* to mean the same thing. Despite its science-fictional implications, entity was one term in previous versions that I liked. Oh well. (AutoCAD veterans are likely to continue to use the word entity, both out of habit and to show how veteran they are.)

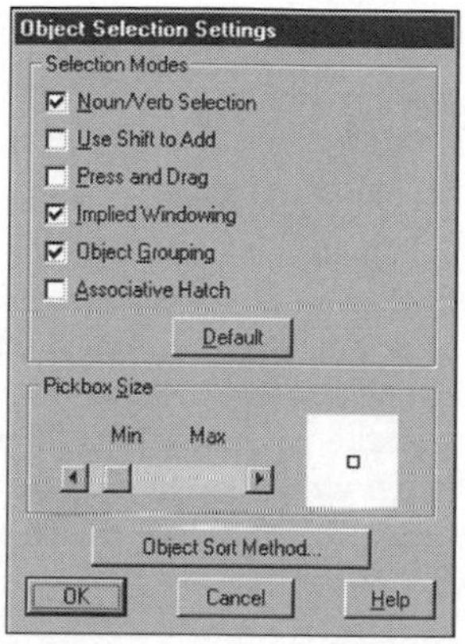

Figure 3-1:
The Object
Selection
Settings
dialog box.

2. **Click the Noun/Verb Selection check box to turn on this setting (if currently off).**

   The setting is on if a check mark appears in the check box, as shown in Figure 3-1. (In this figure, for example, Use Shift to Add and Press and Drag are turned off.)

3. **Turn on Use Shift to Add.**

4. **Turn on Press and Drag.**

5. **Turn on Implied Windowing.**

6. **Turn on Object Grouping.**

7. **Leave Associative Hatch alone for now.**

   I look at Associative Hatch more closely in Chapter 13.

8. **Click the OK button to accept the changes and close the dialog box.**

The good news: The Selection Modes area of the Object Selection Settings dialog box also contains a Default button. Clicking Default makes these settings revert back to the original AutoCAD default settings. (By the way, the default settings are Noun/Verb Selection, Implied Windowing, and Object Grouping on and Use Shift to Add and Press and Drag off, as shown in Figure 3-1.) The bad news: The Undo command doesn't work for the Default button, so write down your current settings before clicking Default if you think that you may need them again. Even more bad news: Not every dialog box includes a Default button, so don't get used to it.

Macintosh user's gloat note

If you're a longtime Mac user, you're no doubt feeling smug right now. And you're right; everything described here as "how Windows works" and "the right way to do things" was first popularized by the Macintosh and such programs as MacWrite and MacPaint, starting waaaay back in 1984. But this book addresses Windows users because that's where the action is in CAD these days. (Sorry to be the one to say this, but I was an Apple employee for seven years — and no, I didn't break any mirrors in 1990 just before I was hired at Apple.)

Maybe the next generation of the PowerPC chip will change things, and the next release of AutoCAD will come out for the Macintosh first — or at least second. Until then, any Mac users reading this book must settle for feeling slightly superior whenever user interface considerations are mentioned . . . and also hope for a bargain on a Windows 95 PC to run AutoCAD Release 14 on.

Setting selection settings from the command line

You're likely to change these selection settings only infrequently, so using the menus to set them is probably your best bet. When you want to change your settings a year from now, you're far more likely to remember how to do so from the menus if you did it that way in the first place. But if you're a real keyboard fan, just follow these steps to set selection settings from the command line:

1. **At the command line, type** PICKFIRST 1 **and then press Enter to turn on <u>N</u>oun/Verb Selection.**

2. **Type** PICKADD 0 **and press Enter to turn on <u>U</u>se Shift to Add.**

   (And don't ask me why, but 0 means *on* for the Use Shift to Add option, but it means *off* for all the other options. That means, of course, that if you want to turn off any of these options by using the command line, type the appropriate command and a 0 instead of a 1 — except for PICKADD, in which case . . . well, you get the idea.)

3. **Type** PICKDRAG 1 **and press Enter to turn on <u>P</u>ress and Drag.**

4. **Type** PICKAUTO 1 **and press Enter to turn on <u>I</u>mplied Windowing.**

5. **Type** PICKSTYLE 1 **and press Enter to turn on <u>O</u>bject Grouping.**

Making it work the AutoCAD way

If you want AutoCAD to work the way it always has, Release 14 lets you do that, too. If you're familiar enough with AutoCAD to want the old settings, you're probably aware of how to change them too. Follow the preceding instructions to bring up the Object Selection Settings dialog, but make the settings almost opposite:

- ✔ <u>N</u>oun/Verb Selection off.
- ✔ <u>U</u>se Shift to Add off.
- ✔ <u>P</u>ress and Drag off.

Don't stay completely in the Stone Age; turn Implied Windowing and Object Grouping on and learn to use them, as described in Chapter 7.

If you want to enter these commands from the command line, enter these commands:

```
PICKFIRST 0
PICKADD 1
PICKDRAG 0
PICKAUTO 1
PICKSTYLE 1
```

(Those last two commands turn implied windowing and object grouping on; if you really have to have them off, enter 0 instead.)

Getting saved

You know all those little things in life you wish you'd done way back when you had the chance: filling out your taxes before midnight on April 15; getting your brakes fixed before that nasty little accident; backing up your hard disk before it crashes forever. Well, setting the *save interval* is another one of these little things.

AutoCAD saves your drawing whenever a designated number of minutes has passed since your last save. If you save your drawing yourself before the automatic save kicks in, the save timer starts over again from that point. If you work for a while, making changes in your drawing, but then stop using the keyboard or mouse, however, AutoCAD actually stops checking to determine whether the specified amount of minutes has passed and, consequently, doesn't save your drawing anymore. So make sure that you save your drawing yourself if you're planning to step away from your machine for a while. Otherwise, you risk lost data if the power goes out while the AutoCAD automatic save takes its own little R&R break.

Here's the quick version for setting this option: To change the save interval by using the menus in AutoCAD Release 14, choose Tools⇨Preferences⇨ General tab. Check the Automatic save check box, and enter any number of minutes between saves that suits your fancy. (If you choose just a few minutes, your data will be safer, but you'll have to wait frequently while the save happens; if you choose too many minutes, you may lose a lot of work when a problem occurs.) Click OK to accept the change.

To change the save interval by using the command line, type **SAVETIME** at the command line and press Enter. However you enter the SAVETIME command, the completed sequence appears on the command line as follows:

```
Command: SAVETIME
New value for SAVETIME <120>: 10
```

AutoCAD offers a default value for many options at the command prompt. If you simply press Enter at the prompt instead of typing something, AutoCAD uses the default. The default value appears on the command line in angle brackets (< >). The <120> in the preceding line, for example, means that 120 minutes is the default value here.

If you try to enter SAVETIME 10, AutoCAD treats the spacebar as a return character. (This arrangement is a time-saver for AutoCAD power users, because the spacebar is easier to find than the Enter key.) It then gives you the prompt for the number of minutes, accepts 10 as the response, and completes the command. So entering the command as SAVETIME 10 ends up working, but the visual feedback you get is a little confusing at first.

After you enter the SAVETIME command, AutoCAD prompts you for the save interval, and then it automatically saves the drawing anytime you wait longer than that interval between saves. Ten minutes is usually a good choice, but any interval you choose will work. AutoCAD saves the drawing in the Windows Temp directory (C:\Windows\Temp) under the name AUTO.SV$.

Keyboard and mouse activity is what drives the mechanism that performs the saves automatically, which is why the automatic saves cease taking place if you walk away from your computer for a while. This is kind of like having a remote control that works only on weekdays; using it solves part of your problem, but not all of it. So always — always! — save your drawing before you ever walk away from your computer for any reason! AutoCAD users work too hard to go losing their efforts to a power outage.

Getting a grip

Grips are little handles that show up on an object after you select it. Grips enable you to grab an object and manipulate it. Grips are cool. Having grips turned on is a Good Thing.

Like so many other features in AutoCAD (sigh), grips don't always work exactly as you'd expect them to. Chapter 8 discusses grip editing in detail. For now, however, you just need to know how to turn them on. You can do this by following these steps:

1. **From the Tools menu, choose Grips. Or type** ddGRips **on the command line and press Enter.**

   The Grips dialog box appears, as shown in Figure 3-2.

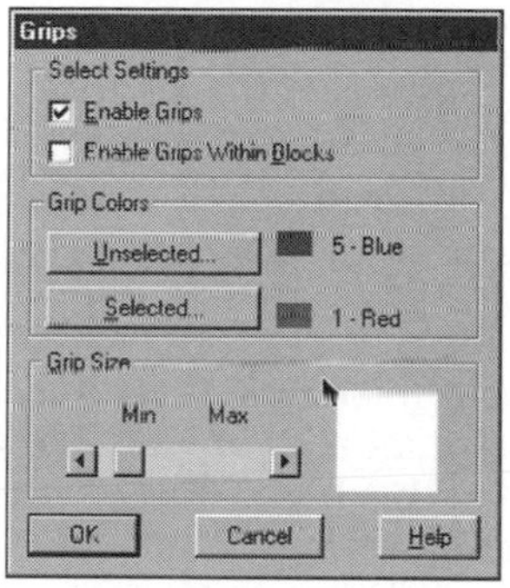

Figure 3-2:
Getting a
grip on tho
Grips dialog
box.

2. **Click the Enable Grips check box to turn on this feature (if it's not already on).**

3. **Click the Enable Grips Within Blocks check box to turn off this feature (if it's not already off).**

   You can turn this option back on later if you need to edit within a block. (See Chapter 15 for more about playing with blocks.) An empty check box means that the feature is turned off, as shown in Figure 3-2.

If you want, you can also change the Grip Colors in the Grips dialog box. Grip colors help identify whether a grip is on and ready for selection (blue) or on and already chosen as a handle (red). Unselected grips are also called cool grips and should be kept in a background color such as the default blue. Selected grips are called hot grips and should be flagged with an attention-getting color such as the default red. Choose either of the Grip Colors icons, Unselected or Selected, to open the Select Color dialog box and change the color to what you want. The Grip Size, too, can be changed by moving the slider box near the bottom of the Grips dialog box from Min to Max; the example window to the left of the size bar shows you the size increases or decreases of the grips as you change this option.

You can also use the command line to enable and turn off grips — especially if you're an experienced AutoCAD for DOS user who is sometimes inflicted with "GUI fatigue" and you need to go back to the old-style AutoCAD user interface as a remedy. The following steps describe the keyboard commands you use to turn grips on and grips-in-blocks off:

1. **At the command line, type** GRIPS 1, **and then press Enter.**

   This command turns on grips. To turn them off, you use a 0 instead of a 1.

2. **Type** GRIPBLOCK 0, **and then press Enter.**

   This command turns off grips within blocks; to turn them back on, you use a 1 with the command instead of a 0.

Making AutoCAD Quicker on the Draw

You can spend the rest of your career fine-tuning how AutoCAD draws — if you really want to, that is. You don't want to, of course, or you'd be reading *AutoCAD Disassembled: Vol. XXIII* instead of this book. But you do need to know how to set a couple of drawing-related settings to do much of anything. This section tackles those particular settings, providing you with just enough info to get you started, and the book harps on them again later as necessary.

Cosmetic surgery via third-party applications

Third-party applications can make a big difference in the appearance of AutoCAD; they can add menus and dialog boxes and set customization defaults in specific ways, which may be matters of substance or merely of style. If you use a third-party application, some of the information in this book may not apply directly to your working environment. If so, look for visible differences and adjust around them as needed.

Turning on running object snaps

In most drawings, different objects touch each other, usually at specific points such as the endpoint of a line, the center of a circle, or the intersection of two existing objects. Drawing becomes much easier if these points act as *hot spots* for the mouse pointer. That is, the mouse pointer is pulled toward specific kinds of points, which enables you to more easily draw objects so that they align correctly with each other. *Object snaps* give you the flexibility to control which points on each object draw the cursor to them.

There are even two types of object snaps. A *single* object snap lasts for just one mouse click. You turn it on by right-clicking the mouse to make the AutoCAD cursor menu appear. Then choose the object snap you want from the cursor menu; for instance, the Midpoint object snap. Then pick a point — it can be an endpoint, or some other point. The Midpoint object snap will then be automatically canceled.

A *running* object snap is similar, but it lasts longer. You can turn on any number of running object snaps at once. All the running object snaps you select stay on until you turn them off, either one at a time, or by turning off the running object snaps feature. (To turn running object snaps on and off, click the word SNAP in the status bar.) You can still use single object snaps whether or not running object snaps are on.

Don't feel bad if you become confused over the difference between the *snap grid* and *object snaps*, or between *single* object snaps and *running* object snaps. Because they all have *snap* in their names, the distinction can sometimes seem a little tricky. (Kinda like if you're cooking and you ask your significant other for the thyme; if he or she says "5:30" instead of handing you a jar of spice, it's not really his fault.) The snap grid makes objects snap to points a predefined distance apart in the drawing area, while object snaps force points that you select to snap to certain locations on other objects. But don't worry: The more you use AutoCAD, the less often these terms confuse you.

Okay, back to the subject. If you're a new user, listen up, because object snaps are really important. If you don't use object snaps, you can draw lines that *look* as though they connect, but they don't *really* connect. As you build up your drawing, these nasty little unconnected lines can cause you more and more problems — and they show you up as a novice if someone has to come in and fix your drawing later. What's more, that glitch is just in two-dimensional (2D) drawings. In three-dimensional (3D) drawings, unconnected objects that look as though they're touching from one point of view may actually be inches, meters, or even miles apart when viewed from a different angle.

This discrepancy becomes evident because, without the benefit of object snaps, lines can too easily be set up at totally different distances from one another — and they show it! — when you add in that oh-so-important third dimension. So use your object snaps to avoid this unfortunate problem; they enable you to draw connecting lines quickly and accurately, making such lines much harder for you to mess up, even if you try.

Important object snaps available in AutoCAD include to the endpoint of a line, the midpoint of a line, the intersection of two objects, and the center of a circle. Using object snaps all the time takes a little self-discipline until you get good at using them, so try out the steps in the following section a few times and then use them in your own work whenever possible, until the steps become second nature.

A new feature in AutoCAD Release 14 is the capability to turn the running object snap feature on and off, making the feature much more usable than in Release 13, when you had to turn running object snaps on and off one at a time. (You would typically spend time getting just the right set of running object snaps turned on; then, when you needed them off for a little while, you'd click them off individually and lose the running object snap set you had painstakingly created.)

Using the Osnap Settings dialog box

The most comprehensive way to manage object snaps is by using the Osnap Settings dialog box. Open this dialog box often and use it to control exactly which object snaps are on.

1. **Choose Tools⇨Object Snap Settings, or type** DDOSNAP **on the command line and press Enter.**

   The Running Osnap tab of the Osnap Settings dialog box opens, as shown in Figure 3-3.

   To open the Osnap Settings dialog box by using keyboard shortcuts in Windows, press Alt+T and then N.

2. **Click the different settings check boxes to set the ones you want and clear the ones you don't want.**

   A good initial working set is to have the Endpoint, Midpoint, Center, and Intersection options turned on, as shown in Figure 3-3.

You can use the Clear All button to clear all the current object snap settings and then just click the ones that you want to set. Even if this method takes more mouse clicks in some cases, starting from a clean slate may be quicker than thinking about which snaps are already set when you first open the dialog box and which of those snaps need to be turned off.

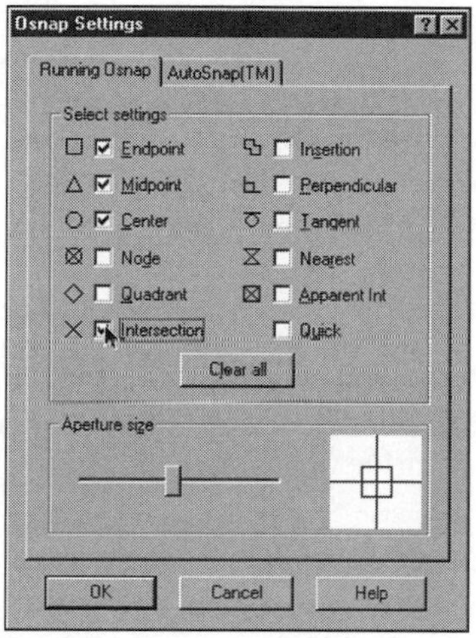

Figure 3-3:
Snap to it
with the
Osnap
Settings
dialog box.

After you've set a group of object snaps, you can turn them on and off easily in Release 14. Just double-click the OSNAP button in the Status bar at the bottom of the screen or press the F3 key. The group of running object snaps that you've selected toggles on and off. (If no running object snaps have been selected, AutoCAD brings up the Osnap Settings dialog to let you set some.)

Setting object snaps by using the command line

You can set and clear object snaps from the command line, too. This procedure is fast after you get good at it, but it's hard to commit to memory. So until you do, follow these steps:

1. **Type '-OSnap on the command line and then press Enter.**

2. **At the command prompt, type the snap modes you want and press Enter.**

   This part is tricky, because you must type in at least the first few letters of the name of each object snap mode you want to use. The following example shows what to type to set the endpoint, midpoint, center, and intersection snaps:

   ```
   Command: '-osnap
   Object snap modes: end, mid, cen, int
   ```

Turning on AutoSnap

AutoSnap is a new feature of Release 14, and a good one. It can change the cursor shape, show a label with the snap name, and even draw the AutoCAD drawing cursor into any snap point that you've set with running object snaps. AutoSnap is like running object snaps on steroids.

AutoSnap is one of those things you have to see to believe and to try to find out whether you like. It's also new, so I'm just going to tell you how to set it up and recommend that you get to know this feature well. After you know how to use both running object snaps and AutoSnap, see whether you agree with me that this feature is worth the price of admission.

Using the Osnap Settings dialog box for AutoSnap

The most comprehensive way to manage AutoSnap is by using the Osnap Settings dialog box. Open this dialog box often and use it to control exactly which object snaps are on.

1. **Choose Tools⇨Object Snap Settings or type** DDOSNAP **on the command line and press Enter. Choose the AutoSnap tab.**

   The AutoSnap tab of the Osnap Settings dialog box opens, as shown in Figure 3-4.

2. **Click Marker to turn the Marker on or off.**

   The Marker is a special shape displayed when the drawing cursor moves over a running object snap point.

3. **Click Magnet to turn the Magnet on or off.**

The Magnet is the feature that pulls your drawing cursor toward the snap point.

The Magnet feature can be wonderful or irritating, depending on what you're trying to do, so be ready to turn this one on and off a lot.

4. **Click SnapTip to turn the SnapTip on or off.**

The SnapTip is a label, like a Windows tool tip, that shows the name of the snap location.

5. **Click Display aperture box to turn the aperture box in the drawing cursor on or off.**

The aperture box is displayed (or not) as a box around the point of the drawing cursor.

6. **Use the Marker size and Marker color settings to change the marker size and color.**

These options control the display of the Marker that appears when the drawing cursor moves over a running object snap point.

7. **Click OK.**

Your changes take effect.

The AutoSnap feature is an excellent example of the ongoing integration of AutoCAD with the Windows 95 user interface and of the benefits that can accrue when everything falls into place. If I weren't so tasteful in my jokes, I'd say it's a Win-Win situation for everyone.

Setting up AutoSnap by using the command line

Setting up AutoSnap by using the command line is actually a good example of the power of the command line combined with new features in Release 14. If you retain nothing else from this section, at least memorize the command for turning the AutoSnap Magnet feature on and off from the command line.

1. **Type AUTOSNAP on the command line and then press Enter.**

AutoCAD responds with this prompt:

```
New value for AUTOSNAP <7>.
```

2. **Type a number for the AutoSnap settings you want.**

Each setting turns off everything that it doesn't turn on. For instance, 1 turns on the Marker and turns off the SnapTip and the Magnet features.

- 0 turns off all AutoSnap features: Marker, SnapTip, Magnet.

- 1 turns on the Marker.

- 2 turns on the SnapTip.
- 3 turns on the Marker and the Snap Tip.
- 4 turns on the Magnet.
- 5 turns on the Magnet and Marker.
- 6 turns on the SnapTip and the Magnet.
- 7 turns on all AutoSnap features: Marker, SnapTip, Magnet.

Enter **AUTOSNAP 3** from the command line to turn on all AutoSnap features except the Magnet; enter **AUTOSNAP 7** to turn on all AutoSnap features including the Magnet.

Getting the layered look

Layers are the most important tool you have in AutoCAD for organizing your drawings. Imagine for just a moment how your body would look if it didn't have a skeleton. (*That* vision should wake you up!) Well, that's exactly what your AutoCAD drawing is like without layers: a pulsating, jumbled mass that can't do very much. Putting different elements of your drawing on different layers, such as text on one layer and dimensions on another, is an important factor in creating perfect AutoCAD drawings.

You needn't make all your layer decisions up front, however, because AutoCAD enables you to add a layer or rename an existing layer at any point in the drawing cycle. (Deleting a layer, however, is harder work.) I suggest that you always create at least a couple of additional layers as you start drawing, however, so that you aren't forced to stick everything in layer 0 and thus end up with a spineless blob of a drawing, like that hapless body without its skeleton. (Blecchh!)

Layers also interact with the AutoCAD drawing updates, called screen refreshes and REGENs, or screen regenerations. A screen refresh occurs quickly and occasionally as you make changes to the drawing; but when too many changes, or certain types of changes, occur, AutoCAD launches a more thorough and time-consuming screen update called a REGEN. The criteria which force a REGEN, and the resulting delay in your work, are too complicated to explain here, but luckily, many fewer REGENs occur in Release 14 than in previous releases of AutoCAD.

As you create new data, it goes on the layer that is designated "current." (Initially, layer 0 is the current layer.) You can make the data on a layer invisible by turning off that layer; you can prevent data on a layer from being updated during a REGEN by freezing it. You can modify or erase data on any layer that's not turned off or frozen.

These possibilities may seem like much ado about nothing if you're new to AutoCAD. But as a drawing gets more complex, seeing what you're doing becomes increasingly harder, and a REGEN of the drawing takes increasingly longer when you make certain kinds of changes. The capability to create and control layers is the single best tool you have to battle this complexity and slowness. It also allows you to plot the drawing different ways — for instance, with and without text showing, or with and without the furniture in a room being displayed.

AutoCAD enables you to specify different colors and linetypes for different objects. You can use this capability to distinguish and organize different types of objects. But the best way to use colors and, in many cases, linetypes is to assign to everything on a specific layer the same color and linetype. That way, you can flag the different layers in your drawing by the colors and linetypes in them.

Layer usage — that is, what exactly goes on each layer — and *layer names* are a big deal in AutoCAD, because drawings from different people don't work well together without a consistent layer usage and naming scheme. If your workplace uses a set of standard layer names, find out what it is and then use it. Otherwise, you need to figure out your own approach and stick with that. Dimensions in your drawings, for example, usually are placed on their own separate layer, and you should always assign that layer a consistent name, such as DIMENSIONS. This way, you can easily add elements of one drawing to another. If you need to share drawings with others, you need only to rename your layers to match their layer names and then get back to work.

The American Institute of Architects has published guidelines for layer use in the architectural and building engineering professions. Check with the AIA for a copy.

Unfortunately, making mistakes in creating layers is far too easy to do, so you need to just keep on practicing until you finally get it right. By following the steps in this section, you can actually create and name a layer and then modify it to use a specific color and linetype. If you're in a hurry to create many layers, you can go ahead and do all the creating and naming first and then make all your color and linetype assignments afterward.

Creating and modifying layers with the Layer & Linetype Properties dialog box

Using the Layer & Linetype Properties dialog box is your best bet to create, edit, and manage layers. It's a little hard to use, however, so make sure that you follow these steps carefully:

1. **Choose Format➪Layer or type** DDLMODES **on the command line and press Enter.**

   The Layer & Linetype Properties dialog box appears, as shown in Figure 3-5. It can take a while to learn what all the icons represent. But don't worry; I explain what all the icons mean, and the AutoCAD tool tips help as well.

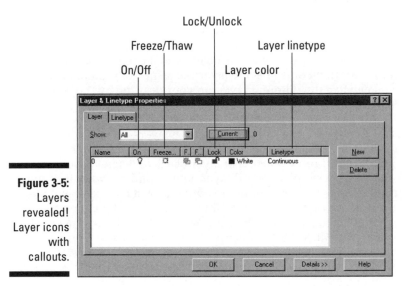

Figure 3-5:
Layers
revealed!
Layer icons
with
callouts.

   You can also open the Layer & Linetype Properties dialog box from the Object Properties toolbar by clicking the Layers icon, the second icon from the far left end of the bar, which displays three stacked planes (geometric planes, not airplanes).

2. **Click the New button to create a new layer.**

3. **Type the new layer's name in the text entry box of the new layer, under the column heading Name.**

   The new layer name appears in the Layer Name list. If, for example, you type **Geometry**, Geometry appears in the list as the name of your new layer.

   The headings at the top of the Layer Name list further describe your layer. The default state for this new layer is On, the Color is White, and the Linetype is Continuous. Now, however, you can modify these settings in the layer.

4. **Repeat to create additional layers.**

   A good starting set of layer names (in addition to 0, of course) may be Geometry, Text, Dimensions, and Underground.

The next few steps apply to any layer. Just use the icon for the layer you want.

You can create multiple new layers quickly by typing commas between the names.

If you intend to share this drawing with others, find out what layer names the other people use and adopt those names.

5. **Click the On/Off lightbulb to keep a layer off after you return to your drawing; click it again to turn the layer back on.**

   If a layer is off, your drawing doesn't display or print it.

   If you click the layer off, the little lightbulb for that layer goes dim.

6. **Click the first Freeze/Thaw button to freeze the selected layer after you return to your drawing; click it again to unfreeze, or Thaw, the layer.**

   If you freeze a layer, your drawing doesn't display it. Unlike with the Off setting, if you update the drawing, you don't regenerate the frozen layer. Because each layer takes time to regenerate, freezing layers saves REGEN time. And if you create a print or plot of the drawing, you don't print the frozen layer.

   If you click the Freeze button, the little sun for that icon goes dim.

7. **Click the second and third Freeze/Thaw icons to freeze the selected layer in the current viewport or in new viewports; click the icons again to unfreeze the layer in specific viewports.**

   If you don't have paper space viewports set up, these icons are grayed out — two less options to worry about.

8. **Click the Lock icon to lock the selected layer; click it again to unlock the drawing.**

   Locking a layer prevents you from modifying the objects on it. You can create new objects on a locked layer, however, and you can display, regenerate, and print the layer.

   If you click the Lock button, the lock icon changes to show the hasp closed rather than open.

9. **Click the Color button to change the color you want to use on the layer.**

   The Select Color dialog box appears. Choose the color you want to use by clicking it in this dialog box. Objects drawn on this layer will be displayed in the color you choose here. The nine Standard Colors listed at the top of the dialog box are the most transferable from one system to another. If you're using a white background in the drawing area, objects drawn in the color named White appear black on-screen.

   If you change the color of a layer, the name of the new color appears under the Color heading in the Layer Name list.

I'm kind of partial to using the shades of gray instead of colors, myself; grays are a more subtle indicator, and they can more clearly indicate relative depth than different colors can. They also print accurately on a noncolor printer and photocopy well on a noncolor copier.

10. Click the Linetype name (not the Linetype tab) to bring up the Layer & Linetype Properties dialog box and change the linetype.

Choose the linetype you want to use from the Loaded linetypes list in the dialog box. Objects drawn on this layer will be displayed in the linetype you choose here. If the linetype you need doesn't appear on this list, you must load it. Click the Load button and choose a linetype to load from the list that appears.

If you change the linetype, the name of the new linetype appears under the Linetype heading in the list of layers.

11. Click a layer's name to select it, and then click the Current button to designate the layer as the Current Layer — that is, the one you'll draw on after you return to your drawing.

The name of the Current Layer appears next to the Current button. Any new objects you create on your drawing are put onto the current layer, but you can edit objects on any layer that's on and not frozen or locked.

12. To exit the Layer & Linetype Properties dialog box after you finish creating layers, click OK.

Figure 3-6 shows the Layer & Linetype Properties dialog box with five new layers in it. The Geometry layer is the first one edited, so it is On and Current; other layers are frozen and locked.

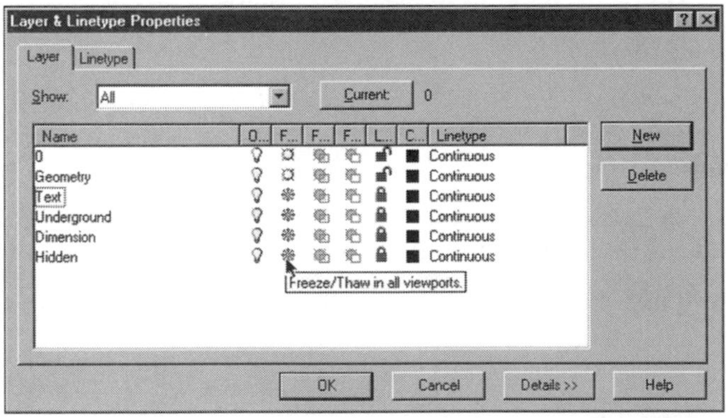

Figure 3-6:
In control of your layers.

As you create new layers, AutoCAD adds them to the existing list in the order in which you create them. You can sort the layers by any layer option simply by clicking on that option's name across the top of the layer list. That's right; even a stray mouse click on the name of one of the options re-sorts the list, in ascending order. To sort them in descending order, just click on the column name again. (No, you can't un-sort them!)

This fact is important to keep in mind, because this surprise re-sorting may make you think that some of your layers have disappeared when actually they've only been scrolled off the part of the layer list that is visible on-screen. And I don't want you to, uh, "resort" to doing anything drastic if this event occurs. Ouch — sorry. For example, if you want to sort the list of layers by name, click the word Name; by color, click the word Color. The list re-sorts to fit.

To work more quickly, create all your layers first by using the New com-mand. Then change the settings by clicking the settings for the layer you want. The Layer & Linetype Properties dialog box immediately updates all the highlighted layers with their new settings.

Release 14 has a cool new feature that lets you manage layer properties from the Object Properties toolbar. (Okay, this one was in Release 13 too, but it's worth mentioning again in case you are upgrading from Release 12 or just missed it.) Just click on the layers pull-down list to open it and then click on layer properties to change them! You can change the On/Off, Freeze/Thaw, and Lock/Unlock properties. To change the layer name, color, or linetype, you still have to go to the Layer & Linetype Properties dialog box.

Chapter 4

Setup Comedy

● ●

● ●

*W*ell, you've heard of standup comedy, so why not *setup* comedy? (Okay, so it should be *situp* comedy; so sue me.) Unfortunately, AutoCAD setup can too often become a comedy of errors — if not performed correctly.

AutoCAD does a great deal for you. But the pleasure it provides is not without an occasional jolt of pain. People who most often feel that pain haven't set up their drawings correctly. Although not fatal, this affliction can cause you to hate any and all of the following: yourself, your boss, your client, and, above all, AutoCAD. The remedy is uncomplicated: Know the steps to set up your drawing correctly. Doing right by your setup saves you trouble down the road.

If you're upgrading from a previous release of AutoCAD, you may be wondering what's new about drawing setup. In Release 14, AutoCAD adds a new dialog box for setup that you see whenever you open a new file or start AutoCAD without specifying what file to open. This Start Up dialog box is described in detail later in this chapter. Equally important is understanding the importance of good file setup practices. Unless you're a whiz at setup and have already figured out the Start Up dialog box, read this chapter.

In Release 14, AutoCAD provides setup help in the form of wizards and templates. The templates are fine, if you know how to use them. However, the wizards don't set up your drawing well. To find out how to use the wizards and templates appropriately, see the section "Start Me Up?," near the end of this chapter.

You need to set up AutoCAD correctly, partly because AutoCAD is so flexible and partly because, well, you're doing *CAD* — computer-aided design. In this context, the following three key reasons help explain why AutoCAD drawing setup is important:

- ✔ **Smart Paper:** The one thing that can do the most to make using AutoCAD fun is to work on a drawing correctly set up so that your screen acts like paper, only smarter. When drawing on real paper, you have to constantly translate between units on the paper and the real-life units of the object you're drawing. But when drawing in AutoCAD, you can draw directly in real-life units — feet and inches, meters, or whatever you use. AutoCAD can then calculate distances and dimensions for you and add them to the drawing. You can make the mouse pointer snap directly to "hot spots" on-screen, and a visible, resizeable grid gives you a better sense for the scale of your drawing. This smart paper function, however, works well only if you tell AutoCAD how you set up your specific drawing. AutoCAD can't really do its job until you tell it how to work.

- ✔ **Dumb Paper:** Creating a great drawing on-screen that doesn't fit well on paper is all too easy. After you finish creating your drawing on the smart paper AutoCAD provides on-screen, you must print it out on the dumb paper used for thousands of years. Then you must deal with the fact that people use certain standard paper sizes and drawing scales. (Most people also like everything to fit neatly on one sheet of paper.) If you set up AutoCAD correctly, good printing results automatically; if not, printing time can become one colossal hassle.

- ✔ **It Ain't Easy:** AutoCAD provides setup wizards and templates for you, but they don't work well unless you understand them. This particular deficiency, though improved in Release 14, is still one of the weakest areas in AutoCAD. You must figure out on your own how to make the program work right. If you just plunge in without carefully setting it up, your drawing and printing efforts are likely to wind up a real mess. You may, in fact, end up with a virtually unprintable drawing (and probably mutter a few unprintable words in the process, too).

Fortunately, although the steps to performing your setup correctly are overly complex, you can master them with a little attention and practice. If you're somewhat familiar with AutoCAD, skip to the end of this chapter and use the section "Seven Not-So-Deadly Steps to Setup" — as well as Appendix B — to help you in your setup work. If you're new, read through this chapter once and then use the setup section and Appendix B for reference.

While you're working in AutoCAD, always keep in mind what your final output looks like on real paper. Even your first printed drawings should look just like hand-drawn ones — only better.

So, You're Really in a Hurry?

Tying together all the elements necessary for an acceptable drawing — the size of the actual objects you're drawing, the size of the paper you print on, and other important quantities, such as the grid display and snap grid you use — is in no way an easy task. (See the section "Making Your Screen Smart," later in this chapter, for details on grid and snap.)

Understanding all the pieces that contribute to the "look" of your drawing when you print it out and the "feel" of AutoCAD as you use it to create different kinds of drawings is important. However, you may already know how these different elements work, and you just need a quick guide to setting up AutoCAD correctly. Or you may be in a really big hurry and don't have time to understand it all just yet. If so, you've come to the right place.

Use Tables 4-1 and 4-2 to determine the correct settings for the major setup options in AutoCAD. (These tables are just examples for some smaller sheet sizes that you're likely to use for check plots; for more comprehensive information, go to Appendix B.) Then go to Table 4-5 at the end of this chapter to find the AutoCAD options and commands that control these settings. In between, you can page through more detailed explanations of the key AutoCAD setup options. Come back to these sections when you want or need to know more.

Under *Limits* in Table 4-1, Table 4-2, or in Appendix B, find the area that comfortably encloses the size of the object(s) you want to draw. Then coordinate that area with the *Paper Size* you plan to use and the *Drawing Scale* to which you want to draw the printout. Taking all these elements into account should result in a single set of figures that you can use to set up your drawing. How to use the numbers in these tables is explained in more detail in the rest of this chapter and in Appendix B.

Table 4-1	**Picking Limits — Architectural Units, Horizontal Orientation**				
Paper Size	*Drawing Scale*	*Limits*	*Grid*	*Snap*	*Linetype & Dimension Scale*
8½"x11"	¼" = 1'	44' x 34'	4'	6"	48
8½"x11"	¼" = 1'	22' x 17'	2'	2"	24
8½"x11"	1" = 1'	11' x 8½'	1'	1"	12
11"x17"	¼" = 1'	68' x 44'	4'	6"	48
11"x17"	½" = 1'	34' x 22'	2'	2"	24
11"x17"	1" = 1'	17' x 11'	1'	1"	12

Table 4-2		Picking Limits — Mechanical and Other Units, Horizontal Orientation			
Paper Size	*Drawing Scale*	*Limits*	*Grid*	*Snap*	*Linetype & Dimension Scale*
8½"x11"	1cm = 1m	25m x 20m	1m	50cm	100
8½"x11"	5cm = 1m	5m x 4m	20cm	10cm	20
8½"x11"	10cm = 1m	2.5m x 2m	10cm	5cm	10
11"x17"	1cm = 1m	40m x 25m	1m	50cm	100
11"x17"	5cm = 1m	8m x 5m	20cm	10cm	20
11"x17"	10cm = 1m	4m x 2.5m	10cm	5cm	10

The number in the Linetype & Dimension Scale column is actually the *drawing scale factor* for the drawing — that is, the conversion factor between any measurement in the drawing and the real-world object it represents. If the Linetype and Dimension Scale, or drawing scale factor, is 96, for example, then a 2"-long element in your drawing represents a 192"-, or 16'-, long object in the real world.

If your lines come out with the dots and dashes seemingly too large, cut the linetype scale in half.

Don't just use one of the wizards in the AutoCAD Start Up dialog box and then start drawing. Your drawing is likely to be at a non-standard scale and, therefore, difficult for others to comprehend. If you later try to change these settings, you may have to make complicated adjustments to AutoCAD and your drawing to make your drawing easy to modify and print.

If you're really in a hurry, find an existing drawing that's already at the correct scale and intended to print on the paper size you plan to use. Make a copy of that drawing and then modify the copy to create the drawing you want.

Drawing Scale Basics

The single most important item in AutoCAD setup is setting up your drawing so that it prints correctly. That means that the drawing fits nicely on the chosen paper size, leaving room for the *title block* (an area that describes drawing facts, such as the drafter's name and company name). The drawing can't be so large that it spills over onto another sheet nor so small as to leave the paper dominated by white space. Text and dimensions must be large enough to be readable but not so large as to overshadow the drawing itself.

The key element in making your drawing fit onto the paper is the drawing scale. The drawing scale is a ratio that converts the actual dimensions of the object you're representing into the dimensions that fit best on paper. However, don't use just any scale; use a recognized, easy-to-remember scale, such as 1" = 1' or $^1/_8$" = 1'. (Anyone who has done much drafting recognizes the value of the metric system.) The size of the paper you're drawing on, combined with the scale you're using, determines the maximum size of a real-world object that you can fit onto the paper.

Table 4-3 shows the maximum object size that can fit on a number of different paper sizes at several popular drawing scales. To use the table, determine the dimensions of a rectangle that can enclose the object you're drawing. Then find the paper size and units (English or metric) that you want to use and look under *Largest Object* to find the corresponding rectangle that is just large enough to hold your object. Read across to see the drawing scale to use.

Table 4-3 Drawing Scales, Horizontal Orientation, A-Size Paper

Paper Size	Drawing Scale (English units)	Largest Object	Drawing Scale (Metric units)	Largest Object
8$^1/_2$"x11"	1" = 1'	11' x 8$^1/_2$'	10cm = 1m	2.5m x 2m
	$^1/_2$" = 1'	22' x 17'	5cm = 1m	5m x 4m
	$^1/_4$" = 1'	44' x 34'	1cm = 1m	25m x 20m
	$^1/_8$" = 1'	88' x 68'	5mm = 1m	50m x 40m
	$^1/_{16}$" = 1'	176' x 136'	1mm = 1m	250m x 200m
11"x17"	1" = 1'	17' x 11'	10cm = 1m	4m x 2.5m
	$^1/_2$" = 1'	34' x 22'	5cm = 1m	8m x 5m
	$^1/_4$" = 1'	68' x 44'	1cm = 1m	40m x 25m
	$^1/_8$" = 1'	136' x 88'	5mm = 1m	80m x 50m
	$^1/_{16}$" = 1'	272' x 176'	1mm = 1m	400m x 250m

The table doesn't set aside room on the paper for a title block, because the size and placement of title blocks can vary widely, so choose a scale that leaves enough room on the paper for your title block. If none of the entries in the table are close to what you need, don't worry; more-complete tables that include additional information can be found in Appendix B.

A few thoughts on paper

You may already know what you need to about the paper sizes used in your profession and in your office's printers and plotters; but if not, here are a few important facts.

The standard paper sizes are lettered A, B, C, D, and E. Their sizes, using ANSI standards prevalent in the U.S., are as follows:

- $A = 8^{1}/_{2}$" x 11" (standard letter-size paper in the U.S.)

- $B = 11$" x 17"

- $C = 17$" x 22"

- $D = 22$" x 34"

- $E = 34$" x 44"

ANSI sizes are different from both architectural and ISO international standards. An architectural D sheet is 24" x 36", for example. Make adjustments as needed for your actual paper sizes.

Knowing the following relationships makes using the tables later in this chapter — as well as switching among paper sizes — easier for you:

- C paper is double the length and width of A paper.

- D paper is double the length and width of B paper.

- E paper is double the length and width of C paper.

Because printing to a large printer, such as an E-sized inkjet printer or pen plotter, is expensive and time-consuming, you may often find yourself sending *check prints* to a standard office printer as a test. (The words *print* and *plot* are now used more or less interchangeably; *plotting* is often used to refer to any printing that creates a large format, such as D or E.)

To maintain correct proportions and layout, you can make check prints for C or E paper on standard A paper (for example, $8^{1}/_{2}$" x 11" copier paper) and check prints for D paper on standard B legal paper. Reading some of the lettering may be hard if printing this small, but such a printout preserves the correct proportions of your drawing.

An 11" x 17" laser or inkjet printer makes a great, economical CAD output device, especially for the small office. You can do reduced-size plots for checking in-house, and have a service bureau do the final, full-size plots. (Bill the full-size plots to your client!) Most 11" x 17" printers will print on 8 1/2" x 11" paper as well, so one device can serve both your CAD and general printing needs.

Taking Your Measurements

The type of units used for measuring distances and angles may well be something that you can set and then forget about for the duration of a project, if not longer. (For example, if all your work is on building plans, you may rarely need to change units.) But getting them right whenever you do set them is important. You may also need to change the precision with which AutoCAD displays units and the direction in which AutoCAD measures angles. The program provides a handy dialog box for changing units, and you can make changes from the command line as well.

Choosing your units

The *units* used within a drawing are the same units of measurement the real world uses. You draw an eight-foot-high line, for example, to indicate the height of a wall and an eight-inch-high line to indicate the cutout for a doggie door (for a Dachshund, naturally). The on-screen line may actually be only two inches long, but AutoCAD indicates that it is eight feet long if that's how you set up your drawing. This way of working is easy and natural when you understand that your drawing is printed at a scale factor.

For units, you choose a *type* of unit — Scientific, Decimal, Engineering, Architectural, and Fractional — and a *precision* of measurement. Engineering and Architectural units are in feet and inches; Engineering units are decimal, and Architectural units are fractional. For unitless measurements, including metric measurements, use one of the other types of units: Scientific, Decimal, or Fractional. You can change the type or precision of units later without causing much trouble in your drawing.

You can choose and change the type of units you use in your drawing by changing settings in the Units Control dialog box. To access this dialog box to choose units (and control how angles are measured), follow these steps:

1. **Choose Format⇨Units from the menu bar; or type** ddUNits **at the command line and press Enter.**

    The Units Control dialog box appears, as shown in Figure 4-1.

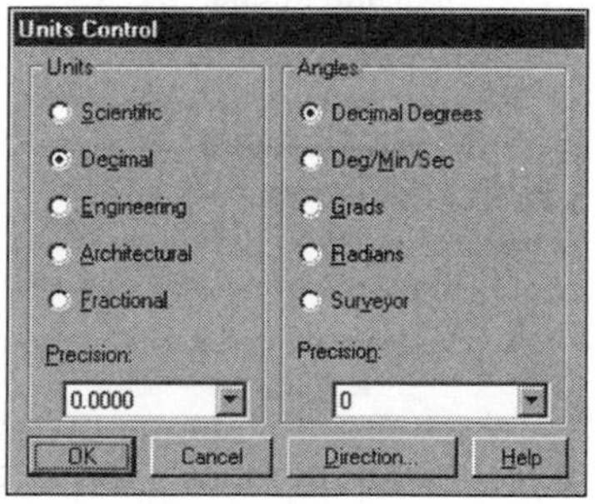

Figure 4-1:
The Units
Control
dialog box.

2. Choose from the Units area the unit option you want for your drawing.

You can choose a unit by clicking the round circle in front of the unit-type name. (These circles are called *radio buttons* or *option buttons* in computerese, if you didn't already know that.) As you select different options, the appearance of the text in the Precision drop-down list box changes to reflect exactly how AutoCAD displays that choice on-screen:

S̲cientific:	0.0000E+01
De̲cimal:	0.0000
E̲ngineering:	0'-0.0000"
A̲rchitectural:	0'-01/16"
F̲ractional:	01/16

The default choice is Decimal, because it's unitless (in case you don't like all those little inch and foot marks all over your drawing). But choose the type of unit representation that is appropriate for your own work. Engineering and Architectural units are displayed in feet and inches; the other units have no dimensions and work well for either feet or inches or metric units, as you prefer.

AutoCAD can "think" in inches! If you're using Engineering or Architectural units (feet and inches), AutoCAD understands any coordinate you enter as a number of inches.

Be able to swiftly find the ' (apostrophe) character on your keyboard so that you can quickly specify feet if that's what you mean.

3. From the P̲recision list box, choose the degree of precision you want.

For Architectural and Fractional units, the choices are fractions, such as 0, $^1/_2$, $^1/_4$, and so on. (Figure 4-2 shows the precision choices for Architectural units.) For the other three types of units, the choices offered represent the number of decimal places you can use.

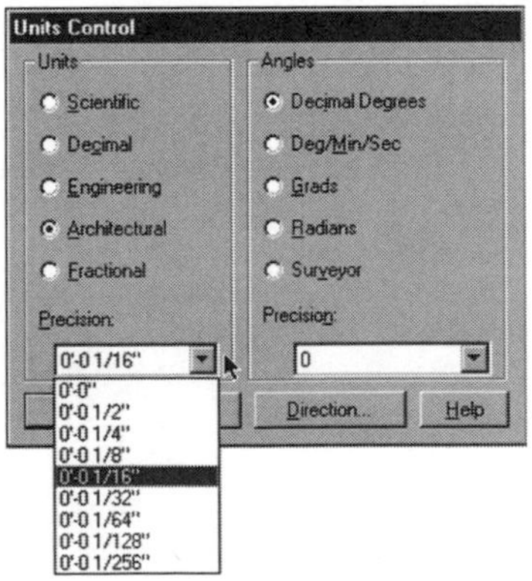

Figure 4-2:
Precision
choices for
Architectural
units.

Too much precision actually slows down cursor response time in a drawing, because AutoCAD tries to calculate where the cursor is to an increasing number of decimal places. A grosser — that is, less precise — precision setting helps AutoCAD move faster. It also makes the numbers displayed in the status bar and dialog boxes, and the default precision in dimension text, more readable. So be gross for now; you can always act a little less gross later.

4. Click OK to exit the dialog box and lock in your unit choices.

If you really like using the command line, you can set units with the UNITS command. Try it from the keyboard and memorize the keystrokes to make the changes you want quickly.

Calculatin' all the angles

In AutoCAD, you also specify *angular units* — the way in which angles are measured, such as a circle having 360 degrees — and the direction in which to draw them. If you use decimal degrees, want to use a precision of one degree (no fractions of a degree), treat a horizontal line pointing to the right as an angle of zero degrees (as in architecture), and measure angles counter-clockwise (as in architecture), you need make no changes here. Otherwise, fire away.

In AutoCAD, you can specify the units in which AutoCAD measures angles. You choose a *type* of angular unit — *Decimal Degrees* (the most common), *Deg/Min/Sec* (useful mainly when you're planning a sea voyage), *Grads, Radians,* and *Surveyor* — and a *precision* of measurement. You can also choose the *direction* in which angles are measured. If you set these options now but change your mind after you start your drawing, you can change angular units, precision, and direction later without causing much trouble for your drawing.

The easiest way to set and change angular units and direction is by using the Units Control dialog box. To use the dialog box to control how angles are measured, follow these steps:

1. Choose Format⇨Units from the menu bar; or type ddUNits at the command line and press Enter.

The Units Control dialog box appears. (Refer to Figure 4-1.)

2. Choose from the Angles area of the dialog box the angular units you want to use in your drawing.

Just click the round circle — the radio button — in front of the unit you want to choose. As you select different options, the appearance of the text in the Precision drop-down list box changes to reflect how AutoCAD displays that choice, as follows:

Dec<u>i</u>mal Degrees:	0
Deg/<u>M</u>in/Sec:	0d
<u>G</u>rads:	0g
<u>R</u>adians:	0r
Sur<u>v</u>eyor:	N 0d E

The default choice is Decimal Degrees, because it needs no unit designation (again, no little measurement marks all over your drawing). You should, however, choose whichever angular unit you need.

3. **From the Precisio<u>n</u> drop-down list box, choose the degree of precision you want for your drawing.**

   For Deg/Min/Sec and Surveyor units, the choices are whole degrees; degrees and minutes; degrees, minutes, and seconds; and degrees, minutes, and seconds plus additional decimal places of precision for the seconds (see Figure 4-3). For the other three units, the choices are the number of decimal places you can use.

   Be able to find the ' (apostrophe) and " (quotes) characters swiftly on your keyboard so that you can quickly specify minutes and seconds.

4. **To change the base direction from which AutoCAD measures angles or to change the orientation of angular measurement (clockwise or counterclockwise), click the <u>D</u>irection button below the Precisio<u>n</u> drop-down list.**

   The Direction Control dialog box appears, as shown in Figure 4-4.

5. **Choose the Angle 0 Direction you want: <u>E</u>ast, <u>N</u>orth, <u>W</u>est, <u>S</u>outh, or <u>O</u>ther.**

   The Angle 0 Direction is the direction that AutoCAD uses as 0 for angular measurements. East is to the right on-screen, North is up, West is left, and South is down. Architects, for example, tend to use East as the Angle 0 Direction; that way, flat things are at 0 degrees and straight up is 90 degrees, which fits architectural usage. A few others tend to use North as the Angle 0 Direction, which fits compass measurement, a generally well-understood usage. You can choose a preset direction, choose Other to select a direction on-screen, or type in a specific direction.

6. **Choose the direction in which AutoCAD measures angles: <u>C</u>ounter-Clockwise or C<u>l</u>ockwise.**

   Architects and others tend to use a counterclockwise measurement so that angles are measured "from the ground up"; it's rare to use clockwise.

7. **Click OK to exit the dialog box and activate your choices.**

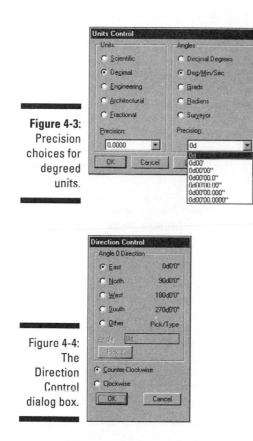

Figure 4-3:
Precision
choices for
degreed
units.

Figure 4-4:
The
Direction
Control
dialog box.

As with linear units, you can change angular units with the UNITS command, If you frequently change angular units, run the UNITS command from the keyboard and experiment with the options. Memorize the keystrokes to make the changes you need quickly.

Set Some Limits!

Your second chore in making AutoCAD really perform for you (after setting your drawing's units of measurement, as described in the preceding sections) is to communicate to AutoCAD how you want it to behave by setting some more of the famous AutoCAD system variables. When the system variables are set correctly, they help you create a drawing that prints comfortably onto the paper you're using, at the correct scale.

One important setup step is to set the *limits* of your drawing correctly. The limits define the size and shape of a rectangular box into which your drawing goes. This rectangular box should represent the dimensions of the paper you plan to print to, adjusted by the drawing scale you're using. That way, you can work in AutoCAD in units that fit the real-world object or area that you're drawing. Equally important is the fact that anything you draw within the limits, when they're correctly set, automatically fits on the paper at print time.

To know what to set the limits to, use Table 4-3 or Appendix B. Then follow the instructions in this section to set the limits.

Don't just set the limits to something "reasonable," such as a box that encloses the object you're drawing; you may not be able to get external elements such as dimensions, text, and the title block arranged correctly for successful printing.

Notice that you can start the LIMITS command from a menu choice but that all the action takes place on the command line; in spite of the importance of the topic, AutoCAD has no dialog box for setting limits, although the Plot Preview dialog box may prove useful for checking limits and paper size. So just follow these steps to set your drawing limits:

1. **Choose Format➪Drawing Limits from the menu bar to start the LIMITS command; or type LIMITS on the command line and press Enter.**

   The LIMITS command appears on the command line, and the command line displays the following at the bottom of the screen:

   ```
   Command: '_limits
   Reset Model space limits:
   ON/OFF/<Lower left corner> <0'-0",0'-0">:
   ```

   The value at the end of the last line of the prompt is the default value for the lower-left corner of the drawing limits; it appears according to the units and precision that you selected in the Units Control dialog box — for example, 0'- 0" if you selected Architectural units with precision to the nearest inch.

2. **Type the lower-left corner of the limits you want to use and press Enter.**

   The usual value to enter at this point is **0,0**. (That is, type a zero, a comma, and then another zero, with no spaces.) Or you can just press Enter to accept the default value. You can adjust the limits later if you want.

AutoCAD now prompts you for the upper-right corner of the limits:

```
Upper right corner <1'-0",0'-9">:
```

3. **Type the upper-right corner of the limits you want to use and press Enter.**

   Use the Limits column in Table 4-1, Table 4-2, or Appendix B to pick an upper-right limit that works for your drawing size, scale factor, and paper size.

   If you enter measurements in feet and not inches, you must also enter the foot designator, such as **6'**; otherwise, AutoCAD assumes that you mean inches.

After you enter the limits, AutoCAD restricts your drawing work to an area of the screen that is proportional to the limits you entered; for example, if the X and Y limits are the same, you're limited to drawing in a square. As you move the cursor, AutoCAD displays the cursor's coordinates relative to the lower-left and upper-right corners you entered.

Making Your Screen Smart

So just what does it mean for a computer screen to be smart? No, not knowing how to tie its shoelaces or spell *cat*. Basically, a smart computer screen helps you do what you want. Now you can set up a *grid* to show you where you are within the limits and a *snap interval* that creates "hot spots" in the drawing area that are easier to draw to.

The *grid* is simply a set of visible, evenly spaced dots that give some orientation as to how your drawing places its objects in relation to one another on-screen.

The *snap interval* is a bit trickier to set. The snap interval attracts the mouse cursor to invisible hot spots a certain distance apart on-screen, enabling you to easily align objects a predetermined distance apart. For example, if you're designing a soccer field, having a snap interval of one meter may make good sense.

The relationship between the grid and the snap interval should be close. In other words, the grid and the snap interval should either be the same distance apart, or the snap interval should be an even fraction of the grid distance ($1/2$, $1/4$, or $1/12$ of the grid distance, for English units; or *orders of magnitude,* for metric units). In this way, the grid serves as a visual reminder of the snap interval.

Technically savvy people love to say "order of magnitude," a term which simply means "a factor of ten." A dollar is an order of magnitude more valuable than a dime, and two orders of magnitude less valuable than a hundred-dollar bill. Now you can toss around the phrase *order of magnitude,* too!

You nearly always want a grid in your drawing because it's so useful in orienting objects to one another. (You can turn it on and off by clicking the GRID button in the status bar, or by pressing the function key, F7.) You may not always want to use a snap interval, however, because some drawings, such as a contour map, don't contain objects that align on specific points. (However, if you're designing a building, not having a snap interval that works may be a bad sign. You may get a thumbs up from the client, but a thumbs down from the general contractor who has to build the thing.)

You can set your grid to work in one of two ways: to help with your drawing or to help with your printout. For a grid that helps with your drawing, set the grid points a logical number of measurement units apart. Grid points, for example, may be 30 feet (10 yards) apart on a drawing of a football field. A grid that helps with your printout is different; you space this kind of grid so that a grid square represents a one-inch square on your final printout.

In either case, set the snap interval at the same value or any even division of it: One-half, one-fourth, and one-twelfth work well for architecture; one-half and one-tenth work well for mechanical drawings and for other disciplines. Good starting points for grid and snap intervals for specific drawings are provided in Tables 4-1 and 4-2, earlier in this chapter, and in Appendix B.

Setting grid and snap intervals in the Drawing Aids dialog box

If you're just finding out about grid spacing and snap intervals, use the Drawing Aids dialog box at first. By using the dialog box, you can quickly note and adjust the relationship between the grid and snap intervals. You're likely to want to change these settings often, however; if you do, you may also want to know how to use the command line to set them, as described in the next section.

To set the grid and the snap intervals by using the Drawing Aids dialog box, follow these steps:

1. **Choose Tools⇨Drawing Aids from the menu bar; or type** DDRmodes **on the command line and press Enter.**

   The Drawing Aids dialog box appears (see Figure 4-5).

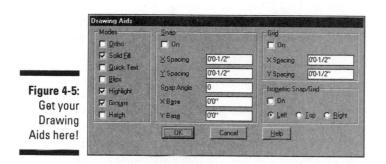

Figure 4-5:
Get your
Drawing
Aids here!

The dialog box has four parts, but you only need to concern yourself with the Snap and Grid sections. Some of the other settings are nerd stuff that you can probably live a long time without ever needing to think twice about; others are covered later in this book.

2. Click the On check box in the Grid section to turn on Grid.

Clicking this box creates a grid with spacing between grid points that is initially set to the snap distance, as described in Step 4.

3. Enter the X Spacing for the grid in the accompanying text box.

Use Table 4-1, Table 4-2, or Appendix B to select a grid spacing that maps to one plotted inch, based on your drawing size, scale factor, and paper size. Or just enter a value that makes sense to you in relation to the size of the objects you're drawing and your screen area; you probably want to have at least a 10 x 10 grid to start.

The Y spacing automatically changes to equal the X spacing. Don't change it; having the X and Y spacing equal creates a square grid, which is just what you want for now. (Maybe later you'll want a different X value in your grid, but this setting is fine 'til then.)

X measures horizontal distance; Y measures vertical distance. The AutoCAD drawing area shows an X and Y legend in case you forget. Legend has it that the mathematician René Descartes devised this scheme after watching a fly walk on a patterned ceiling. (This story would be better if he had thought it up while watching horses graze on a freshly mowed lawn, but I don't think you can put Descartes before the horse. . . .)

4. Click the On check box in the Snap section to turn on Snap.

This action creates default snaps half a unit apart.

5. Enter the X Spacing for the snap interval in the accompanying text box.

Use Table 4-1, Table 4-2, or Appendix B to select a snap spacing that works best for your drawing, or just enter a value that makes sense to you; any value that's an even fraction of the grid spacing works.

The Y spacing automatically changes to equal the X spacing. Don't change it; having them the same creates a square snap grid, which is just what you want for now.

The array of snap points is sometimes referred to as the *snap grid*. This term makes sense, because the snap points do form a grid, but it's easy to get confused between the snap grid and the other grid. What to call that one? The *visible grid* is a good name, because its purpose is to be seen. So if you use the term *snap grid* for your snaps, call the other grid the *visible grid*.

As long as you have the Drawing Aids dialog box open, you may as well make sure to turn off Blips (in the Modes section) if they're on. The Blips setting determines whether AutoCAD leaves little blips on-screen to mark points you select as you draw. One common reason for doing a redraw is to get rid of blips, however, and starting a redraw takes a moment — time you don't need to waste. So turn off Blips right now by clicking the check box to remove the check mark (if one is there) — unless, of course, you really like them.

Setting grid and snap intervals from the command line

If you need to change the visible grid and the snap grid often — for example, if you switch frequently between detail work on a small part of your drawing and large-scale work on the whole thing at once — knowing how to change grid and snap settings from the command line is definitely worth the effort. Follow these steps to use the command line to change these settings:

1. **Type GRID at the command line and press Enter.**

   The following prompt appears:

   ```
   Grid spacing(X) or ON/OFF/Snap/Aspect/ <0.5000>:
   ```

2. **Type the value for the grid spacing at the prompt and press Enter.**

   Use the suggested values from Table 4-1, Table 4-2, or the more-complete list in Appendix B.

   When you press Enter, the grid appears.

   If you're using Architectural or Engineering units, indicate feet by entering an apostrophe after the number, unless you're sure that you want a grid spacing in inches. (Fine for a light switch, but maybe not so good for the Los Angeles Coliseum seismic retrofit!)

3. **Type** SNap **at the command line and press Enter.**

   The following prompt appears:

   ```
   Snap spacing or ON/OFF/Aspect/Rotate/Style <0.50000>:
   ```

   Don't worry about the options on the command line labeled Aspect, Rotate, and Style; you can look them up in your AutoCAD manual in the unlikely event that you ever need them.

4. **Type the value for the snap spacing at the prompt and then press Enter.**

   Use the suggested values from Table 4-1, Table 4-2, or the more-complete list in Appendix B.

   After you press Enter, your cursor begins to snap to invisible "hot spots" that are separated by the snap distance.

Use an even division of the grid spacing for your snap setting. Values of $1/2$, $1/4$, and $1/12$ of the grid spacing work well, for example, if you're using feet and inches; values of $1/2$ and $1/10$ of the grid spacing work well if you're using metric units or miles.

You can quickly turn on or off the grid and snap spacings by entering the commands **GRID ON**, **GRID OFF**, **SNap ON**, and **SNap OFF** at the command line.

You can also double-click the snap button in the status bar to toggle snap on and off; the same goes for the grid button and the grid setting.

Press F7 to toggle the grid setting on and off; press F9 to toggle the snap spacing on and off.

Scaling, Scaling, over the Bounding Main . . .

Even though you know from the tables earlier in this chapter what scale your drawing is in, AutoCAD doesn't know the scale until you tell it. This situation is fine as long as you're just drawing shapes, but you're likely to want to use different *linetypes* (patterns that make some lines look different from others) and to want to add *dimensions* (measurements that show the size of the things you're drawing).

To help AutoCAD handle these additional elements correctly, you need to tell it your *scale factor* — how much it should magnify or shrink the appearance of linetypes in your drawing. If AutoCAD doesn't know what scale factor to use, dimensions can come out very tiny or very large, and line patterns can look waaaay too big or too small.

The scale factor that works best for linetypes is found in a system variable called LTSCALE (as in LineType SCALE). The scaling factor that works best for dimensions is found in a system variable called DIMSCALE. Chapter 2 offers more information on system variables.

You can start the LTSCALE command from a menu choice, but you can finish it only from the command line. You can also set the linetype scale in the Layers & Linetype Properties dialog box. You can set DIMSCALE from the command line or through a complicated dimensioning dialog box. This section describes how to set them both from the command line, for simplicity's sake. You can change either of these settings at any time.

When you change the dimension scale from the command line, it overrides the dimension scale in the currently active dimension style. To find out how to update the dimension style, see Chapter 10.

To set the dimension scale and linetype scale from the command line, follow these steps:

1. **Type** DIMSCALE **on the command line and press Enter.**

   AutoCAD responds with a prompt asking you for the dimension scale. The value already listed at the end of the prompt is the current dimension scale setting (the default), as shown in the following example:

   ```
   New value for DIMSCALE <1.0000>:
   ```

   DIMSCALE is only the most important of the dozens of variables that affect how dimensions look. Because DIMSCALE affects many of the other variables, it may be the only one you need (if you're lucky). To delve further into this complex topic, see Chapter 10.

2. **Type the value you want for the dimension scale on the command line and press Enter.**

   This value is the scaling factor for dimensions that's appropriate for your drawing, as listed in Tables 4-1 and 4-2 and Appendix B.

3. **Type** LTScale **on the command line and press Enter.**

   AutoCAD responds with a prompt, asking you for the scale factor. The value at the end of the prompt is the current linetype scale setting, as in the following example:

   ```
   New scale factor <1.0000>:
   ```

4. **Type the value you want for the linetype scale on the command line and press Enter.**

   This value is the scaling factor for linetypes that's appropriate for your drawing, as listed in Tables 4-1 and 4-2 and Appendix B. (You may want to use a somewhat smaller factor, such as half the scaling factor in the drawing; experiment with the linetype you've chosen.)

Print a couple of check prints of your drawing at an early stage — before you draw many objects — to make sure that everything works out the way you expect. Include dimensions, text, a couple of different linetypes, and graphics to test all the key elements of your drawing.

Start Me Up?

The Start Up dialog box (shown in Figure 4-6) comes up every time you start AutoCAD by double-clicking on the AutoCAD program icon. A very similar dialog box called Create New Drawing (only the Open a Drawing button is missing) comes up whenever you choose File⇨New in AutoCAD. (To get the same reaction as when you click the Open a Drawing button, choose File⇨ Open.) These two dialog boxes are new with AutoCAD Release 14 and are an attempt to ease the all-too-difficult process of setting up an AutoCAD drawing.

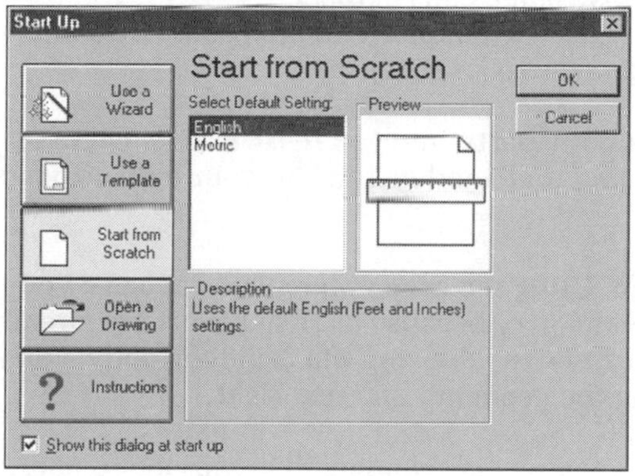

Figure 4-6:
Do get me started.

The Start Up dialog box looks kind of funny — more like a little application than a dialog box. The banner across the top of the dialog box changes, depending on which button you click. But it is indeed a dialog box, one that you see quite often as you use AutoCAD.

The Start Up dialog box can be a big help or a big hindrance, depending on how you use it. Its options vary greatly in their usefulness.

(Start from) scratch where it itches

Eleanor Roosevelt was famous for advising people to "scratch where it itches." That's kind of what you're doing when you use the Start from Scratch option — that is, you do whatever you want, without any help from anyone. AutoCAD just comes up with a blank document.

This blank document is set up with the drawing area representing an area 12 units wide by 9 high and a drawing scale of 1, which means that the drawing area pretty well represents an A-size, $8^1/2$"-x-11" piece of paper in *landscape,* or horizontal, orientation.

If you choose this option, immediately use the setup options in the preceding sections to get your drawing set up appropriately, and you'll be in great shape.

Starting the drawing from scratch is like starting a new drawing in Release 12 or Release 13 with the default ACAD.DWG prototype drawing. Because Release 14 has templates, as described below, it uses the template drawing ACAD.DWT instead.

Use a template of doom

Using a template is actually a great idea. A *template* is simply a drawing that you can't edit, and whose name ends in the letters DWT; when you try to open it, you open a *copy* of the template. You're prompted for a new filename, and the original stays unchanged.

So templates serve as body parts, and you're Dr. Frankenstein — you make a copy of the original and then modify it to suit your evil purposes. Sounds like fun, huh?

Well, templates are fun. Using the correct template can save you hours of time and much needless worry because all the options are already set correctly for you. You know the drawing will print correctly; you just have to worry about getting the geometry and text right.

The only problem with templates is finding the right one to use. AutoCAD isn't much help here. The good news is that AutoCAD gives you a bunch of templates; the bad news is that it doesn't tell you anything about them. Also, all the templates provided with AutoCAD Release 14, except ACAD.DWT and ACADISO.DWT, use paper space; to learn how to use paper space, see Chapter 13.

To help you, I'm providing a description of exactly how to start with a template and a table of what all the templates that AutoCAD Release 14 provides are actually like. This way, you can zoom to the exact template you want.

1. **Close AutoCAD and restart it by double-clicking on the AutoCAD icon or by choosing AutoCAD from the Start menu.**

   The Start Up dialog box appears.

You can accomplish the same thing by choosing File⇨New from within AutoCAD. If so, the dialog box that appears is the same, except that it's called Create New Drawing and it doesn't have a button labeled Open a Drawing.

2. Click the Use a Template button.

The center of the dialog box changes to display three areas: Select a Template, Preview, and Template Description.

- *Select a Template* presents a list of templates that come with AutoCAD. Table 4-4 lists a description of each template.

- *Preview* shows a small thumbnail sketch of what the currently highlighted template looks like.

- *Template Description* gives a brief description of what the template contains.

3. Highlight the template name you want to look at in the scrolling list.

The Preview and Template Description change to reflect the highlighted template.

4. Click OK or double-click the template name to open the template you choose.

A new drawing with no name appears. (The template you opened remains unchanged.)

5. Save the file under a new name.

Take the time to save the drawing to the appropriate name and location now so you can worry about getting your drawing right.

6. Make needed changes.

For most of the templates that come with AutoCAD, you need to consider changing the units, the limits, grid and snap settings, linetype scale, and dimension scale. See the section "Seven Not-So-Deadly Steps to Setup," later in this chapter.

7. Consider saving the file as a template.

If you'll need other drawings in the future similar to the current one, consider saving your modified template as a template in its own right. See the section "Creating Terrific Templates," later in this chapter.

Find or create templates for the main types of drawings that you do. Perfect them over time. You'll save yourself hours of setup hassles, and the quality of your work will go up. Instructions on how to set up templates appear later in this chapter.

Table 4-4			Templates That Come with AutoCAD			
Template Name	**Paper Size**	**Drawing Scale**	**Limits**	**Units**	**Grid**	**Snap**
acad.dwt	A	1=1	12 x 9	Decimal	.5	.5
acadiso.dwt	A	1=1	420 x 290	Decimal	10	10
ansi_a.dwt	A	1=1	11 x 8.5	Decimal	.25	.25
ansi_b.dwt	B	1=1	17 x 11	Decimal	.25	.25
ansi_c.dwt	C	1=1	17 x 22	Decimal	.25	.25
ansi_d.dwt	D	1=1	22 x 34	Decimal	.25	.25
ansi_e.dwt	E	1=1	34 x 44	Decimal	.25	.25
ansi_v.dwt	A	1=1	8.5 x 11	Decimal	.25	.25
archeng.dwt	D	1=1	36 x 24	Decimal	.25	.25
din_a0.dwt	a0	1=1	1189 x 841	Decimal	10	10
din_a1.dwt	a1	1=1	841 x 594	Decimal	10	10
din_a2.dwt	a2	1=1	594 x 420	Decimal	10	10
din_a3.dwt	a3	1=1	420 x 297	Decimal	10	10
din_a4.dwt	a4	1=1	210 x 297	Decimal	10	10
gs24x36.dwt	D	1=1	34.5 x 23	Decimal	.25	.25
iso_a0.dwt	a0	1=1	1189 x 841	Decimal	5	5
iso_a1.dwt	a1	1=1	841 x 594	Decimal	5	5
iso_a2.dwt	a2	1=1	594 x 420	Decimal	5	5
iso_a3.dwt	a3	1=1	420 x 297	Decimal	5	5
iso_a4.dwt	a4	1=1	210 x 297	Decimal	5	5
jis_a0.dwtt	a0	1=1	1189 x 841	Decimal	10	10
jis_a1.dwt	a1	1=1	841 x 594	Decimal	10	10
jis_a2.dwt	a2	1=1	594 x 420	Decimal	10	10
jis_a3.dwt	a3	1=1	420 x 297	Decimal	10	10
jis_a4l.dwt	a4	1=1	297 x 210	Decimal	10	10
jis_a4r.dwt	a4	1=1	210 x 297	Decimal	5	5

L-type Scale	Dim'n Scale	Title Block	Description
1	1	None	Normal template file (English standard)
1	1	None	Normal template file (Metric standard)
1	1	Top & bottom	ANSI A (landscape) title block and border
1	1	Top & bottom	ANSI B title block and border
1	1	Top & bottom	ANSI C title block and border
1	1	Top & bottom	ANSI D title block and border
1	1	Top & bottom	ANSI E title block and border
1	1	Top & bottom	ANSI V (portrait) title block and border
1	1	Right	Architectural 24" x 36" title block and border
1	1	Lower right corner	DIN A0 title block and border
1	1	Lower right corner	DIN A1 title block and border
1	1	Lower right corner	DIN A2 title block and border
1	1	Lower right corner	DIN A3 title block and border
1	1	Bottom	DIN A4 title block and border (portrait mode)
1	1	Right edge	Generic 24" x 36" title block and border
1	1	Right corners	ISO A0 title block and border
1	1	Right corners	ISO A1 title block and border
1	1	Right corners	ISO A2 title block and border
1	1	Right corners	ISO A3 title block and border
1	1	Right corners	ISO A4 title block and border (portrait mode)
20	1	Lower corners	JIS A0 title block and border (Japanese)
20	1	Lower corners	JIS A1 title block and border
20	1	Lower corners	JIS A2 title block and border
20	1	Lower corners	JIS A3 title block and border
20	1	Lower corners	JIS A4 title block and border
1	1	Top and bottom	JIS A4 title block and border (portrait mode)

Use a (not so?) wonderful wizard

One of the most promising features in Release 14 is the Setup Wizards in the Start Up dialog box. Given how hard it can be to set up an AutoCAD drawing so that everything fits and it prints successfully, the wizards seem very promising indeed.

To use a wizard, just click the Use a Wizard button in the Start Up dialog box or the Create New Drawing dialog box. Then choose Quick Setup or Advanced Setup. (Figure 4-7 shows the choice between the two.) The appropriate wizard starts.

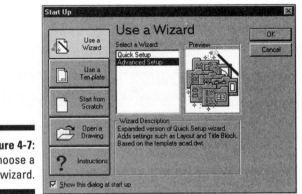

Figure 4-7:
Choose a
wizard.

The good news is, the wizards set up several parameters for you:

- ✔ **Quick Setup Wizard:** Sets up units and prompts you for the drawing area to represent
- ✔ **Advanced Setup Wizard:** Adds angular units, title block, and paper space layout questions

The bad news is, neither wizard ever asks you the paper size nor the drawing scale. This omission might be okay if the wizards assumed some standard paper size and then calculated an appropriate drawing scale. But instead, the wizards invent a drawing scale that doesn't fit any standard.

Unfortunately, a drawing with a nonstandard drawing scale is almost useless. Trying to fix the drawing scale is more trouble than just following the steps in this chapter to set up your drawing.

Hopefully, the setup wizards will be improved in a future release of AutoCAD. Until then, you're best off avoiding them and advising others to do so, too.

Get a drawing open

Opening an existing drawing is something you do every day. AutoCAD Release 14 makes finding the drawing you need easier than in previous releases.

You can use one of two dialog boxes to find files:

- ✔ The Select File dialog box enables you to locate a file whose name and location you know.

- ✔ The Browse/Search dialog box enables you to do more speculative searching — to find a file whose location you don't know or to preview many files to see whether one that meets your needs is available. You reach the Browse/Search dialog box by choosing the Find File option within the Select File dialog box.

The shortcut for creating a new drawing is Ctrl+N; for opening an existing drawing, the shortcut is Ctrl+O.

Getting a select-ed file

To select a file to open, click the Open a Drawing button in the Start Up dialog box. A short list of recent files appears. If this list doesn't go back far enough to include the file you want, click the More files button or choose File⇨Open from the AutoCAD menu bar. The Select File dialog box, shown in Figure 4-8, appears.

List/details buttons   Preview box

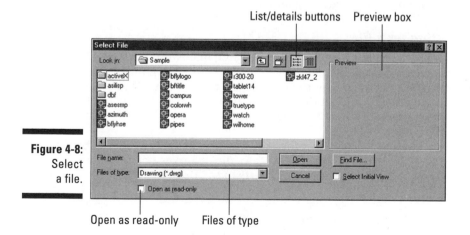

Figure 4-8:
Select
a file.

Open as read-only   Files of type

The Select File dialog box is a standard Windows "Open File" dialog box, with some special features. Try clicking all the different buttons and options now so that you know what capabilities are available when you need them. Include the Browse/Search dialog box and its Browse and Search tabs, described in the following list, in your experimenting.

Some of the standard and special features of the Select File dialog box that are of special interest to AutoCAD users include:

- **List/Details:** This pair of buttons enables you to toggle between a view of filenames only and a view of filename, type, size, modification date, and more. In the Details view, you can sort by a different column, such as modification date, just by clicking on the column heading. Double-click to reverse the sort order.

- **Preview:** This preview window is larger than the ones in the Start Up or Create New Drawing dialog boxes but smaller than the largest preview available in the Find File dialog box. It shows a preview of any Release 13 or Release 14 drawing file you've highlighted.

- **Files of type:** You can choose drawing (DWG) files, interchange format (DXF) files, or template (DWT) files.

- **Open as read-only:** Click this check box to open a file as read-only. When in doubt, use this option, especially if you're opening someone else's drawing!

Use these options to help find the file you need. But if you can't find the right file with the Select File dialog box, the Browse/Search dialog box offers even more powerful searching options.

Browsing for a file

To use the Browse tab of the Browse/Search dialog box, click the Find File button in the Select File dialog box. The Browse/Search dialog box, as shown in Figure 4-9, appears, with the Browse tab at the front. (If you have previously used the Search option, the Search tab may be chosen. Click the Browse tab to bring it to the forefront.)

Browse lets you see files by previews. Most of the features of the Browse tab are either standard features of Windows dialog boxes or the same as in the Select File dialog box. The coolest parts of the Browse dialog box are the resizeable previews and the network connection options:

- **Size:** This option lets you change the size of previews and includes the capability to specify the largest preview area of any file searching mechanism in AutoCAD. Figure 4-9 shows the Browse tab with this largest option selected.

> ✔ **Network:** This option brings up another dialog box that enables you to specify network drives to search on. It even has an option that automatically reconnects you to the drive each time you start up — a real time-saver when you're using a drive on an ongoing basis, such as when you join a new project.

If the Browse tab isn't enough to help you track down that file, it's time to go to your last resort: the Search tab.

The Network dialog box is the standard Windows 95/Windows NT 4.0 Map Network Drive dialog box, which you may see used outside of AutoCAD.

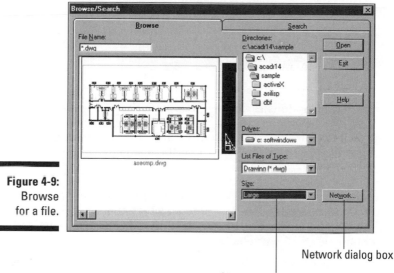

Figure 4-9:
Browse
for a file.

Network dialog box

Size drop-down list box

Searching for a file

To use the Search tab of the Browse/Search dialog box, click the Find File button in the Select File dialog box. The Browse/Search dialog box appears, with the Browse tab at the front. Click on the Search tab to bring it to the front. The Search tab is shown in Figure 4-10.

File list   Date & Time

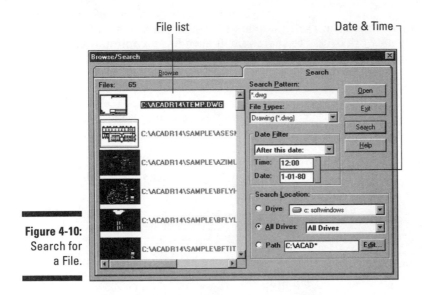

Figure 4-10:
Search for
a File.

Search gives you some options regarding the search pattern or location, but the main options that Search has that the regular Select File dialog box doesn't have are a *filter,* for removing files by date, and a different kind of display. I give the date filter a thumbs up, and the file display a thumbs down:

✔ **Date Filter:** The date filter enables you to specify a beginning date and time for the search — the date and time on which the file was created. I'd prefer that it let me choose to search by modification date instead, but this option is still very valuable.

✔ **File display:** The display of files shows preview images of the drawings in a size that's too small to see much but that doesn't leave enough room to see the entire pathname and filename. You have to scroll horizontally and vertically to see everything, and you can almost never see a file's entire pathname and filename at once.

If you frequently have a hard time finding the files you need, consider creating some kind of record of files you've worked on. If you were to print an A-size view of each file you did significant work on; wrote the filename, date, and a couple of notes on the printout; and stuck that page in a file by chronological order, you'd be better able to find files than 90 percent of your coworkers.

Creating Terrific Templates

I bet you didn't notice this fact, but every drawing you create in AutoCAD is based on a *template* — a file that AutoCAD uses as the base for the initial drawing — whether or not you choose the Use a Template option in the Start Up or Create a New Drawing dialog boxes. Templates are a new feature in AutoCAD Release 14 that enables you to create special files for use as a "master" that is then modified to create individual drawings. (Templates are an upgraded replacement for *prototypes,* a previously existing feature.) Templates have a special filename extension, DWT, and descriptions that are displayed when searching for a file.

To save yourself a great deal of time going forward, create a new template every time you set up a drawing so that you can reuse it later. After you finish the initial setup work on a new drawing, save that drawing as a template. Eventually, you'll have a template for each paper size and scale factor combination that you use. You may also want to include a basic set of layers and a suitably scaled title block in each template.

After you save your drawing as a template, save it again under its regular name in the directory you want. Then you can go back to working on the drawing.

You can initiate the save process from either the menus or the command line. In either case, you use the Save As dialog box to save your work. Follow these steps to save your drawing as a template:

1. **Choose File⇨Save As from the menu bar; or type** SAVEAS **at the command line and press Enter.**

   The Save Drawing As dialog box appears, as shown in Figure 4-11.

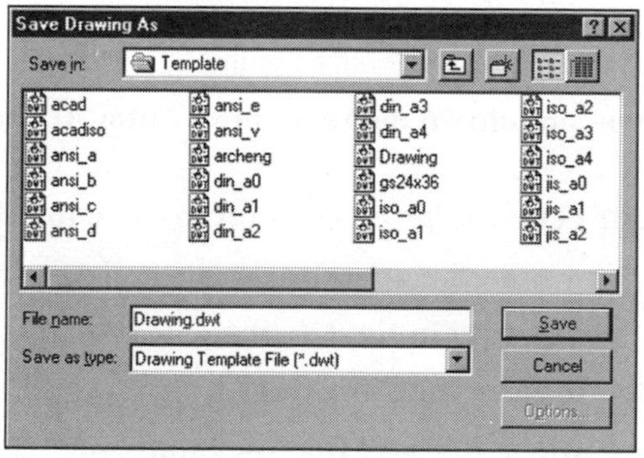

Figure 4-11:
Saving a
drawing as
a template.

2. **From the Save as type pull-down menu, choose Drawing Template File (*.dwt).**

3. **Navigate to the subdirectory where you want to store the drawing.**

   You probably want to create a subdirectory just to hold template drawings.

4. **Enter the name of the drawing in the File name text box. Add .DWT at the end of the filename.**

   A name such as ESIZ48SC.DWT may seem cryptic at first glance, but a name that includes the paper size (ESIZ, or E size) and scaling factor (48SC) actually may help you find the template you need later.

   Because AutoCAD Release 14 runs only on Windows 95 and Windows NT, both of which support long filenames, you may be tempted to use a long filename for your AutoCAD Release 14 files. That's fine, because Release 14 drawings can only be opened by people who are also running 32-bit versions of Windows, which support long filenames. But if you save the file to an earlier version of AutoCAD, be sure to give it a filename using the DOS 8.3 pattern. (An eight-character filename followed by a three-character extension, such as BUDSMITH.DWG.)

5. **Click the Save button to save your drawing.**

   The drawing is saved as a template. A dialog box for the template description appears.

6. **Enter the template file description and measurement units (English or Metric).**

   Enter the key info now; otherwise, you may never record it.

7. **Click OK to save the file.**

8. **To save your drawing as a regular drawing, choose File⇨Save As from the menu bar; or type** SAVEAS **at the command line and press Enter.**

   The Save Drawing As dialog box appears again.

9. **From the Save as type pull-down menu, choose AutoCAD Release 14 Drawing (*.dwg).**

10. **Navigate to the subdirectory where you want to store the drawing.**

    Use a different directory than the one with your template drawings.

11. **Enter the name of the drawing in the File name text box.**

12. **Click the Save button to save your drawing.**

    The file is saved. Now, when you save it in the future, the regular file, not the template file, gets updated.

Seven Not-So-Deadly Steps to Setup

Of the hundreds of commands available to you in AutoCAD, you really need concern yourself with only seven commands for setting up your drawing correctly. Use Table 4-5 to find both menu-driven and command line versions of these seven basic steps to setup.

Table 4-5	Seven Serviceable Setup Steps	
Step	*Menus/Dialog Boxes**	*Command Line*
Units & Angles	Format⇨Units; or DDUNITS command	UNITS command
Limits	Format⇨Drawing Limits	LIMITS command
Grid	Tools⇨Drawing Aids; or DDRMODES command	GRID command
Snap	Tools⇨Drawing Aids; or DDRMODES command	SNAP command
Linetype scale	Format⇨Linetype; or DDLTYPE command	LTSCALE command
Dimension scale	Format⇨Dimension Style, Geometry button; or DDIM command	DIMSCALE command
Save template drawing	File⇨Save As; or SAVEAS command	SAVEAS command

* The commands that start with "DD" access dialog boxes;
  other commands work on the command line.

After you know the basic steps of setup, you can get off to a much better start on your AutoCAD drawings. Just keep in mind the following tips:

✔ Saving your drawing as a template requires no special procedures; just save it with the extension DWT, and save it someplace away from your regular drawings.

✔ For the linetype scale and dimension scale, use the values that you find in Table 4-1 or Table 4-2, earlier in the chapter, or in the more-complete list in Appendix B.

Part II
Let There Be Lines

The 5th Wave

By Rich Tennant

In this part . . .

Setting up the program correctly makes AutoCAD work better, but all the setup in the world doesn't get your drawing done. Points, lines, circles, and other elements of geometry make up the heart of your drawing. And AutoCAD offers many different ways to draw, including, for the first time, the ability for the cursor to pull you toward object snap points. After you draw your lines, you usually must go back and make a few changes in them. And in the process, you probably need to zoom in and out and pan all around to see how the entire drawing is coming together, a process that is much enhanced in Release 14. Editing and viewing your work also are important parts of the drawing process; this part covers it all.

Chapter 5

Ready, Set, Draw!

*Y*ou're never off the hook entirely when it comes to AutoCAD setup, so this chapter starts out with a quick look at the minimal amount of setup you need to create a simple drawing in AutoCAD. Then it's off to the races with some of the more meaty aspects of CAD: drawing from the command line, undoing what you draw, and a look at a couple of different ways to control how the objects you draw on-screen appear and how you can best organize them.

Basic drawing is one of the least-changed aspects of AutoCAD in Release 14, but you have a little less setup work to do in the new version because some of the default settings are now Windows-appropriate instead of being compatible with old-style AutoCAD. (For information on how to return these settings to the old-school approach, see Chapter 3.) If you're looking for features that are new with Release 14, you only need to skim this chapter and look for the Release 14 icons. But if you're new to AutoCAD with this release, the whole chapter is especially valuable to you.

Snappy Setup

The easiest way to set up your drawing correctly is to use an existing drawing that's as similar as possible to the one you're going to create. This fact helps explain why so many drawings look so much alike and why offices often insist upon strict standards concerning the drawings created on a project. You can actually waste far more time perfecting an AutoCAD drawing — or trying to rescue a problematic one — than you would creating a hand-drawn one. So using a copycat approach — that is, starting with an existing drawing to use as a template for your new one, as described in Chapter 4 — often is a good idea.

But many times you may just need to start from scratch to fit the specific needs of your drawing or to avoid inheriting junk that *your* ever-so-special drawing simply doesn't need. This section, therefore, helps you quickly set up a couple of key settings. For the complete story on AutoCAD and drawing setup, see Chapters 3 and 4.

Setting selection settings . . . selecting set- . . . er, whatever

Set your selection settings as described in this section to make AutoCAD behave like a standard Windows application. You need to set your selection settings only once, so these steps use a dialog box instead of the command line.

To set your selection settings to Windows style, follow these steps:

1. **Choose Tools⇨Selection from the menu bar.**

   The Object Selection Settings dialog box appears.

2. **Click the following check boxes as needed to turn on each selection setting:**

   • Noun/Verb Selection

   • Use Shift to Add

   • Press and Drag

   • Implied Windowing

   • Object Grouping

3. **Click OK to exit the dialog box and put your settings into effect in your drawings.**

Note: If you're an experienced AutoCAD user and you don't want to change to the more modern way of operating, be aware that the balance of this book assumes that you use the Windows-style settings. You may need to be flexible in interpreting the detailed instructions in some of these procedures if you still use the old AutoCAD-style settings. See Chapter 3 for more information on keeping the old-style settings.

Getting a grip on your drawing

AutoCAD *grips* (little handles that show up on objects after you select the objects) are different from grips found in other drawing packages, but they're also powerful and flexible. You can easily turn them on and off from the command line by following these steps:

1. **To turn on grips, simply type** GRIPS 1 **on the command line and press Enter.**

2. **To turn off grips, type** GRIPS 0 **on the command line and press Enter.**

Zooming in on the results

After your other settings are, well, *set,* you can use the ZOOM command to zoom in on the drawing so that your screen displays the entire grid. (*Zooming* just gives you a closer-up or farther-away view of your drawing.)

Having your screen display your entire grid as you start your drawing can be pretty useful, and you probably want to zoom out to that view at various times during your work so that you can examine your entire drawing at once. Two commands give you a view of the entire grid: The first command zooms out so that the grid fills your drawing area; the second command zooms out an additional 10 percent to give you a little working room around the edges of the drawing. Both commands require that you type ZOOM on the command line, but that similarity shouldn't confuse you at all if you simply follow these steps:

1. **Type** Zoom **on the command line and press Enter.**

2. **To show your entire grid on-screen, type** ALL **at the prompt and press Enter.**

   AutoCAD displays the words Regenerating drawing, and then a new command prompt appears.

3. **Type** Zoom **on the command line a second time and press Enter.**

4. **At the prompt, type** .9X **to give yourself a little working space, and press Enter again.**

The following example shows the command line with these commands entered:

```
Command: ZOOM
All/Center/Dynamic/Extents/Left/Previous/Vmax/Window/
          <Scale(X/XP)>: ALL
Regenerating drawing.
Command: ZOOM
All/Center/Dynamic/Extents/Left/Previous/Vmax/Window/
          <Scale(X/XP)>: .9X
```

In this example and elsewhere in AutoCAD, just press the spacebar at the command prompt, or press Enter, to repeat the preceding command.

How to Draw

The rudest shock for the novice user of AutoCAD is the level of complexity involved in using AutoCAD as opposed to using most other drawing programs. (Well, actually the rudest shock is probably the price — *ten times* what a standard drawing program costs; the *second* rudest shock is the additional complexity.) The difficult setup procedures and numerous methods of controlling what's happening on-screen in AutoCAD can be quite daunting without help. At no point is the program's complexity more apparent than when you're simply trying to draw something — *anything!* — on-screen. But the power of AutoCAD makes the price and initial learning curve worthwhile; the additional power of add-on programs for specific needs, available from Autodesk and other companies as well, make AutoCAD invaluable.

In AutoCAD, you can draw either by using the mouse or by entering commands from the command line. Each drawing option offers its own special advantages. But to really make AutoCAD sing, you want to use a combination of the two methods. The command line is good for entering data about the initial part of the drawing and its main elements; the mouse is good for adding more elements that depend on the initial ones, for editing, and for adding text, dimensions, and annotations.

One of the few changes in the look of AutoCAD in Release 14 is the new look and feel of the cursor. The cursor crosshairs now occupy 5 percent of the screen by default, instead of extending to the edges of the drawing area. And the cursor changes shape to reflect the object snap point that it's approaching.

Drawing on command

Whenever AutoCAD users talk about using the command line to "enter geometry," they mean something quite different from merely using the command line to enter commands. You can enter commands from the command line any time if you want; in fact, how you enter commands in AutoCAD is just a matter of deciding which of the following methods is fastest for you to use and easiest for you to remember:

- ✔ Use the mouse to choose the command from a menu.
- ✔ Use Windows keyboard shortcuts to choose the command from a menu.
- ✔ Use the mouse to click an icon to launch the command.
- ✔ Use the keyboard to enter the command from the command line.

Entering geometry from the command line, on the other hand, means using the command line to specify the actual coordinates of points on your drawing. This method enables you to draw complicated shapes, with great accuracy, without ever picking up the mouse. (Unless you become really, really confused in placing your points on-screen, in which case your drawing is likely to wind up looking like particularly ugly graffiti.)

Experienced AutoCAD users can undoubtedly work faster than rank novices, especially when creating a new drawing, because they are quite accustomed to using the command line to quickly enter coordinates for their drawing. Entering drawing coordinates from the command line effectively, in the lofty manner of these AutoCAD experts, requires that you master the following different ways to enter keyboard coordinates:

- ✔ Absolute entry of X,Y coordinates
- ✔ Relative entry of X,Y coordinates
- ✔ Relative entry of polar coordinates

X,Y coordinates are two-dimensional coordinates defined by the Cartesian coordinate system. A specific point, called the *origin,* is defined as being 0,0. Other points are defined by moving first in an *X,* or right/left, direction, and then in a *Y,* or up/down, direction.

You define the X,Y coordinates on-screen when you specify a drawing's limits; limits make the on-screen coordinates meaningful to the drawing you create by scaling them to a paper size. The grid you define shows some of the points in the X,Y map, and the snap grid you define — if you turn on the snap grid — tells you which points in the X,Y map you can select with the mouse.

The following sections further define the two types of X,Y coordinates as well as the third type of coordinates — polar coordinates.

If you're new to AutoCAD or just not yet familiar with all the different types of coordinate entry, try doing the following examples yourself; knowing all the different ways to enter geometry is a good way to improve your productivity with AutoCAD.

Absolute coordinates

Absolute coordinates are an unvarying description of a point's location. For relative coordinates and polar coordinates, described below, you need to enter a special symbol with the numbers to specify the coordinate type; but with absolute coordinates, you just enter the numbers. If the lower-left corner of your drawing is 0,0, for example, the absolute coordinates 2,1 take you 2 units to the right of the lower-left corner and 1 unit above the corner. No matter where on-screen you're working at a given time, the absolute coordinates 2,1 describe that same location. If you try to draw a line from 2,1 to 2,1, it doesn't go anywhere; it starts and ends at the same point.

The following example displays the commands you would enter on the command line to draw a three-unit-wide square starting at 2,4 by using absolute coordinates:

```
Command: LINE
From point: 2,4
To point: 5,4
To point: 5,7
To point: 2,7
To point: C
```

Instead of entering point coordinates such as 2,4 from the keyboard, you can enter them by clicking at the appropriate point on-screen with the mouse.

You can always complete a line command for a triangle, square, or other shape by typing **C**, for *close*, at the command prompt. The C closes the shape.

In case you've forgotten my advice from waaay back in Chapter 3, do *not* use spaces on the command line, such as between point coordinates, because AutoCAD interprets them as returns. A definite no-no!

Figure 5-1 shows the screen with a square drawn on it by using absolute coordinate commands.

From 2,7 to 2,4

From 5,7 to 2,7   From 5,4 to 5,7

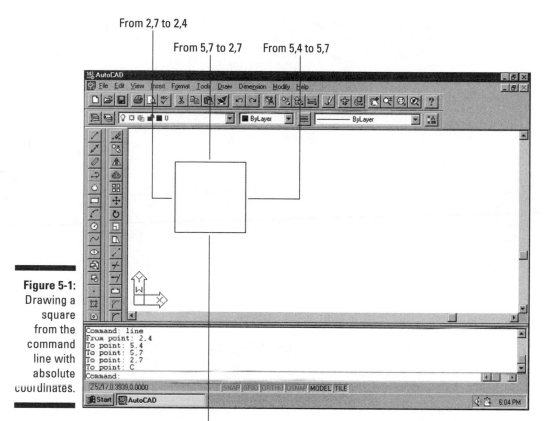

From 2,4 to 5,4

Figure 5-1:
Drawing a
square
from the
command
line with
absolute
coordinates.

Relative coordinates

Relative coordinates describe where a point is in relation to the previous
point you specified. A set of relative coordinates is designated by preceding
the coordinates with the @ symbol. If the first point you specify is **0,0**, for
example, you can move to 2,1 from the command line two ways: by entering
the absolute coordinates **2,1** or by entering the relative coordinates **@2,1**.
Now if, at this point (pun intended), you enter the absolute coordinates **2,1**
again, you don't go anywhere new; but if you enter the relative coordinates
@2,1, you move right two units and up one.

The relative coordinates described here use the X and Y displacement from
the previous point; for relative coordinates that use an angle and a displacement, see the next section.

The following example displays the commands you would enter on the command line to draw a four-unit-wide, two-unit-high rectangle starting at 6,6 by using relative coordinates:

```
Command: LINE
From point: 6,6
To point: @4,0
To point: @0,2
To point: @-4,0
To point: C
```

You can always complete a line command for a triangle, square, or other shape by typing **C**, for *close*, on the command line. The C closes the shape. (Sorry to repeat this note from the previous page, but plenty of people use this book as a reference and therefore miss some of the context.)

Figure 5-2 shows the screen with a rectangle drawn on it by using relative coordinate commands.

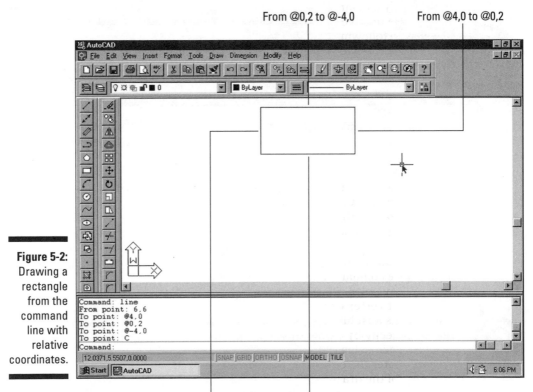

Figure 5-2: Drawing a rectangle from the command line with relative coordinates.

Polar coordinates

Polar coordinates are always relative, because they describe the angle and distance of one point from the previous point. The angles you enter for polar coordinates depend on the angle direction you specify; the default in AutoCAD assumes that an angle straight up is 90 degrees, an angle to the right is 0 degrees, an angle to the left is 180 degrees, and an angle straight down is 270 degrees. This default setting represents the most commonly used angle directions.

To change the angle direction to something different, such as designating straight up as 0 degrees, type **ddUNIts** on the command line and press Enter to open the Units Control dialog box. Then click the Direction button in the dialog box. Chapter 4 contains more detail on changing angles this way.

The odd thing about polar coordinates is that, although they specify a point relative to the last point you entered, the *angle* you enter is absolute. No matter the direction of the last line segment you draw, the polar coordinates stay the same — just as you specified in the Units Control dialog box.

You specify a polar coordinate on the command line by using the @ symbol to indicate relative coordinates and the less-than symbol (<) to indicate an angle. The following example displays the commands necessary to draw an equilateral triangle, three units on a side, starting from the coordinates 5,5 and using polar coordinates:

```
Command: LINE
From point: 5,5
To point: @3<0
To point: @3<120
To point: C
```

You can always complete a line command for a triangle, square, or other shape by typing **C**, for *close*, on the command line. The C closes the shape. (Sorry to repeat this note yet again, but as we mentioned before, plenty of people use this book as a reference and therefore miss some of the context.)

Figure 5-3 shows the screen with a triangle drawn on it by using polar coordinate commands. Drawing the second side of the triangle demonstrates why polar coordinates are so important, because entering the uppermost vertex of the triangle exactly, either by using the mouse or by entering its absolute coordinates, is nearly impossible. Some points that are easy to specify by using polar coordinates are difficult or impossible to specify when using only absolute coordinates. By using polar coordinates, you can enter the exact point needed for the drawing and preserve the integrity of the drawing.

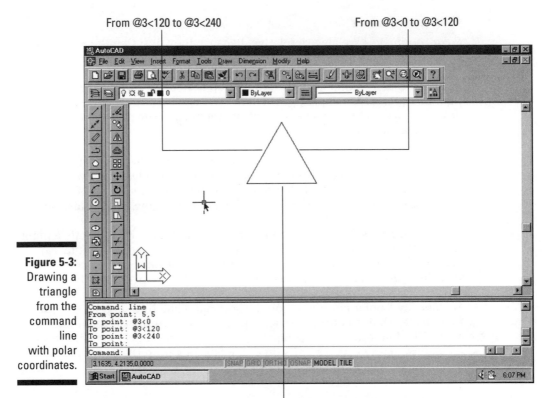

From @3<120 to @3<240   From @3<0 to @3<120

Figure 5-3:
Drawing a
triangle
from the
command
line
with polar
coordinates.

From 5,5 to @3<0

Getting the look right

Wanting different objects in your drawing to look different is a pretty natural
desire. A different look — different colors, lineweights, or linetypes — can
communicate important information about the characteristics of the object
being drawn, about what other objects it may be like, or even about the
relative depth of objects within a drawing. (That is, which *real-world* objects
are above or in front of one another; the drawn objects are, of course, all flat
and only as far from your nose as the screen or paper. Maybe I've been
spending too long looking at a screen myself. . . .)

The most commonly used ways that AutoCAD enables you to make objects
look different from one another are through changes to the *color* of an object
or to the *linetype* of an object:

✔ *Linetype* describes the thickness and the pattern of filled-in and empty spaces in a line. A thin line is distinguishable from a thick line, for example, and a solid line is easily distinguishable from a dotted line.

✔ *Color* is also used to differentiate objects, but more for on-screen differentiation than for any differentiation on the printout. That's mainly because most CAD drawings are either printed in black and white in the first place or are eventually photocopied into a black-and-white version, or are reproduced as a blueline print that others in the creation process must understand. So in most cases, plan to use color mainly to communicate nice-to-have information rather than must-have information.

Though color often "disappears" in the process of printing or reproducing a drawing, AutoCAD offers another way to distinguish lines. In the Plot dialog box, as described in Chapter 12, you can assign colors to different linewidths. This setting allows lines that are differentiated by color on-screen to be differentiated by thickness on the plot.

Users of AutoCAD assign linetype, color, and linewidth distinctions according to conventions that make them valuable. Linetypes most often indicate different types of objects; color, as often as not, indicates the layer that an object is on. (Color is then translated into linewidth at printing time.) Sometimes the linetype, the color, and the layer mean exactly the same thing; you may draw all the trees in your drawing in dashed lines, in green, on the Foliage layer. But you can also use layers to subdivide a category; you may subdivide the foliage into Trees, Bushes, and Grass layers, for example, all of which are green and all drawn with the same linetype.

You can also specify linetypes and colors for each individual object you create, which at first seems like a good idea because it gives you a great deal of control. But this practice can quickly become cumbersome if you must assign separate linetypes and colors for each type of object, as well as remember *why* you made all the decisions for each object. Sometimes, however, you simply find it necessary to be that specific, and if that's the case, AutoCAD quite handily supports this capability; just make sure that you use it as sparingly as you can. (Or you may need a whole 'nother computer just to keep track of what all the colors and linetypes for all your different objects mean.)

Many professions and projects develop detailed standards for how to use linetypes and layers. Linetypes are very important in helping the users of your drawing understand just what you're doing; layers are very important for sharing drawings with others currently working on the project or who may later want to reuse your work. Determine what standards, if any, exist for your profession and follow them relentlessly; doing so makes it possible for you to reuse your current work in later work that you do.

Using that layered look

In the following example, you create two layers by using different linetypes and colors and then draw objects on these layers. The objects in this example are the outline of a swimming pool and the water in the pool (but you can plug your own names into these basic steps at any point to create your own drawings). You use the Layer & Linetype Properties dialog box in this example; the setup steps at the beginning of this chapter describe how to create layers entirely from the command line if you want to do that instead.

In Release 12 and Release 13, you use the Layer Control dialog box for this procedure; in Release 14, you use the Layer tab of the new Layer & Linetype Properties dialog box. (Although writing "the Layer tab of the . . ." all the time is clumsy, putting these related functions in one dialog box does make sense.) Also new is the capability to modify layer properties through the layer control drop-down menu in the Object Properties toolbar; you don't have to come back to the dialog box to lock or unlock a layer, for example.

Follow these steps as a guide to creating layers for different linetypes and colors:

1. **Choose Format⇨Layer from the menu bar; or type** DDLMODES **at the command line and press Enter.**

   The Layer & Linetype Properties dialog box appears with the Layer tab selected, as shown in Figure 5-4. A new drawing has only one layer, Layer 0. You need to add the layers you need for your drawing.

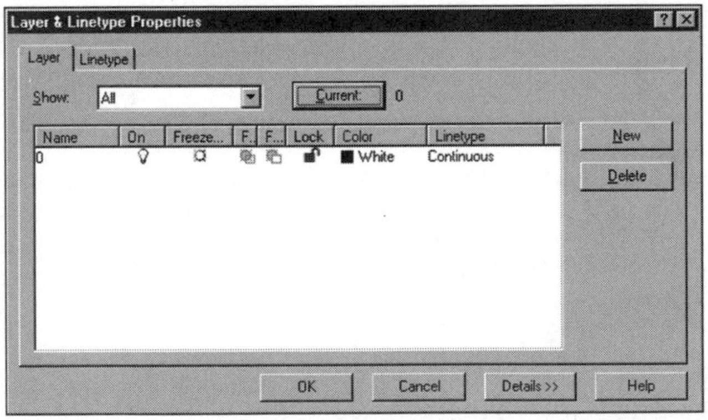

Figure 5-4:
The Layer tab of the Layer & Linetype Properties dialog box with only Layer 0 defined.

2. **Click the New button to create a new layer.**

   A new layer appears. It's given the name Layer1, but the new name is highlighted and selected so that you can easily type a new name to replace Layer1.

3. **Type a name,** Concrete **in this example, as the name for the new layer.**

In Release 14, AutoCAD automatically converts the layer name to an initial capital letter followed by lowercase letters. Try typing the name in all caps or all lowercase letters and watch what happens to it after you type it.

4. **On the same line as the new layer, click the color block or color name,** White, **of the new layer.**

The Select Color dialog box appears, as shown in Figure 5-5.

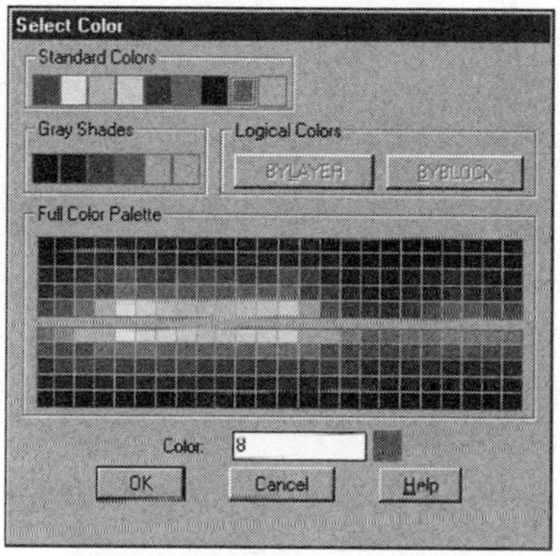

Figure 5-5:
The Select Color dialog box, with the color gray selected in the Standard Colors list.

5. **Click a color to select it as the color for this layer and then click OK.**

For the Concrete example, click gray, the eighth color from the left in the Standard Colors list.

The colors available on your system may be different from those on mine, so the exact appearance of your Select Color dialog box also may be different than that shown in the figure. But that's okay; just pick any of the Standard Colors that you want from the list on your system.

The Layer & Linetype Properties dialog box reappears. In the Name list, the Color for the Concrete layer changes to 8, which is the color number for gray. (This number also appears in the Color text box at the bottom of the Select Color dialog box after you select the color.)

6. **On the same line as the new layer, click the Linetype name of the new layer.**

In this case, the Linetype name is Continuous.

The Select Linetype dialog box appears, as shown in Figure 5-6.

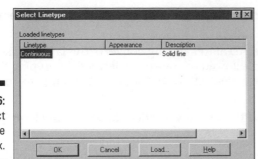

Figure 5-6:
The Select
Linetype
dialog box.

If you already loaded the linetypes you need for your drawing, the
Select Linetype dialog box displays them in the Loaded linetypes list.
If not, click the Load button and select the linetype file and linetype
you need. For this example, the linetype file is ACAD.LIN, in the subdirectory \ACADR14\SUPPORT (on my machine, at least), and the
linetype needed is Border. You can also load the linetype Divide2 at
this time, because you can use that linetype to indicate water in the
swimming pool.

7. **Click** Border **in the Loaded linetypes list to highlight and select it as
the linetype for the Concrete layer and then click OK.**

After you click OK, the Select Linetype dialog box disappears, returning
you to the Layer & Linetype Properties dialog box. In the Name list, the
Linetype for the Concrete layer changes to Border, the linetype you just
selected.

In previous releases of AutoCAD, the highlighting of selected items and
the way in which multiple-item selections were made was handled much
differently than in other Windows programs. In Release 14, highlighting
and multiple-item selections are very Windows-like, making selection
easier and more consistent.

8. **Repeat Steps 2 through 7 to create another layer called Water with
the standard color cyan (light blue) and the linetype Divide2.**

The Layer & Linetype Properties dialog box reappears with your two
new layers set up.

9. **Click OK to accept the new layer settings.**

Objective properties

In previous releases of AutoCAD, you use the Object Creation Modes dialog
box to change colors, linetypes, and other settings. If you're an experienced
AutoCAD user, you probably have typed DDEMODES from the command line
many times to bring up this dialog box. But now you don't have to bring up
this dialog box anymore; it's gone! In Release 14, most of the functions of
the Object Creation Modes dialog box have been moved into the Object

Properties toolbar, where they're much more readily available. For more information on what happened to the functions of the Object Creation Modes dialog box, see the topic DDEMODES in the AutoCAD Help system.

In Release 14, get in the habit of using the Object Properties toolbar to specify linetypes and colors for specific objects. It's available easily and is quick to use after you've done it a few times. Figure 5-7 shows the Object Properties toolbar and the parts of it that I cover in this section. (You've heard of *MTV Unplugged*? Well, we have Object Properties undocked!)

Figure 5-7:
Highlights of the Object Properties toolbar, undocked.

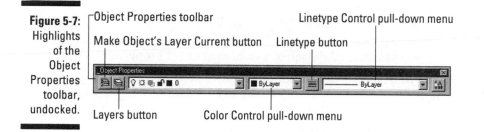

You can also specify linetype and color attributes from the command line. In many cases, you may want to change the linetype and color, draw a few objects, and then return to the color and linetype assigned to the layer you're working on.

ByLayer is the default setting for both colors and linetypes. This setting enables you to automatically use the color or linetype defined for a layer on objects in that layer. If an object has ByLayer assigned as its color, for example, and is on a layer assigned the color green, that object is shown in green. If you later change the layer's color to, say, red, all objects on the layer that are assigned ByLayer as their color attribute instantly become red as well.

In the following example, you do your drawing on Layer 0, the default layer for new objects in the standard AutoCAD drawing. You change the color and linetype by using the Object Properties toolbar; then you use the command line to change the color and linetype back to those of ByLayer. The steps in this example can serve as a guide for you to follow in creating your own objects.

To change the color and linetype of an object, follow these steps:

1. **In the Object Properties toolbar, click the Color Control pull-down menu in the middle of the toolbar.**

   The Color Control menu appears, as shown in Figure 5-8. It contains the standard colors plus any additional colors you have selected in this drawing.

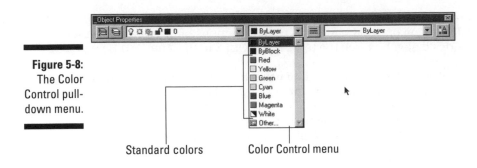

Figure 5-8:
The Color
Control pull-
down menu.

Standard colors   Color Control menu

2. Click the color that you want to use for your object.

The pull-down menu pulls back up, and the color name you selected appears in the Color Control area of the Object Properties toolbar.

To bring up the Select Color dialog box from the Color Control pull-down menu and choose a different color than those already on the list, choose the last item in the list.

3. Click the Linetype Control pull-down menu.

The Linetype Control menu appears, as shown in Figure 5-9. It contains all the linetypes you have loaded for use in the current drawing plus ByLayer, which assigns the linetype of the current layer, and ByBlock, which is for use with blocks and which you should avoid — at least until you read about blocks in Chapter 14.

Figure 5-9:
The
Linetype
Control
pull-down
menu.

Loaded linetypes

4. Click the linetype that you want to use for your object.

At this point, you can draw the object or objects that use the color and linetype you specified. After you finish, you can use the command line to change the color and linetype back to the default ByLayer attribute.

5. At the command line, type -LineType and press Enter.

6. To change the linetype, type SET at the prompt and press Enter.

7. At the prompt, type BYLAYER as the linetype and press Enter.

8. Press Enter again to complete the command.

9. **At the command line, type** COLOR **and press Enter.**

10. **At the prompt, type** BYLAYER **again as the color and then press Enter.**

The following lines show the commands and prompts you enter to set both the linetype and the color back to ByLayer:

```
Command: LINETYPE
?/Create/Load/Set: SET
New object linetype (or ?) <BYLAYER>: BYLAYER
?/Create/Load/Set: <Enter>
Command: COLOR
New object color <BYLAYER>: BYLAYER <Enter>
```

The Way You UNDO the Things You Do

One of the biggest problems in drafting is the sheer ease involved in thoroughly messing up an otherwise great drawing just by mismeasuring something or drawing an errant line or two. In a paper-and-pencil drawing, fixing such a mistake may requires so much erasing and redrawing as to basically be irreparable. But with AutoCAD, you can fix most mistakes. (Not all, mind you, but hey, you can't have everything!)

The mistakes that you *can* fix in AutoCAD are mostly errors of *commission;* that is, you commit an act you shouldn't have. You may, for example, draw a square in the middle of a complex drawing and then realize — ackkkk! — you should have drawn a circle instead. Well, no problem. Mistakes such as these are easy to fix in AutoCAD; these types of mistakes, in fact, are what the UNDO command was designed for. (Da da da da ta-daaa!)

But before I discuss this modern wonder of CAD, I must take time to mention the horror of (pause for effect) the mistakes you *can't* fix easily in AutoCAD! (Cue thunder and lightning.) These mistakes are mostly errors of *omission;* in other words, you neglect to perform a setup step or set a mode setting incorrectly, and, as a result, your drawing becomes very testy to work with. If you complete a complicated drawing but neglect to set limits correctly, for example, you may find that creating a printout of your drawing that looks at all fetching becomes very, very hard. You may need to rearrange the elements in your drawing considerably or even perform complicated manipulations in paper space (described in Chapter 13) just to get a decent-looking printout.

To help you repair either kind of error, AutoCAD provides a powerful UNDO/REDO feature. Unlike the undo capabilities of many other programs, the AutoCAD UNDO does — or undoes — almost anything you want, up to and including the following feats of design derring-do:

 ✔ UNDO goes back a nearly unlimited number of steps, all the way back to the beginning of the current drawing session.

 ✔ UNDO is not affected by saves; you can save your drawing and still undo actions performed before the save.

 ✔ UNDO affects almost all commands. The undo capabilities of some programs affect only specific commands; AutoCAD UNDO not only undoes items you actually draw but also mode settings, layer creation, and more.

 ✔ UNDO offers several different options for handling groups of commands or erasing several commands simultaneously.

This section describes the most useful features of the AutoCAD UNDO capability, those you need 99.9 percent of the time. For more details and information on other, less useful features, especially should an emergency arise, check the AutoCAD online Help facility or the AutoCAD manuals.

The AutoCAD UNDO does not work for all AutoCAD commands and does not reverse changes made to all system variables. Among the important commands AutoCAD can't undo are the following:

 ✔ CONFIG, used to configure AutoCAD.

 ✔ NEW or OPEN, used to create or access drawings.

 ✔ PSOUT, QSAVE, SAVE, and SAVEAS, used to save drawings to disk.

 ✔ PLOT, used to plot a drawing. (Because creating an UNDO command that makes the printer pick up a sheet of paper and erase it would be pretty difficult!)

If you're using the UNDO command to fix a complicated or long-ago mistake, consider saving your drawing to a different name before starting the UNDO process. You may want to save some parts of your work but not others, and having an additional copy of the messed-up drawing can help you do so.

AutoCAD provides two kinds of UNDO commands for reversing a single step. The more common command is *U*, short for UNDO (well, what did you expect — Unicorn?), and the less common command is *OOPS* (for obvious reasons).

Typing **U**, as described in this chapter, undoes a single step; typing out UNDO at the command line brings up several options, which you will rarely need. Experiment with the Undo command if you do need to use them.

OOPS reverses the last ERASE command. Just enter **OOPS** at the command line after you accidentally use ERASE to . . . uh, well, erase something, or some things. OOPS instantly reverses the effect of that ERASE. (This command also works if you simply change your mind, rather than making an out-and-out mistake.)

The ERASE command can be started by typing **Erase** at the command line or by clicking on the Erase button, the button that looks like a pencil with an eraser at the top of the Modify toolbar.

The UNDO command, however, does much more. The simplest way to use UNDO is to just keep undoing your previous actions until you work your way back to your mistake. To UNDO and REDO a command sequence a single step at a time, follow these steps:

1. **Use one of the single-step UNDO commands.**

   Your choices include the following actions:

   - Choose Edit⇨Undo from the menu bar.
   - Press Ctrl+Z.
   - Type **Undo** at the command line and press Enter.
   - On the standard toolbar, click the icon that displays a curved arrow pointing to the left.

The UNDO capability works even across saves of your drawing. It does not, however, work after you close your drawing and then reopen it. Think twice, therefore, before you close any drawing; you may later wish you had undone something in it first. And then it's too late.

2. **Think carefully now, before doing anything else, about whether you really wanted to perform an UNDO operation.**

   This warning is a *very important* one: The AutoCAD REDO capability only redoes the *last* step that you undo; unlike the UNDO command (or that annoying Energizer bunny), REDO does *not* just keep on going. In AutoCAD, as in life, you really don't want to undo much without thinking about it first. Otherwise, you can all too easily just keep undoing and undoing — and then realize too late that you've gone too far and undone valuable, even irreplaceable, work. Also, it is far too easy to undo one action, replace it with another, and only then realize that you didn't really want to undo the first action at all. Too late! If you enter another command after using UNDO, REDO doesn't work. Not even a little. So after each individual UNDO you perform, think — *think!* — about what you've just (un)done and make sure that you're truly glad you got rid of it, whatever it was, before you lose the capability to replace it.

3. **If you need to, redo the step by performing a REDO operation.**

   Your choices include the following actions:

   - Choose Edit⇨Redo from the menu bar.
   - Type **REDO** at the command line and press Enter.

• On the standard toolbar, click the icon that displays a curved arrow pointing to the right.

You can redo only *one action*.

Do not try to type **R** at the command line to redo a command. REDO does not work like UNDO in using its initial as the command to activate it. *R,* in fact, is the abbreviation for the REDRAW command, not REDO. If you enter **R** at the command line, not only must you wait while AutoCAD redraws the screen, but you also discover that the REDO command doesn't work anymore, because you executed another command after the UNDO. (If you think that this scenario seems like paying twice for one mistake, you're not alone.)

4. **Use one of the single-step UNDO commands (described in Step 1) again if you want to continue undoing.**

   Continue to choose Edit⇨Undo, press Ctrl+Z, enter **U** at the command line, or click the standard toolbar icon with the arrow curved to the left. Continue to consider, after each UNDO step, whether you're sure that you haven't already undone too much.

The best way to get to know the UNDO capability in AutoCAD is to experiment with it. Create a test drawing with different layers and other settings and create some geometry on-screen. Then use UNDO to back up through your actions, watching what happens as you do so. Experimenting helps you use UNDO intelligently and not overdo it when you really need it — and not overdo UNDO when you really need to REDO.

Chapter 6

Tooling Around in Your Drawing

The main purpose of AutoCAD, of course, is to support computer-aided drafting (what a concept!). And the most important activity in drafting is drawing *geometry* — shapes such as lines, circles, rectangles, and so on. Dimensions, text, and other important parts of the drawing — neat as they are — don't matter much unless the underlying geometry is right.

RELEASE 14

14

AutoCAD offers a small but powerful range of drawing tools. The drawing tool lineup isn't changed in Release 14; it wasn't changed in Release 13, either. What have changed from Release 13 to Release 14 are the toolbars — the *flyouts* that enabled you to access suboptions in the Draw toolbar are gone. (Maybe the AutoCAD programming team went to a San Francisco Giants game and decided to "sacrifice flyouts." Sorry. . . .) Instead, you start the command from the Draw toolbar and then enter options in the command line. Also, the Draw menu from Release 13 for DOS, with its *submenus,* has been integrated into Release 14, even though Release 14 is Windows-only. (A submenu is a secondary menu that is available as an additional choice only after you choose a menu item by highlighting it. I just want to make sure that you know that a submenu isn't what the crew of a submarine uses to decide on dinner.)

In this chapter, you find out how to get the most out of the AutoCAD drawing tools. You also discover — in detail — how to get what you want out of the AutoCAD user interface, whether you use the menus, the toolbars, or the command line. The tips and tricks you find in this chapter, in fact, help you navigate through all of AutoCAD.

The AutoCAD Drawing Tools

AutoCAD features relatively few types of objects to draw, but the types that the program does offer are quite powerful. For descriptive purposes, this chapter divides the drawing tools into the following three groups:

- ✓ **Lines**
- ✓ **Points and shapes**
- ✓ **Curves**

Third-party add-on packages that run with AutoCAD often add extra drawing tools to the mix; see the documentation that comes with the add-on program for information on such tools.

Using the command line is nearly unavoidable when drawing. You can start drawing commands from the Draw menu, which gives you submenus from which to choose options, but this method is slow. You can also use the Draw toolbar, but it simply types the initial command on the command line for you; you must then enter additional options on the command line yourself. The examples in this chapter, therefore, just cut right to the chase and show you how to do things from the command line. You can start the commands any way you like, though.

Table 6-1 offers an overview of most of the drawing tools native in AutoCAD, without the 3D-related commands. It describes the tools' major options and shows you how to access them from either the command line, the Draw menu, or the Draw toolbar. Use the table for an initial survey of what's available and as a quick refresher course if you're working along and suddenly find yourself at a loss for the command to access the tool you need. (Oh, and don't worry just yet if not all the terms on the table are familiar to you; they all become clear as you read through the chapter and use the commands. Trust me.)

Table 6-1	AutoCAD Drawing Tools and Commands			
Tool Entry	*Command*	*Major Options*	*Toolbar Icon*	*Draw Menu*
Line	LINE	Start, end points	Line	Line
Ray	RAY	Start point, point through which ray passes		Ray
Construction line	XLINE	Two points on line	Construction line	Construction line

Tool Entry	Command	Major Options	Toolbar Icon	Draw Menu
Multiline	MLINE	Justification, scale, style	Multiline	Multiline
Polyline	PLINE	Vertices	Polyline	Polyline
3D Polyline	3DPOLY	Vertices		3D Polyline
Polygon	POLYGON	Number of sides, inscribed/ circumscribed	Polygon	Polygon
Rectangle	RECTANG	Two corners	Rectangle	Rectangle
Arc	ARC	Various methods of definition	Arc	Arc; submenu for definition methods
Circle	CIRCLE	Three points, two points, tangent	Circle	Circle; submenu for definition methods
Donut	DONUT	Inside, outside diameters		Donut
Spline	SPLINE	Convert polyline or create new	Spline	Spline
Ellipse	ELLIPSE	Arc, center, axis	Ellipse	Ellipse; submenu for definition methods
Point	POINT	Point style	Point	Point; submenu for definition methods
Sketch	SKETCH	Increment, pen, erase, connect		

Flyouts and secondary menus

A *flyout* is not something sticky that you hang up on hot days to catch bugs and then toss out after it's full of the nasty beasties. A feature of some AutoCAD Release 14 toolbar icons, a flyout is an additional row or column of icons that appears, or *flies out,* after you click a particular icon. All the toolbar icons with little triangular pointers on them have flyouts.

In Release 14, however, flyouts have been removed from all the Draw toolbar icons. If you want to avoid the command line by *choosing* suboptions instead of *typing* them, you need to use the Draw menu instead. Figure 6-1 shows the Draw menu with options for an arc.

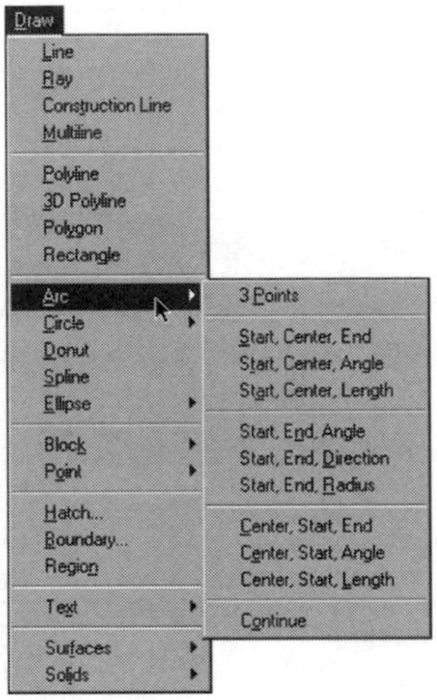

Figure 6-1:
The Draw
menu and
arc options.

To use a submenu, simply highlight the menu item you're interested in. (Any menu item with a submenu has a little right-pointing triangle next to it.) The submenu then appears next to the item. Drag the mouse straight across into the submenu; if you miss and drag the mouse up or down too far before you reach the submenu, the submenu disappears.

Commands versus the (ooey!) GUI

So what's your best course: to enter drawing commands from the command line or to choose them from the menus or toolbars in the graphical user interface — or the *GUI*, as those of us fond of sticky treats like to call it? I recommend that you memorize the command line entries for the drawing commands you use most. Choosing from the Draw menu is slow, especially if you must locate options on a secondary menu. Using the toolbar icons just starts the command and doesn't let you specify options; you usually need to finish the command at the command line. The drawing commands you enter at the command line enable you to keep your hands almost entirely on the keyboard, speeding your work. Also, the drawing commands are almost completely consistent across the different versions and different releases of AutoCAD, so if you ever move among versions, knowing these commands reduces your learning curve considerably.

So, as I've told you I've-forgotten-how-many times before (and will keep telling you until you commit it firmly to memory), *use the command line for frequently used options, and use the menus and toolbars for less frequently used ones!*

This chapter is filled with "Keyboard" icons to point out paragraphs that tell you how to create shapes from the command line. Go through and try them all. Getting a feel for working from the command line now puts you on the road to much faster work in AutoCAD later.

Toeing the Lines

You can create a rough drawing of just about anything by using only straight lines, so they're worth tackling first. The following two line commands are the most important ones you use in AutoCAD:

- ✔ **Lines**
- ✔ **Polylines**

The following additional line commands are also available in AutoCAD:

- ✔ **Rays**
- ✔ **Infinite lines**
- ✔ **Multilines**
- ✔ **Sketches**

The sections that follow describe each of these line-related commands.

AutoCAD mostly uses the term "construction line" to describe a line with no beginning or endpoint, but I use "infinite line" instead because it's more descriptive.

Lines (lines, everywhere a line . . .)

A *line* in AutoCAD is actually a series of one or more connected line segments. Each *segment*, or piece of a line with endpoints, is a separate object. This construction doesn't seem like a big deal until you try to move or otherwise edit a multi-segment line and find that you must select each and every piece of it. To avoid such a hassle, use polylines, described later in this chapter, instead of lines when you want the connected segments to be a single object.

Your first few attempts to draw a line in AutoCAD can be very confusing, because AutoCAD keeps prompting you for additional points. A *point* in AutoCAD can be either an endpoint, which marks the location of the end of an object, or a true *point*, a single spot that's not a part of anything else. CAD programs compose many objects in multiple connected line segments, so AutoCAD just keeps asking you for more points until you tell it to stop by pressing Escape, the spacebar, or Enter.

The LINE command doesn't offer any major options; it uses the currently selected linetype and color. The linetype selected is especially important; if the linetype is noncontinuous and the line bends often (compared to the distance between dots and dashes in the line), the line can be pretty hard to follow. Setting the linetype size to an appropriate value, as described in Chapter 5, is important in making a noncontinuous line visible as it bends around.

Creating a line

The three different ways to tell AutoCAD to create a line are as follows:

- ✔ Type **Line** on the command line and press Enter.
- ✔ Click the Line icon on the Draw toolbar.
- ✔ Choose Draw⇨Line from the menu bar.

Line example

The following example shows all the commands you need to enter on the command line to create a square made up of individual line segments:

```
Command: LINE
From point: 2,2
To point: 5,5
To point: 5,8
To point: 2,8
To point: C
```

Ortho mode is an important AutoCAD mode that affects lines and polylines. If ortho mode is on, you can draw lines only straight up, straight down, directly left, or directly right — and in no other direction. You can turn ortho mode on and off in the middle of a line command by clicking the word ORTHO in the status bar; by pressing the function key F8; or by preceding the ortho command with an apostrophe, as in **'ORTHO ON**. Entering the command **'ORTHO OFF** turns off ortho mode and enables you to draw lines in any direction. (The apostrophe makes the command *transparent,* meaning that you can enter it in the middle of another command.)

Polylines (wanna crackerline?)

A *polyline,* in its simplest form, is just like a line — that is, a series of connected line segments. Polylines, however, can include arcs as well as line segments. But no matter how many line segments and arcs it encompasses, a polyline (as a whole) is still one object. Plus, polylines offer options that regular lines lack: You can control the width of each segment or even specify a *halfwidth* that causes the polyline to taper along its length. (But *never* call your boss a halfwidth, even if he or she tapers along his or her length — whatever *that* means.)

After you create a polyline, you can use the PEDIT command to edit it, or you can convert the polyline to a collection of line and arc segments by using the EXPLODE command — although you lose the width defined for each segment when you explode a polyline.

Creating a Polyline

The three different ways to tell AutoCAD to create a polyline are as described in the following list:

- ✔ Type **PLINE** on the command line and press Enter.
- ✔ Click the Polyline icon on the Draw toolbar.
- ✔ Choose Draw⇨Polyline from the menu bar.

Polyline example

The following example shows the commands you enter on the command line to create a polyline with a straight segment, an arc, and another straight segment:

```
Command: PLINE
From point: 3,2
Current line-width is 0.0000
Arc/Close/Halfwidth/Length/Undo/Width/<Endpoint of line>:
      3,6
rc/Close/Halfwidth/Length/Undo/Width/<Endpoint of line>: A
Angle/CEnter/CLose/Direction/Halfwidth/Line/Radius/Second
      pt/Undo/Width/<Endpoint of arc>: 4,6
Angle/CEnter/CLose/Direction/Halfwidth/Line/Radius/Second
      pt/Undo/Width/<Endpoint of arc>: L
Arc/Close/Halfwidth/Length/Undo/Width/<Endpoint of line>:
      4,2
Arc/Close/Halfwidth/Length/Undo/Width/<Endpoint of line>:
      C<Enter>
```

Figure 6-2 shows the polyline — a single object — created by these commands.

Initial line segment   Arc   Final line segment

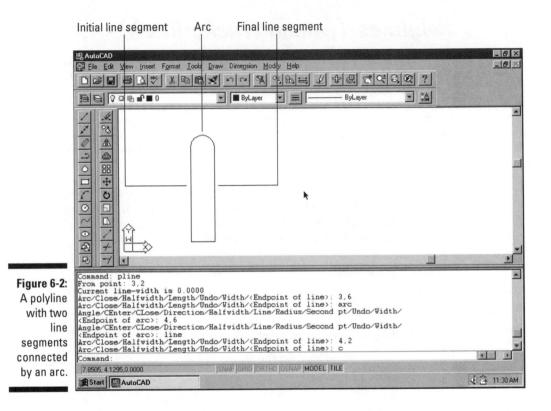

Figure 6-2:
A polyline
with two
line
segments
connected
by an arc.

Rays and infinite lines (Buck Rogers, watch out!)

You can use both *rays* and *infinite lines,* also known as *xlines,* mainly as guides to construction as you create your drawing, because no real-world object that you represent in a drawing can contain a true ray or infinite line. (Nothing in real life goes on forever, although some things — hopefully not this book — may seem to!) Even if you want to depict a ray or infinite line in your drawing, you simply use a line segment with one or two arrowheads to get the idea across.

Rays are easy to draw; you just define a starting point and then a second point through which the ray passes. AutoCAD then keeps prompting you for more of these second points, or *through points*, so that you can draw as many rays as you want that start at the same point as the first one. You can't, however, enter an angle to specify how many angular units to offset the current ray from the previous one, which would be fun.

Infinite lines are more complex. For an infinite line, you can specify not only a *from* and a *to* point but also whether the infinite line is horizontal through a single point, vertical through a single point, and so on. Figure 6-3 shows horizontal and vertical infinite lines. Rays and infinite lines both plot only to the outside edges of the drawing as defined by its limits (or by the edges of the outermost objects, if one or more objects lies outside the limits).

If you're using XLINEs and RAYs as construction lines (such as temporary or reference lines that you don't want to plot), draw them on a separate layer so that you can turn that layer off before plotting.

Creating a ray

The two different ways to tell AutoCAD to create a ray are as follows:

✔ Type **RAY** on the command line and press Enter.

✔ Choose <u>D</u>raw⇨<u>R</u>ay from the menu bar.

In Release 14, rays are one of several commands that are no longer available from an icon in the toolbar. If you want to draw rays fast, use the command line or the Windows shortcut for rays, Alt+D, R.

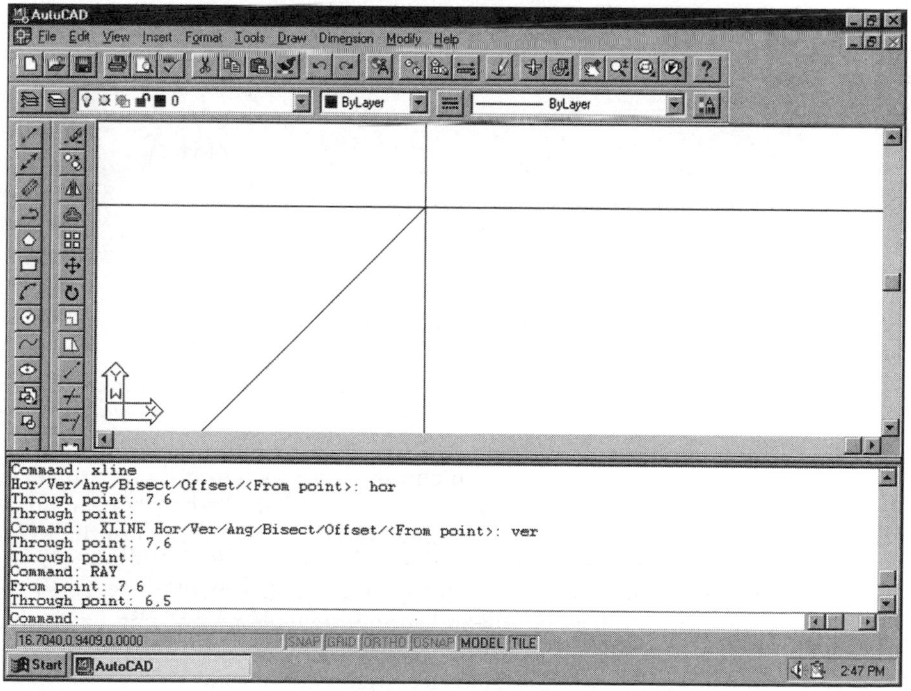

Figure 6-3:
Horizontal and vertical infinite lines and a ray.

Ray example

The following example shows the commands you enter at the command line to create a ray from point 3,6 through point 7,8, and on into infinity:

```
Command: RAY
From point: 3,6
Through point: 7,8
Through point: <Enter>
```

Creating an infinite line

The way to tell AutoCAD to create an infinite line is to either

- ✔ Type **XLine** on the command line and press Enter.
- ✔ Choose <u>D</u>raw⇨<u>M</u>ultiline from the menu.
- ✔ Click the Multiline icon on the Draw toolbar.

Infinite line example

The following example shows the commands you enter on the command line to create a horizontal and a vertical infinite line through point 7,6:

```
Command: XLINE
Hor/Ver/Ang/Bisect/Offset/<From point>: V
Through point: 7,6
Through point: <Enter>
Command: XLINE
Hor/Ver/Ang/Bisect/Offset/<From point>: H
Through point: 7,6
Through point: <Enter>
```

Multilines (lines aplenty)

Multilines are specialized types of lines that actually consist of several parallel lines — up to 16 — seen as one object. You can use the default style multiline, which includes two elements, or you can create your own, adding additional elements as you choose. Your own multilines can vary in the presence or absence of *joints* that appear at each corner and in the style of *end cap* that appears at the beginning and end of the multiline. Multilines that cross each other can create patterns to represent specific elements. Multilines are useful in architectural drawings and in drawing construction elements such as piping and geopolitical elements such as borders. For example, drawing a river by entering a single multiline, which then appears on-screen as two lines, saves a great deal of time.

If you want to use a multiline style other than the standard, two-line style, you must load or define it in advance. And if you want to modify the standard style before using it, you must also do so in advance. Use the MLSTYLE command on the command line to load and modify multiline styles. This command opens the Multiline Styles dialog box. Getting into the Multiline Styles dialog box isn't anything you're very likely to do, however, so just see the AutoCAD documentation for details on how to use this dialog box to create new styles and modify existing ones if you ever need to.

You can draw multilines, in either the standard style or a new style you define, by using one of the following options:

- ✔ **Top, Zero, Bottom:** Specifies whether the cursor location indicates the top line of the multilines, a spot in the middle (zero) of the lines, or the bottom line.
- ✔ **Scale:** Determines the distance between lines.

Creating a multiline

You can tell AutoCAD to create a multiline by using an already loaded multiline style or the standard default style in the following three ways:

- ✔ Type **MLine** on the command line and press Enter.
- ✔ Click the Multiline icon on the Draw toolbar.
- ✔ Choose Draw➪Multiline from the menu bar.

Multiline example

The following example shows the commands you can enter on the command line to create a multiline:

```
Command: MLINE
From point: 2,2
From point: 5,9
From point: 7,11
From point: <Enter>
```

Scoring Points . . . and Shapes

Points and *shapes* are AutoCAD objects that enclose or mark a location in space and aren't curved. The following three types of objects, all of which are important, are available in this category:

 ✔ **Points**
 ✔ **Rectangles**
 ✔ **Polygons**

The following sections describe each type of object and how to create it.

Shape is an AutoCAD object type that is less and less used. It's used here as a generic word for points, rectangles, and polygons.

Points (game, set, and match!)

Although simple in real life (and in other drawing programs), *points* in AutoCAD are complex. Before drawing a point, you must specify the *point style* and *point size;* otherwise, you're stuck with the default. (And the default may not appear as you want it to on-screen or on a plot, so specify your points *before* you start drawing.)

You can use points not only to represent small objects, but also for construction purposes. You may, for example, want to create a point as something you can snap to while doing a drawing and then get rid of later. To get object snaps to snap to points, choose the Node option.

You can specify how a point is drawn, as well as its size, by using either commands entered on the command line or the Point Style dialog box. The command line commands, PDMODE and PDSIZE, are complex and use arbitrary and hard-to-remember values. (The default for PDMODE is 0, which displays as a one-pixel dot.) Unless you plan on using points frequently and really love the keyboard, I suggest that you use the dialog box instead.

DDPTYPE is the command that opens the Point Style dialog box (see Figure 6-4). You can access it from the menus by choosing Format⇨Point Style. The first line in the dialog box shows the actual point styles available. The second, third, and fourth lines add surrounding shapes to the point — a circle (second line), square (third line), or circle-in-square (fourth line).

You can also specify the Point Size in the Point Style dialog box. You can specify the point size as a percentage of the screen size (which means that the point always appears on-screen) by clicking the Set Size Relative to Screen option button, or as a number of drawing units (which means that the point always appears on your printout) by clicking the Set Size in Absolute Units option button. You may want to specify point styles in screen units while working on your drawing so that they can't disappear from the screen and then respecify them in absolute units before printing so that they're sure to appear in the plot.

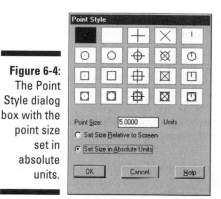

Figure 6-4:
The Point
Style dialog
box with the
point size
set in
absolute
units.

Specify your point as a percentage of screen size if it's a temporary point and you don't need it to appear in printouts; specify the point as a fixed number of drawing units if it's permanent.

After you specify the point style, actually placing the point on-screen is easy; the following sections show you how to do this task.

Creating a point

You can create a point by using any of the following methods:

- ✔ Type **POint** on the command line and press Enter.
- ✔ Click the Point icon on the Draw toolbar.
- ✔ Choose Draw➪Point from the menu bar (with submenu).

Point example

The following example shows you the commands to enter on the command line to create a point:

```
Command: POINT
Point: 2,2 <or pick a point>
```

Rectangles (oh, what a tangled wreck . . .)

The RECTANG command is a fairly recent addition to AutoCAD, first appearing in Release 12. (Yes, that fact may seem surprising to those of you who have been drawing rectangles in MacDraw since 1984, or in other programs since shortly after, but it's true.) Rectangles are really rather simple to create, which is nice; just pick a corner, move the mouse, and pick another corner. You don't even have any options to bother with. And you don't need to hold down the mouse cursor and drag it anywhere to create a rectangle either; just click in one corner, move the mouse to the opposite corner, and click there, too.

Rectangles and polygons in AutoCAD are really just polylines that are specified in a way that's appropriate to the shape you're creating.

Unlike in other drawing programs, you don't click and drag the mouse to draw lines or create rectangles in AutoCAD; instead, after choosing the appropriate command for the object you want to draw, you click and release the mouse at the point on screen where you want the drawing to begin, and then you do so again at the second point, where you want it to end.

If you choose the Press and Drag option in the Object Selection Settings dialog box at the time you set up AutoCAD, because you wanted AutoCAD to function like other programs when drawing objects, forget it; that setup choice affects how you *select* objects, but not how you *draw* them. See Chapter 3 for details.

Creating a rectangle

You can tell AutoCAD to create a rectangle by using the following methods:

- ✔ Type **RECtang** on the command line and press Enter.
- ✔ Click the Rectangle icon on the Draw toolbar.
- ✔ Choose <u>D</u>raw⇨Rectangle from the menu bar.

Rectangle example

The following example shows you the commands to enter on the command line to create a rectangle:

```
Command: RECTANG
Chamfer/Elevation/Fillet/Thickness/Width/<First corner>:
        4,7
Chamfer/Elevation/Fillet/Thickness/Width/<Other corner>:
        7,4
```

If you really want to eliminate clean-up work at the end of the drawing process and dramatically reduce your odds of creating an unprintable drawing (and then saying unprintable things), start your work by making a rough drawing that contains nothing but rectangles to represent the drawing's major parts. Put the rectangles on their own layer so that you can hide or get rid of it later. Set the correct limits and so on, but don't worry about actually drawing anything; just put rectangles of about the right size anywhere that geometry or text are to go. Print the result to see how it looks. You can get a good idea of the final look of your drawing in a short period of time by using this method.

Polygons (so next time, lock the cage . . .)

Moving from rectangles to *polygons* is much like moving from the very simple to the almost too complex for words — except maybe a few we can't print here. Creating a triangle, a pentagon, or another polygonal shape in AutoCAD can readily be considered a minor feat of engineering in and of itself. The process involved in creating a polygon is exact, however, and relates well to what "real" drafters do. But if all your previous drawing experience is with a drawing package rather than with a drafting board, drawing AutoCAD polygons can be a real pain.

To create a polygon, follow these steps:

1. **Type** POLygon **on the command line and press Enter.**

   AutoCAD prompts you for the number of sides you want on your polygon.

2. **Type at the prompt the number of sides you want for your polygon, and press Enter.**

   If you want to draw a triangle, for example, you type **3** at this prompt. AutoCAD then prompts you to specify either the center of the polygon (the default) or the edge of the polygon.

3. **Specify at the prompt whether you want to draw an edge of a polygon or specify the center point of the polygon.**

   You need to type **E** at this prompt and press Enter to specify that you want to draw an edge, and then continue on with Step 4. If you want to use the center point of the polygon, skip to the unnumbered paragraph immediately before Step 5.

   Now here's where you can really get in trouble, so follow along closely.

4. **At the prompt, type the coordinates for the first point of an edge for the polygon you want to create and press Enter.**

   AutoCAD automatically creates a polygon with the specified number of sides — a triangle, square, pentagon, or whatever. This polygon is then resized according to the coordinate you enter in the following step.

5. **At the prompt, type the coordinates for the second endpoint of the edge of your polygon and press Enter.**

   After you specify the second endpoint of the edge, you're done. Whatever shape you're creating is exactly *equilateral* (all sides the same length), so that second endpoint had better be in the right spot; otherwise, you can easily create a pentagon that looks as if its base is horizontal but is really tilted slightly right or left. If you want a *nonequilateral* shape, such as a right triangle, you must edit your equilateral triangle — or draw a polyline — to get it.

Creating a polygon by specifying its number of sides and what circle it surrounds or is circumscribed by is relatively easy. The circle is used to define either the distance from the polygon's center to the middle of each side — a *circumscribed polygon* — or to each *vertex,* or corner — an *inscribed polygon.* After entering the number of sides for your polygon, as described in Step 2, you click a point on-screen or enter coordinates for the center of the polygon at the following prompt *instead* of entering an E to specify a polygon edge (as described in Step 3, if you're on edge — as you may actually be at this point).

6. **To specify using the center point of the polygon for your drawing, type the coordinates for the center of the polygon, or pick the center point by clicking in the drawing area with the mouse, and then press Enter.**

   Now you must tell AutoCAD whether the polygon is *inscribed in* a circle or *circumscribed around* a circle; inscribed within a circle is the default setting.

7. **At the prompt, type C if you want the polygon circumscribed around a circle and then press Enter; if you want the polygon inscribed in a circle, type I at the prompt and press Enter or just press Enter.**

   Finally, you must enter the radius of the circle, either by entering a number from the keyboard or by clicking a point on-screen. If you use the keyboard to enter a number at the command line, a polygon of the right size and with a horizontal base appears. If you pick a point, the polygon's exact alignment depends on the point you pick. Again, if you use this latter method, you can easily end up with a slightly misaligned shape.

8. **At the prompt, type the value you want for the radius of the circle and press Enter.**

   AutoCAD draws the polygon.

If you want to turn your equilateral polygon into a nonequilateral one, you must grab the offending corner and drag it to the right spot on-screen to make the shape you want. You can find more information about this particular task in Chapter 7.

Use POLYGON with 4 sides and the Circumscribed option to draw a rectangle centered on a point.

Creating a polygon

You can tell AutoCAD to create a polygon by using any of the following methods:

- Type **POLygon** on the command line and press Enter.
- Click the Polygon icon on the Draw toolbar.
- Choose Draw⇨Polygon from the menu bar.

Polygon examples

The following example shows you the commands to enter at the command line to create a polygon by specifying its *bounding*, or inscribed, circle:

```
Command: POLYGON
Number of sides: 3
Edge/<Center of polygon>: 4,8
Inscribed in circle/Circumscribed about circle (I/C) <I>: I
Radius of circle: 2
```

The following example shows you the commands to enter on the command line to create a polygon, as shown in Figure 6-5:

```
Command: POLYGON
Number of sides: 5
Edge/<Center of polygon>: E
First endpoint of edge: 7,3
Second endpoint of edge: 9,3
```

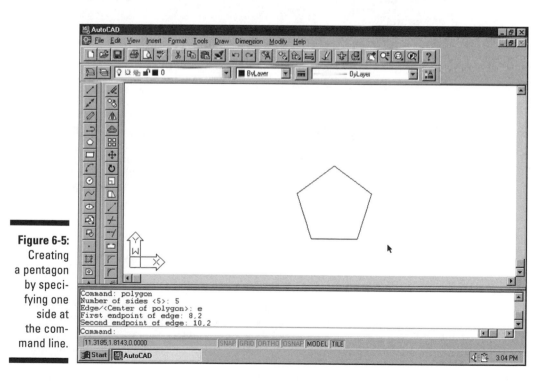

Figure 6-5: Creating a pentagon by specifying one side at the command line.

(Throwing) Curves

AutoCAD features a strong selection of curved objects for your drawing needs, as well as many ways to define them. Because you're provided with so many ways to create curves, and because getting them to the right spot requires a fair amount of thought, you may want to consider drawing all your curved objects at once for a while, especially if you're an inexperienced AutoCAD user, until you get good at creating and placing them. The important curve-shaped objects for most AutoCAD users are as follows:

- Circles
- Arcs

Other curved objects available in AutoCAD that are not as important to most users as circles and arcs are:

- Ellipses
- Splines
- Donuts

The following sections describe each command. You probably need to practice drawing all these shapes, however, except perhaps circles, if you really want to get them right.

(Will he go round in) circles . . .

AutoCAD offers an easy way to draw circles in AutoCAD, and it also offers . . . *other* ways. The easy way is to define the center point of the circle and then to define the radius or diameter. You can also define a circle by entering one of the following options of the command (for those "other" ways):

- **3P:** Represents any three points on the circumference.
- **2P:** Represents the endpoints of a diameter of the circle.
- **TTR:** Represents two tangents and a radius.

Any of these commands can be useful for getting just the right circle into just the right spot on-screen, but you may find yourself doing what I do, which is creating the circle you want by using the center point/radius method and then moving it to just the right spot, as described in Chapter 7.

Creating a circle

You can tell AutoCAD to create a circle by using any of the following methods:

✔ Type **Circle** on the command line and press Enter.

✔ Click the Circle icon on the Draw toolbar.

✔ Choose <u>D</u>raw⇨<u>C</u>ircle from the menu bar (with submenus).

Circle example

The following example shows you the commands to enter on the command line to create a circle from a center point and radius:

```
Command: CIRCLE
3P/2P/TTR/<Center point>: 7,7
Diameter/<Radius>: <4.0000>: 2
```

You can also type **D**, and then enter the diameter, if that's more convenient.

Arcs (the 'erald angels sing . . .)

Arcs are, quite simply, pieces of circles. By the time you finish finding out about all the many ways to define arcs, you just may end up drawing a circle where you want an arc and then using correction fluid to cover over everything but the desired arc on your printout.

As with circles, AutoCAD offers you an easy way to define arcs. Just specify three points on-screen to define the arc, easy as one-two-three. These points tell AutoCAD where to start the arc, how much to curve it, and where to end it.

Sounds pretty easy, right? So where's the problem? Well, the trouble is that you often must specify arcs more exactly than is possible by using this method. AutoCAD helps you specify such arcs, true, but the procedure ain't easy.

You can start your arc by specifying the center of the arc or the start point. If you specify the center, AutoCAD asks you to specify the start point of the arc. AutoCAD defines arcs counter-clockwise, so pick a start point in a clockwise direction from the end point. After you specify the center and start point, AutoCAD presents several options you can choose, including the following:

✔ **Angle:** This option specifies the angle used by the arc. A 180-degree angle, for example, is a semicircle.

✔ **Length of chord:** This option specifies the length of the straight line connecting the endpoints of the arc. If you know the exact length, select Length of chord as the option you want.

✔ **Endpoint:** This option specifies where the arc ends. It's the default option and is often the easiest to use.

If you specify the start point as the first option, you then can choose among the following three command line options as well:

- ✔ **Center:** This option takes you back to the preceding options: Enter Angle, Length of chord, or Endpoint.

- ✔ **End:** This option specifies the endpoint of the arc. You then need to define the angle the arc covers, its direction, its radius, or its center point.

- ✔ **Second point:** This is the default option. The second point you choose is not the endpoint; instead, it's a point on the arc that, along with the start and endpoints, defines the arc's curvature — that is, how much it curves. After you enter the second point, you must enter an endpoint to complete the arc.

Creating an arc

You can tell AutoCAD to create an arc by using any of the following methods:

- ✔ Type **Arc** on the command line and press Enter.

- ✔ Click the Arc icon on the Draw toolbar.

- ✔ Choose <u>D</u>raw⇨<u>A</u>rc from the menu bar (with submenus for different ways to define the arc).

Arc examples

The following example shows you the commands to enter on the command line to create an arc by specifying three points on the arc:

```
Command: ARC
Center/<Start point>: 1,1
Center,End/<Second point>: 2,2
End point: 3,1
```

The following example shows the commands to enter on the command line to create an arc starting from the center and specifying an angle, as shown in Figure 6-6:

```
Command: ARC
Center/<Start point>: C
Center: 4,4
Start point: 6,4
Angle/Length of chord/<End point>: ANGLE
Included angle: 90
```

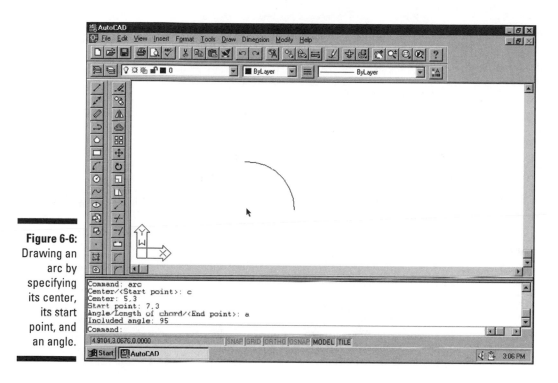

Figure 6-6:
Drawing an
arc by
specifying
its center,
its start
point, and
an angle.

Ellipses (S. Grant?)

An *ellipse*, like an arc, is complex to draw. An ellipse is like a warped circle with a *major* (long) axis and a *minor* (short) axis to determine its length, width, and degree of curvature. After you start to draw an ellipse, AutoCAD presents the following options at the prompts on the command line:

- **Arc:** This option generates an elliptical arc rather than a full ellipse. You define an elliptical arc just as you do a full ellipse. The following methods for creating an ellipse apply to either.

- **Center:** This option requires that you define the center of the ellipse and then the endpoint of an axis. You can then either enter the distance of the other axis or specify that a rotation around the major axis defines the ellipse. If you choose the latter, you can enter (or drag the ellipse to) a specific rotation for the second axis that, in turn, completely defines the ellipse.

- **Isocircle:** This option creates an *isometric circle* — something you're unlikely to use; check the AutoCAD documentation if you need details.

- **Axis endpoint 1:** This option requires that you define one axis by entering its end points and the other by entering a distance or rotation.

These options are confusing to master by reading; try creating an ellipse to get a feel for drawing one. If you need to draw an ellipse, you're likely to specify it by using one of these methods.

Creating an ellipse

You can tell AutoCAD to create an ellipse by using any of the following methods:

- Type **ELlipse** on the command line and press Enter.
- Click the Ellipse icon on the Draw toolbar.
- Choose <u>D</u>raw⇨<u>E</u>llipse from the menu bar (with submenu for definition methods).

Ellipse example

The following example shows you the commands to enter on the command line to create an ellipse:

```
Command: ELLIPSE
Arc/Center/<Axis endpoint 1>: 4,4
Axis endpoint 2: 8,4
<Other axis distance>/Rotation: .25
```

Other curved objects

A *spline* is a curve that passes near or through a number of points in a smooth way. You're unlikely to need splines when getting started with AutoCAD. See the AutoCAD documentation when you're finally ready to vent your spline.

Creating a *donut* (hold the coffee, please) is a simple way to define a single object that consists of two concentric circles with the space between them filled. But watch out; drawing a donut is likely to draw some cops, too! (Sorry. . . .) Creating a donut can be a time-saver in some cases, but the command for doing so is certainly not the most important one to memorize. In fact, you're unlikely to use the DONUT command much; if you do need it, you can usually figure it out through trial and error (donuts work much like circles) or see the AutoCAD documentation for details.

You can create a filled circle with the DONUT command; specify an inside diameter of zero. Try this one for yourself!

Chapter 7

Edit It

· ·

· ·

This chapter describes working with existing objects in AutoCAD. The two preceding chapters discuss how to draw in AutoCAD and use the AutoCAD drawing tools. In this chapter, I describe two ways you work with existing objects: One way is to use existing objects as a reference point for adding more geometry; another way is to modify existing objects. In your actual work, you move back and forth among creating brand-new geometry, adding other related geometry to it, and modifying what you've created, which means that you use the information in this group of three chapters interchangeably as well.

Editing may be the function that's most difficult to master and use in AutoCAD. Editing in any version of AutoCAD is really different from the editing you do in other programs — and some of the AutoCAD commands are inconsistent with one another. Users who have a historical perspective of AutoCAD updates over the last several years, however, recognize that editing in AutoCAD has come a long way since the program's early days; for most of your work, you can now actually use editing techniques that are similar to, if somewhat more complicated than, those of many other programs. As for those folks who may not be as familiar with AutoCAD (the rest of you) — well, you may find yourself checking this book, your AutoCAD books and manuals, and other sources every now and then for guidance.

After you successfully scale the learning curve for AutoCAD editing, you can do almost anything you want with your drawings — much more so than is possible in other, less powerful programs. So stick with AutoCAD until it all starts to make sense.

Snapping to Attention

One of the main features of any CAD program is the capability to *snap to objects*. No, this feature doesn't refer to something you do with your fingers; *object snap* is the capability to make newly created objects align correctly with existing ones. For example, you often want a new object to join the end, center, corner, or other particular point of an existing object. When the program helps you find and connect with such a point, that's object snapping.

AutoCAD Release 14 has new capabilities for two snap-related features that are explained in the next sections: *running object snap,* which AutoCAD has had for several releases, and *AutoSnap,* a new feature in Release 14. Though each has a substantial learning curve, these features work both separately and together to make creating accurate drawings quick and easy.

Single object snaps

Single object snaps enable you to quickly connect the next point on the object you're drawing to any of several particular points on a nearby object. Object snaps are most easily accessed by the Cursor menu, shown in Figure 7-1. To bring up the Cursor menu, hold down the Shift key while right-clicking your mouse.

If you have a three-button mouse, clicking the middle button also brings up the Cursor menu. For those of you still using a digitizer, the third button on the digitizer puck does the same thing.

Figure 7-1:
Hold down
Shift while
right-
clicking to
see the
Cursor
menu.

The Cursor menu lists any of several possible snap points for different kinds of objects; choosing the right one for the kind of snap point and the kind of object you want to connect with is up to you. Among the most useful snap points are the *endpoint* or *midpoint* of a line or arc; the *center* or *tangent* of an arc or circle (not a rectangle or square!); and the *perpendicular* of a line, circle, or arc.

For a complete description of snap points, press F1 in AutoCAD to bring up the Help system; choose Help topics and enter the topic **Default Cursor Menu**.

If you haven't used object snaps before, take some time to experiment with them; they can save you a great deal of time and are the key to running object snaps and AutoSnap as well.

The Cursor menu, like so much else in AutoCAD, is customizable; see the AutoCAD Release 14 documentation for more information.

Trying object snaps

To get a feel for using object snaps, try the following example, which simply draws a circle overlaying the end of a rectangle.

1. **Type** RECtang **at the command line and press Enter.**

2. **Click any two points to draw the rectangle.**

   A rectangle appears on your screen.

3. **Type** Circle **at the command line and press Enter.**

4. **Hold down the Shift key and press the right mouse button.**

   The Cursor menu appears.

5. **Choose <u>M</u>idpoint from the Cursor menu.**

   The Cursor menu disappears.

6. **Move the cursor over any side of the rectangle.**

   As soon as the box around the cursor touches a line, a yellow box appears at the midpoint of that line.

7. **Click anywhere on the line to place the center of the circle at the midpoint of the side of the rectangle.**

8. **Hold down the Shift key and press the right mouse button.**

   The Cursor menu appears again. Figure 7-2 shows the screen at this point in the exercise.

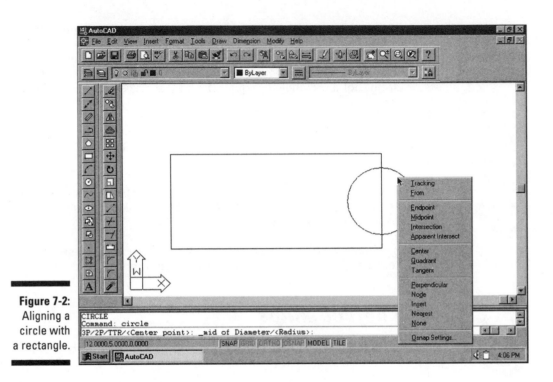

Figure 7-2:
Aligning a
circle with
a rectangle.

9. Choose <u>E</u>ndpoint from the Cursor menu.

The Cursor menu disappears.

10. Move the cursor over the same side of the rectangle again and click.

As soon as the box around the cursor touches the side, a yellow box appears at the endpoint of the side that is nearest the cursor. When you click, the circle is completed, with its center on the midpoint of a side and its radius at the endpoint. The circle command is complete.

You may think that ten steps seem like quite a few to create a simple construction, and it is. But the good news is that objects entered this way are exactly where you need them to be. After you build up some experience with object snaps, they become a fast way to enter exact geometry.

If the object snap you're using permits multiple possible destinations, use the Tab key to cycle among them. For example, if you're connecting to a tangent point of a circle, you have two tangent points to choose from; AutoCAD displays the closest one for you. Press Tab to see the other. This behavior also applies when you have turned on running object snaps, which gives you multiple possible connection points, as explained in the next section.

Running object snaps

If you use object snaps even a little bit, you're likely to find yourself wishing that you could have them on all the time. Although bringing up the Cursor menu is relatively easy, doing so constantly still gets tiresome.

The good news is that you can have object snaps on all the time by using *running object snaps*. With running object snaps, you simply turn on one or more object snaps, and they stay on. The Osnap Settings dialog box for turning running object snaps on and off is shown in Figure 7-3. To bring up this dialog box, choose Tools➪Object Snap Settings from the menu or type **ddOSnap** at the command line.

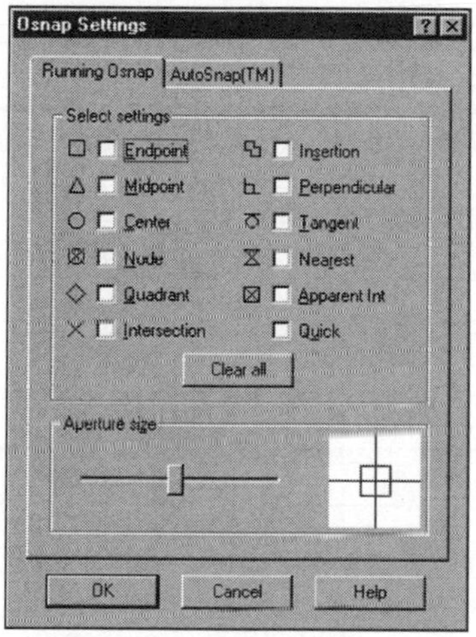

Figure 7-3:
The Osnap
Settings
dialog box.

Running object snaps are nearly always a good thing, but at times you need to get back quickly the capability to draw to a point near, but not on, an object snap point. So the *really* good news is that Release 14 has a quick way to turn running object snaps on and off. Just set your running object snaps with the Osnap Settings dialog box and then double-click the OSNAP button in the status bar to turn them on and off as needed. (If no running object snaps are set, double-clicking the OSNAP button first brings up the Osnap Settings dialog box and then turns on running object snap.)

In addition to the other ways of controlling running object snaps, you can use the Object Snap toolbar. To see the toolbar, just choose View➪Toolbars from the menu. The Object Snap toolbar appears. You can use this toolbar as an alternative quick way to turn on and off individual object snaps. The F3 key also turns object snap on and off.

Try turning on all running object snaps and then turning them on and off as needed. Then just turn off the ones that are actually more trouble than they're worth.

Try using running object snaps to draw. Create a figure with several shapes and then use running object snaps to add geometry that connects with and depends on those shapes. This way, you can start your way up the learning curve at a time when you don't have to concentrate on getting the details of a drawing right.

You can, of course, drive running object snaps from the command line as well. The command is **-OSnap**. However, unlike in most command line activity, the prompt you get doesn't give you the abbreviations for the object snap names. They're shown in Table 7-1.

Table 7-1	Running Object Snap Settings	
Object Snap Name	*Command Line Abbreviation*	*Alt+Key Combination*
Endpoint	END	Alt+T, N, E
Midpoint	MID	Alt+T, N, M
Center	CEN	Alt+T, N, C
Node	NOD	Alt+T, N, N
Quadrant	QUA	Alt+T, N, Q
Intersection	INT	Alt+T, N, I
Insertion	INS	Alt+T, N, S
Perpendicular	PER	Alt+T, N, P
Tangent	TAN	Alt+T, N, T
Nearest	NEA	Alt+T, N, R
Apparent Intersection	APP	Alt+T, N, A
Quick	QUI	Alt+T, N, U
Clear all	NON	Alt+T, N, L
Aperture size	'APERTURE (1–50 pixels)	Alt+T, N, Z (use slider)

In addition to typing at the command line, you can use the keyboard to drive the AutoCAD windows. Just use Alt-plus-key combinations to turn individual running object snaps on and off. The appropriate combinations are also shown in Table 7-1.

The Selective Service

Before you can edit something, you must *select* it. Selecting is the process of telling the computer which object(s) the program is to operate on. The usual reason for selecting an object is so that you can somehow modify it. You may even want to get rid of it entirely. You may also select an item so that you can find out something about it or its properties. For all these reasons, understanding how the selection process works is an important first step in mastering AutoCAD editing.

This section discusses all the different ways that AutoCAD selects objects. Taking the time to discover and experiment with these different methods is really worth the effort, because much of the power of AutoCAD is unavailable to you if you don't know how to select objects correctly. So try to follow closely through this section, and practice — as many times as necessary — any tasks that may at first seem confusing to you. Your work becomes better and faster as a result.

Getting the settings right

To access the most selection options possible in AutoCAD, you must turn on some settings that, by default, remain turned off until you activate them. AutoCAD has evolved over many years from a primitive program containing only a dull, retrograde, small number of ways to select objects to a highly advanced program offering an exciting, forward-looking, large number of ways to select objects. Unfortunately, the default selection settings are mostly the old, primitive ones that you don't want or need most of the time. To access the settings you do want, you must make a few adjustments to get them just right.

The Object Selection Settings dialog box contains all these settings, just ready for you to fix. Just type **ddSElect** at the command line and press Enter or choose Tools⇨Selection from the menus to access the dialog box. Your best bet is to turn on all the options in the dialog box, so click the check boxes as needed to turn on all the options except Associative Hatch; see Chapter 11 for more on that. Figure 7-4 shows how the dialog box looks after you finish. The object selection settings affect the creation of a *selection set*, a group of selected objects. You find more details about this dialog box, its settings, and the system variables that back it up in Chapter 4.

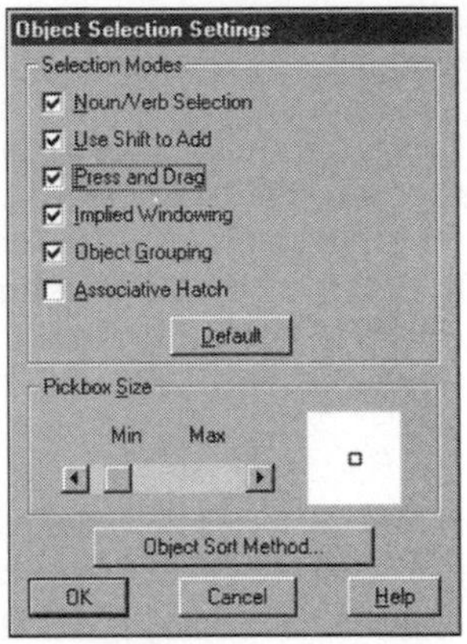

Figure 7-4:
The Object
Selection
Settings
dialog box
with
Windows-
like settings
turned on.

Picking objects one at a time

One way to select objects is to pick (by clicking) them one at a time. The Use Shift to Add option of the Object Selection Settings dialog box, which controls the setting of the PICKADD system variable, controls this option.

If the Use Shift to Add option is off, you build up a selection set just by clicking objects one at a time. In most programs, you can select only one item at a time when using this method; if you select one object and then another, the first object is deselected and the second one selected. Only the object you select last remains selected. But in AutoCAD, with Use Shift to Add turned off, *all* the objects you select, one at a time, remain selected and are added to the set, no matter how many objects you highlight. Whatever command you choose next affects every selected object.

With the Use Shift to Add option turned on, however, things get almost back to normal. If you click one object and then another, only the second object stays selected. You must click an object, *press and hold the Shift key*, and *then* click another object to build up the selection set. As you select more objects with the Shift key held down, you add selections to the set. Be careful, however; with a few of the less frequently used AutoCAD commands, that old, Shiftless style still applies, even with this option turned on. For those commands, pressing Shift is a waste of effort.

The most confusing difference between selected objects in AutoCAD and those in other programs involves *grips* (which are described in detail in the section "Grip editing," later in this chapter). In most other programs, only selected objects display grips, or *handles*, at certain points surrounding the objects. In AutoCAD, however, a selected object retains its grips even *after* you deselect it. To the new user, the object probably looks as though it's still selected. In AutoCAD, the only clue you can trust to indicate whether you've actually selected an object — and that it is still selected — is the dotted appearance that the object acquires. The currently selected object in Figure 7-5, for example, displays the dotted linetype to indicate that it is still selected.

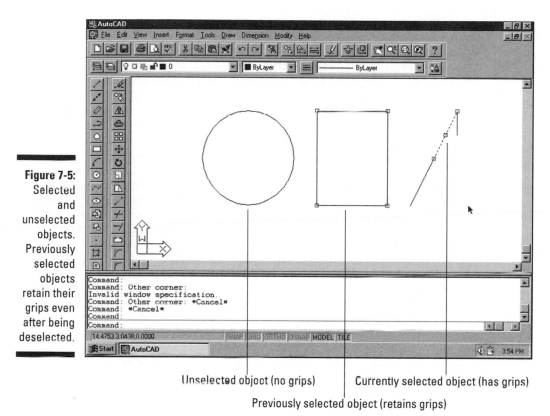

Figure 7-5:
Selected
and
unselected
objects.
Previously
selected
objects
retain their
grips even
after being
deselected.

Unselected object (no grips)   Currently selected object (has grips)

Previously selected object (retains grips)

Never assume that an object is currently selected just because it displays grips. Objects retain grips even when no longer selected.

How much is that object in the window?

The Implied Windowing option in the Object Selection Settings dialog box (backed up by the PICKAUTO system variable) enables a powerful AutoCAD feature called, appropriately enough, *implied windowing*. Leaving out the history lesson, this feature enables you to use two different types of *selection windows* easily — although one type does take a bit of getting used to. A selection window, by the way, is simply a window that you draw — by clicking one corner and then clicking the opposite corner — to select objects within the window. With the Implied Windowing option on, you can either use a *bounding window*, the kind of selection window most other programs use, or a special type of selection window called a *crossing window*. You can determine which type of selection window you use just by varying how you move the mouse.

In most graphics programs, you can select a group of objects by dragging the mouse to create a window around those objects. Everything that's *totally inside* the window is then selected; everything that is only partly in the window or that's entirely outside the window isn't selected. To use this kind of selection window in AutoCAD, just start with the mouse pointer on the *left* side of the objects to be selected, click and hold the mouse button to begin drawing the window, and drag the mouse toward the *right* side of the screen, making sure that you fully enclose in the window that's created every object you want to select. Then release the mouse button. Every object that is now fully enclosed by the bounding window is selected; other objects are not.

With implied windowing, you can also use a crossing window for object selection. Just like the window described in the preceding paragraph, a crossing window also selects objects as you drag a window around them. But with a crossing window, you can also select objects that are only *partially* in the window. A crossing window thus enables you to select large objects that may not be entirely visible on-screen just by capturing a piece of them within your selection window. To use a crossing window in AutoCAD, just start the mouse pointer on the *right* side of the objects to be selected, click and hold the mouse button to begin drawing the window, and then drag your mouse to the *left* side to create the window, making sure that you enclose at least part of any object you want to select within the window. Then release the mouse button. Every object that is fully enclosed by the window or that is partly enclosed by the window is now selected.

Try drawing a bunch of objects, and then try selecting different groups of them by using a combination of crossing windows, bounding windows, the Shift key, and mouse clicks. This exercise is great practice for making you a faster AutoCAD user.

To sum up: To create a *bounding window* in which to select objects that are fully within the window, drag the mouse *from the left side* of the objects *to the right side*. To create a *crossing window* in which to select objects that are fully or partially within the window, drag the mouse *from the right side* of the objects *to the left side*. These two types of selection windows, therefore, are distinguished only by the direction in which you drag the mouse on-screen.

Figures 7-6 and 7-7 show a bounding window and a crossing window, respectively, in action.

If the Press and Drag option in the Object Selection Settings dialog box (also controlled by the PICKDRAG system variable) is turned on (an X appears in its check box), you create any selection window by pressing the mouse button down at the starting corner of the window, dragging the mouse to its destination, and releasing the mouse button at the ending corner of the window, as described in the preceding paragraphs.

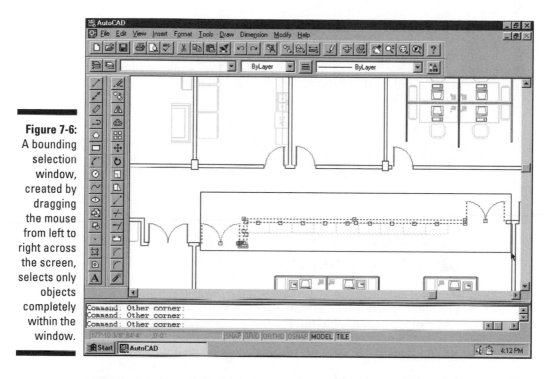

Figure 7-6:
A bounding selection window, created by dragging the mouse from left to right across the screen, selects only objects completely within the window.

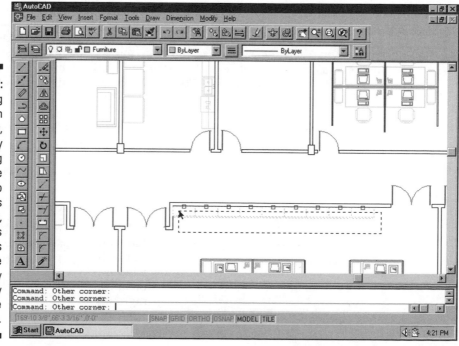

Figure 7-7:
A crossing selection window, created by dragging the mouse from right to left across the screen, selects objects that are completely or partially within the window.

If the Press and Drag setting is turned off (its check box is empty), you create any selection window by clicking and releasing the mouse button in the starting corner of the window, moving the mouse to its destination *without* pressing the button, and then clicking and releasing the mouse button again at the ending corner of the window.

Creating a selection window, as you've no doubt figured out by now, is much like drawing an object; the difference is that, to draw an object, you must first enter a drawing command on the command line and then choose a command from the Draw menu or click a drawing icon on a toolbar. Creating a selection window requires no such preliminary — just click and mouse away!

Selecting objects with the SELECT command

Many selection methods aren't available until after you enter a command — a process called *command-first editing*. (You find more information about command-first editing in the section "Command performances," later in this chapter.) You can gain access to these methods at any time, though, by entering the SELECT command at the command line.

Entering a command that operates on objects or entering the SELECT command enables you to use a very wide range of methods to select objects. After you finish selecting objects and terminate the command, however, the grips and selection highlights disappear. "So what good does that do?" you may wonder. Never fear; the selection you made is now stored as the previous selection set, and you can specify this selection later by typing **PREVIOUS** at the command line. The previously selected objects are then selected — and highlighted — again.

Although selecting objects from the command line has a bewildering number of options, the following are the most important ones:

- **Mouse clicks:** Though it's not listed as an option, just click with the mouse to click objects to add to the selection set.

- **Window:** This option enables you to use a bounding window (as described in the preceding section) to add objects to the selection set.

- **Crossing:** This option enables you to use a crossing window (as described in the preceding section) to add objects to the selection set.

- **Group:** If you previously specified a group of objects, this option enables you to add the group to the selection by entering the group's name at the command line.

✔ **Polygon:** This option enables you to use a polygon, instead of a window, to enclose a group of objects. A *window polygon*, or *WPolygon*,
selects all the objects surrounded by the polygon you create; a *crossing
polygon*, or *CPolygon*, selects all objects surrounded by or crossing the
polygon boundary.

✔ **Fence:** This option is the most fun. A *fence* is basically a *crossing
polyline*; to use it, you just draw a polyline around the screen, through
all the objects you want to select, clicking the mouse after every
line segment; you thereby select every object the polyline touches.
Neat, huh?

✔ **ALL:** This option just selects everything — even objects on layers that
are turned off and therefore not visible on the drawing screen. Objects
on layers that are frozen or locked are not selected. If you really want to
select all the objects in your drawing, turn on all layers before using
ALL! If you want just slightly less than everything, use ALL and then
click the objects you don't want, to remove them from the selection set.

You can use these options in combination or separately.

AutoCAD has been "cleaned up" in a kind of unfriendly way. Some of the
command prompts, with all their options, were starting to look too complicated, so the program now just doesn't show all the options if too many of
them are available. You're supposed to be able to find these missing options
by pressing F1 and using Help, but this task can be time consuming and
distracting. Instead, just enter **?** at the command prompt for these options.
AutoCAD doesn't like the question mark one bit, however — in fact, it
throws a nasty error message at you — but the program then offers the
entire list of options that should have appeared in the first place.

To use the SELECT command from the command line, start by typing
SELECT at the command prompt and then pressing Enter. Then you type the
appropriate designation for any option you want to use (the uppercase
letters that appear in the option name on the prompt). To see the options
for the SELECT command, enter something wrong (such as **?**), and the
options appear on the command line as follows:

```
Command: select
Select objects: ?
*Invalid selection*
Expects a point or
Window/Last/Crossing/BOX/ALL/Fence/WPolygon/CPolygon/Group/
          Add/Remove/Multiple/Previous/Undo/AUto/Single
Select objects:
```

The important options that aren't available elsewhere are ALL, to select all
objects, WPolygon and CPolygon, to create bounding and crossing polygons, and Fence, to draw a polyline through objects you want to select.

If you don't remember how to enter the option you want, type **?** at the prompt; AutoCAD responds with an error message but then lists all the options on the command line.

AutoCAD Release 14 does not have the selection toolbar icon with a flyout for different selection methods that graced (or cluttered, depending on your point of view) the Release 13 for Windows standard toolbar. The SELECT command is only available from the command line.

Getting Editing

AutoCAD uses two styles of editing: *command-first editing* and *selection-first editing*. I don't know about you, but I need a review of how these editing styles work.

With *command-first editing*, you enter a command and then click the objects on which the command works. You're unlikely to be familiar with this style of editing for graphics work unless you're a long-time user of AutoCAD. But command-first editing is common in nongraphical environments such as DOS. Whenever you type **DEL *.*** in DOS, you're issuing a command — **DEL**, for *del*ete — and then choosing the objects on which the command works — ***.***, meaning all the files in the current directory. Command-first editing is the default style of editing in AutoCAD.

In *selection-first editing*, you perform the same steps — in the same order — as you do in Windows-based applications, on the Macintosh, or when using a typical word processor, drawing program, and so on: You select the object first and then choose the command. To delete a line of text in a word processor, for example, you highlight (select) the line and then press the Del (Delete) key. The text you highlight is the object you want to delete, and pressing the Del key is the command. Notice that whether you want to delete, underline, or copy the text, the first act is the same: You highlight the text to select it.

For most of its life, AutoCAD has been a command-driven, command-first program. The selection-first style of editing is a relatively recent addition to the program — one that doesn't yet work in all circumstances. Newer yet is *direct manipulation*. Direct manipulation is a refinement of selection-first editing in which you perform most commands by using the mouse to actually grab the selected object and perform an action on it, such as moving it to a "trash can" icon to delete it or to another on-screen location to reposition it.

AutoCAD supports direct manipulation through a powerful but somewhat complicated technique called *grip editing*. Grips, as you may well know by now, are handles that appear on an object when you select it; you can use the grips to stretch, move, copy, rotate, or otherwise edit the object. The complications arise from the fact that you can do so many things with an object after you select it. (Look for more information on grips in the section "Grip editing," later in this chapter.)

Throughout this book, you use selection-first editing and direct manipulation wherever possible. This style of editing is the style nearly all other programs use, and it's becoming the style that AutoCAD uses more and more. So get to know and use this editing style in AutoCAD as well; you finish your work faster, better, and with less confusion as you move between AutoCAD and other programs. (Hey, why delve into the strange and different when you can stick to the familiar? You can find plenty of other odd challenges in AutoCAD to worry about. I promise.)

The movement over time toward direct-manipulation editing in AutoCAD is clear in the addition of new features such as AutoSnap in Release 14. In the past, users would have done the same kind of thing from the command line. With Release 14, AutoCAD has more options for selection-first editing and direct manipulation than ever before.

Command performances

(Okay, so I lied. I'm going to discuss *this* odd challenge after all.) As I explained in the preceding section, command-first editing is the venerable (no, *not* out-moded . . . at least, not totally) practice of first entering an editing command and then selecting what the command works on. Command-first editing is always available in AutoCAD; unlike selection-first editing, command-first editing can't be turned off.

You're usually better off getting in the habit of using one or the other style of editing most of the time. Command-first editing may actually be a good choice for you if you spend most of your time in AutoCAD, because AutoCAD implements this editing style more consistently throughout the program; command-first editing *always* works. Selection-first editing, on the other hand, is more natural for most people and is the style other programs use, so it's the best choice for many users.

Even if you try to stick with selection-first editing, however, you do need to use command-first editing occasionally. (Command-first editing may, in fact, be your choice if you're an experienced AutoCAD user who doesn't want to switch back and forth from one style to another.) Certain commands stubbornly tend to ignore your previous selection and ask you for a new one. In this case, you need to tell AutoCAD to recover the previous selection by typing **Previous** at the command line, or you need to make a new selection — which means you're back to using command-first editing after all.

The following steps show you how to perform command-first editing by using the CHAMFER command (which chops off a corner or intersection and replaces it with a line segment across the gap):

1. **Use the LINE command, as described in Chapter 6, to create two lines that intersect or that would intersect if extended far enough.**

   After you finish your intersecting (or would-be intersecting) lines, you select the Chamfer command.

2. **Type CHAmfer at the command line and press Enter, or click the Chamfer icon from the Modify floating toolbar.**

3. **Select the first line to be chamfered by clicking the line.**

   If you select the lines to be chamfered *before* you start the CHAMFER command, AutoCAD ignores the selection, and you can't restore it.

4. **Select the second line to be chamfered by clicking the line.**

   AutoCAD chamfers the lines, as shown by the example on the right in Figure 7-8.

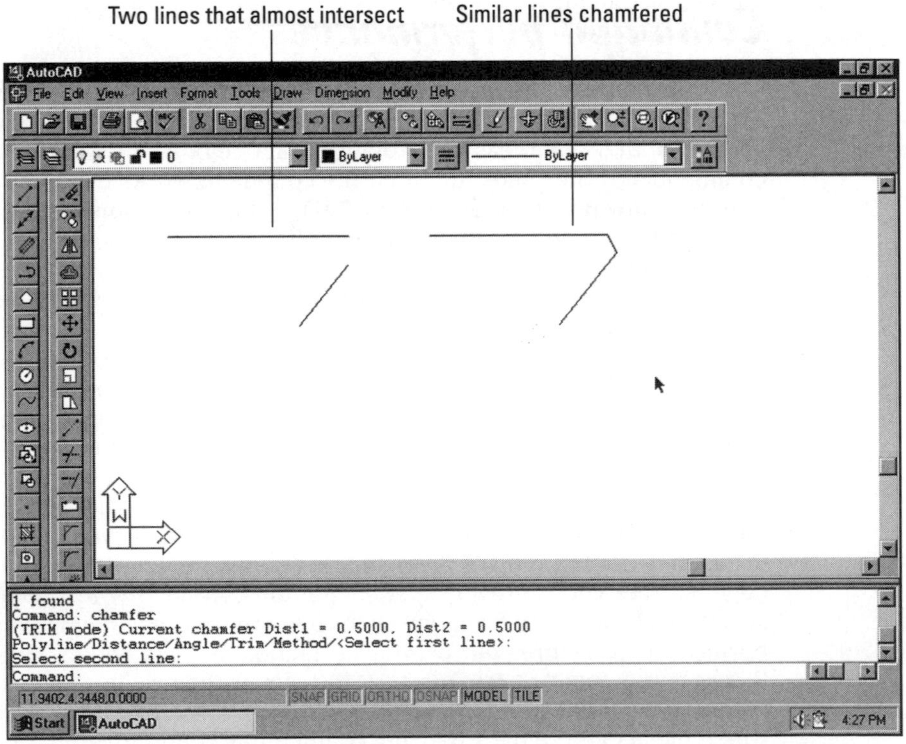

Two lines that almost intersect   Similar lines chamfered

Figure 7-8:
Two sets of almost intersecting lines, with the right-hand set chamfered.

The CHAMFER command is flexible and offers a number of options. In addition to extending lines to their intersection point, the command can force lines to intersect without actually creating a chamfer, add a chamfer without trimming the existing lines, and run other options. Unless you're a more experienced AutoCAD user, however, you probably don't use the CHAMFER command all that often. You can find more about the CHAMFER command in the AutoCAD online Help or reference manual.

Being manipulative

In spite of the ubiquitous nature of command-first editing, selection-first editing and direct manipulation are the preferred ways to edit in AutoCAD for most users. These related methods are closer to how most programs already work now anyway — and (mark my words!) how all programs will eventually work in the future. So from this point on, this book concentrates on these types of editing and simply lumps both selection-first editing and its direct manipulation offspring together under the term "direct manipulation" (to avoid being wordy, of course).

Using direct manipulation to edit, however, may actually require more preparation and forethought than using command-first editing. This additional effort is partly because of the inconsistencies inherent in the way AutoCAD works and partly because of the complexity involved in using direct manipulation for such an exacting application as AutoCAD.

To use direct manipulation, you must engage in a bit of setup work to coax AutoCAD to work differently than it has in the past, stick-in-the-mud that it is. (These setup steps are described in the section "The Selective Service," earlier in this chapter, as well as in Chapter 3.) You must make sure that the Noun/Verb Selection option in the Object Selection Settings dialog box is turned on to enable direct manipulation. The Use Shift to Add and Press and Drag options in this dialog box also support this style of editing, although these features don't work consistently throughout AutoCAD, even after you specify them.

Creating your selection first also may require extra work. To use way-cool selection techniques such as FENCE with direct manipulation, you must enter a drawing command or type the SELECT command on the command line (and press Enter, of course) and then choose the Fence option at the prompt. After you make your selection and press Enter to exit the SELECT command, however, your selection disappears; but you can resurrect the selection for use with a subsequent command by entering P for the Previous option at the command line (it's alive — it's alive!). With some commands, however, not even this roundabout method works; so experiment to discover which of the commands you use demand that you make a selection only *after* the command is entered.

Another difficulty of direct manipulation is that it's hard to use for exacting work such as CAD. You really need to set distances, offsets, and so on exactly right if the drawing you create is a template to be used for construction or manufacturing. You can't just drag a tangent up against a circle, for example; the tangent must touch the circle at one, and only one, point. And in this sort of work, a two-inch square simply *cannot* be $1^{63}/_{64}$ inches on one side and 2 inches on another. Such a glaring disparity just is not acceptable!

Your allies in getting your geometry exactly where you want it in selection-first editing are the *snap grid* and *object snaps*. As described in Chapter 3, the snap grid helps you create objects of just the right size; object snaps help you create objects with just the right relationship to one another. Adjusting the snap grid and using the correct object snaps are extra steps that take some of the ease out of direct manipulation, but if you use them enough, these features become second nature to you.

The following steps show you how to perform selection-first editing, using the ERASE command as an example:

1. **Select the objects you want to erase by using one of the following methods:**

   - Press and hold the Shift key as you click each object.

   - Use a bounding window (drag the mouse from left to right) to enclose the objects.

   - Use a crossing window (drag the mouse from right to left) to enclose or connect with the objects.

   - Type **SELECT** at the command line, press Enter, and at the following prompt choose an option such as ALL, Fence, WPolygon, or CPolygon.

2. **Type Erase at the command line or click the Erase icon on the Modify floating toolbar.**

   If you select your objects by using the SELECT command, you must enter the Previous selection option to select them a second time.

3. **Press Enter to erase the objects.**

Figure 7-9 shows several objects selected by using the fence option just before using the ERASE command to erase them. (Zap!)

The Fence option of the SELECT command ignores whether you turned on the Press and Drag selection option; you must define the fence line by clicking and releasing at each *vertex,* or fence point.

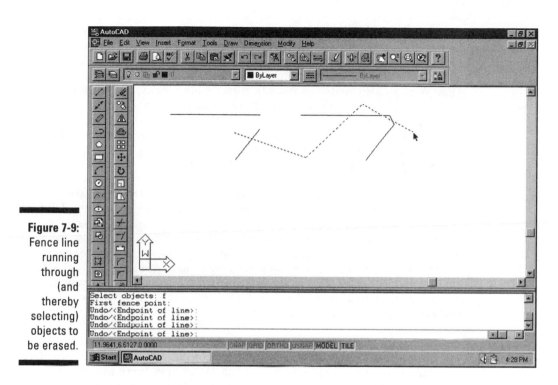

Figure 7-9:
Fence line
running
through
(and
thereby
selecting)
objects to
be erased.

Grip editing

Grip editing is familiar to almost anyone who has ever edited graphics on a
computer — unless your only graphics experience is with a version of
AutoCAD prior to Release 12. If you're an experienced user only of AutoCAD
Release 11 or earlier, you've probably never seen grips. And even if you're
an experienced user of other graphics programs, you've never seen grips in
quite the way AutoCAD uses them. Either way, some explanation is in order.

Grips, as explained earlier in this chapter, are little handles that appear on
an object after you select it. You use these handles in many programs for
direct manipulation of the object. *Direct manipulation*, as used here, involves
the following operations: To move an object, you grab the object's middle
grip and drag that grip; to stretch an object, you grab a corner, or edge grip,
and drag that grip; to move a copy of the object, you hold down the Shift key
while dragging the middle of the object. Even the little frames around the
graphics you import into a word processing program are likely to work
this way.

AutoCAD grips have some differences from the grips used in other programs. First, grips require a little setup wizardry to get them to work just right. The ddGRips command, entered at the command line, opens the Grips dialog box, in which you can click the appropriate check box to enable grips. You can also enable or disable grips within blocks, change the grips' colors, and change the grips' sizes all by clicking the appropriate check boxes in the Grips dialog box, as shown in Chapter 3. None of these options are as important as simply having grips turned on, however. You can turn grips on and off directly by typing the commands **GRIPS 1**, for on, and **GRIPS 0**, for off, directly at the command line.

Another way in which AutoCAD grips are different from those of other programs is in when the AutoCAD grips appear (or, more accurately, fail to disappear). As in other drawing programs, AutoCAD displays grips on a selected object. But unlike the perfectly well-adjusted grips in those other programs, AutoCAD grips *don't go away* after the object they enclose no longer is selected. In fact, they seem to hang around *forever* (much like that annoying *Twilight Zone* theme music keeps running over and over again through your mind after you've heard it one time too many — do-do-do-do, do-do-do-do, do-do — arrrrrggghhh!).

Grips, in fact, remain visible both on *previously selected* and on *currently selected* objects. The persistence of these grips can become really confusing, especially if you're trying to figure out exactly what is currently selected on-screen. This persistence does, however, enable you to use the grips as targets for future editing chores, such as to make one object touch another.

Despite their persistence problem, AutoCAD grips *are*, for sophisticated users, better than the grips found in most other programs, because you can do so much more with them. You can, for example, use AutoCAD grips to move, stretch, or copy an object. You can also use them to rotate an object, scale it to a different size, or *mirror* an object — that is, create one or more copies. In conjunction with the snap grid, object snaps, and the cursor location display, you can use grips for some pretty complex editing chores. Options such as Ortho also affect the workings of grip editing in interesting ways. Finally, grips actually act as *temporary object snaps* themselves, which is why grips remain on an object even after it's deselected — you may want to snap to it.

AutoCAD grips are also better — but correspondingly more complicated — than grips in other programs in that AutoCAD grips come in three varieties: hot, warm, and cold. (I could compare these types to the grip a person may have on a significant other, but that would just be causing trouble.) A *hot grip* is the grip that you use to actually perform an action, such as stretching an object. A *warm grip* is any grip on a selected object that isn't a hot grip (nothing's happening to its object at the moment). A *cold grip* is a grip on an unselected object that only acts as a snap target. Cold grips and warm grips both appear as empty, not-filled-in squares; their default color on-screen is blue. Hot grips, on the other hand, appear on-screen as red, filled-in squares.

What all these grip capabilities really mean to the beginning user, however, is that effectively using grips in AutoCAD requires a fair amount of practice. What can help you the most in finding out how to use grips is simply your determination to do so. If you set your mind to use grips as much and as frequently as possible in your drawings, the little buggers slowly — but surely — yield their secrets to you.

Make sure that the Press and Drag and Use Shift to Add object selection settings are turned on in the Object Selection Settings dialog box before you start these steps! See Chapter 3 for details.

The following steps show you all the different operations in which you can use grips:

1. **Click an object on-screen to give it grips (if you don't already have an object selected).**

   Warm grips appear around the object on-screen.

   Cold grips and warm grips both are empty squares; their default color is blue. They are identical except that warm grips appear on selected objects, cold ones on unselected objects.

2. **Click one of the grips of your selected object to make it hot.**

   The blue, empty square turns to a red, filled-in square. This grip is now hot.

   Grip editing options now appear on the command line. The first option to appear is STRETCH.

3. **Press the spacebar (or press Enter) to cycle through the grip editing options on the command line.**

   The displayed grip editing option changes as you press the spacebar or Enter. The options that appear are, in order, STRETCH, MOVE, ROTATE, SCALE, and MIRROR. The appearance of your selected object changes as you display each option. Choosing STRETCH, for example, causes a stretched version of the object to appear on-screen.

4. **Keep pressing the spacebar (or Enter) until STRETCH (or the option you want) reappears as the grip editing option.**

5. **Drag the hot grip in the direction in which you want to stretch (or otherwise manipulate) your object.**

Figure 7-10 shows a line being "stretched" by its midpoint — which is a fast way to move the line. The dotted line shows what the new location of the line will be after you complete the line command by pressing Enter.

You can experiment with all the grip editing options to find out exactly how they affect a selected object, including using all the options that are available while holding down the Shift key (see the following tip).

If you want to see what a grip editing option does to your object without actually changing it, press and hold the Shift key while dragging the object's grip. Holding down the Shift key during grip editing causes the grip editing action to affect a *copy* of the object rather than the original; the original object remains in place, unchanged. (I guess you can consider this one a Grip Tip.)

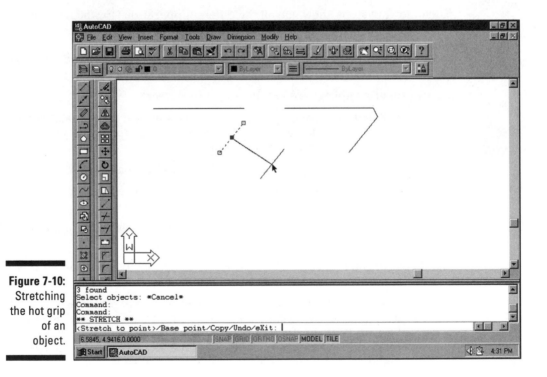

Figure 7-10:
Stretching
the hot grip
of an
object.

Chapter 8

A Zoom with a View

*O*ne of the advantages of AutoCAD is its capability to give you different ways to view your drawing. You can zoom in close, zoom out to a great distance, and pan around. You have several different ways to zoom and pan, which are explained in some detail in this chapter.

Keeping the appearance of the screen in sync with the actual drawing file — having the screen reflect changes as you make them — is the biggest single challenge to the performance of AutoCAD. User frustration over having to wait for redraws of the screen and for full regenerations (REGENs) of the screen image from the drawing database has pushed plenty of AutoCAD-related hardware sales over the years.

In AutoCAD Release 14, the AutoCAD graphics pipeline is redesigned, and the Windows-based AutoCAD Release 14 is now said to perform roughly as fast as the previous speed champ, the DOS-based Release 12. (Which was slow on its own, but quite fast with any of a number of commercially available display drivers.) Release 14 also uses less memory than Release 13 for Windows and has smaller file sizes. This reduction in memory use is a big help, freeing up more room for your drawing to be stored in memory, which improves performance.

AutoCAD Release 14 also performs "just-in-time" loading of the different parts of the program. Only a core group of commands and capabilities loads into memory at startup; other commands (for example, the ACIS kernel, used for solid modeling) aren't loaded until needed. The good news is that just-in-time loading means that AutoCAD Release 14 loads faster and starts off using less memory; the downside is that you may wait while using certain commands for the first time in a session and may experience a simultaneous decrease in available memory.

In addition to the performance improvements in Release 14, you can do certain things to help yourself even more. This chapter describes some of your options for getting more performance out of AutoCAD.

Degenerating and Regenerating

From the AutoCAD point of view, each drawing has two parts. The important part is the DWG (drawing) file, a highly precise database of objects that is stored on disk. AutoCAD uses high-precision numbers to describe the location of each object. The less-important part is the part that you interact with — the on-screen display of the drawing. For the on-screen display, AutoCAD uses less-precise integer numbers that are easy to calculate but less accurate than the numbers used in the DWG file.

The REGEN command does more than the REDRAW command. The REGEN command goes back to the DWG file for information on what objects have changed and need to be displayed with their new positions, colors, or linetypes. It then creates a new display list. The REGEN command also reorganizes the database that makes up the display for better performance and then redraws the current viewport from the new display list. REGEN regenerates the current viewport; REGENALL regenerates all views.

Some changes introduced in Release 14 of AutoCAD greatly reduce the need for redraws and regens. If you leave blips off, you may need to use the REDRAW and REGEN commands only rarely. The performance of these commands is still a big topic for AutoCAD aficionados, however, so you may hear about them more often than you would expect.

In AutoCAD Release 14, you can force a redraw or regen in two quick ways. The first method is to use the REDRAW or REGEN command from the command line. The second way uses two commands, Redraw (which runs the REDRAWALL command), Regen, and Regen All, on the View menu. The menu shortcuts for these commands are Alt+V, R, Alt+V, G and Alt+V, A. The keyboard shortcuts are Redraw, RedrawAll, REgen, and REgenAll.

How to Zoom-Zoom-Zoom on Your Room-Room-Room

Moving your viewpoint in to get a closer view of your drawing data is called *zooming in;* moving your viewpoint back to get a more expansive view is called *zooming out.*

Zooming in and out of your drawing is one of the big advantages that AutoCAD offers over manual drawing. You can do detailed work on tiny little objects and then zoom out and move around rooms, houses, or neighborhoods from an Olympian perspective.

Panning is closely related to zooming. If you zoom in enough that some of your drawing no longer shows up on-screen, you're going to want to pan around — move left, right, up, and down in your drawing — without zooming in and out. AutoCAD makes panning easy with scroll bars and the built-in aerial view.

Both panning and zooming change what is known as the *view*. The view is simply the current location and magnification of the AutoCAD depiction of your drawing. Each time you zoom or pan, you establish a new view. You can give a name to a specific view to make returning to that view easy.

Release 14 now enables real-time pans and zooms with fast switching between them via the cursor menu and support for real-time pans and zooms in paper space and print preview modes. These capabilities make working in AutoCAD more efficient and make "living" in paper space a real possibility for many users. See Chapter 13 for more information.

Release 14 has significantly reduced the degree to which the AutoCAD display-support hogs memory. For details on how this reduction works, see Chapter 1.

Out of the frying pan . . .

Panning isn't complicated, but it is confusing to use until you're comfortable with it. Because panning is integral to the ZOOM DYNAMIC command, one of the most important ways to zoom, I introduce panning first and then show you how to zoom in the next section.

Panning can be as simple or as powerful as you need it to be. The simpler approaches are very intuitive but may bog down with relatively slow performance in highly complex drawings. The more powerful approaches take more effort to master but work fast in almost any drawing.

The first approach to panning in AutoCAD that you should get to know is simply using the *scroll bars*. If you're coming to Release 14 from an early Windows version or a DOS version of AutoCAD, scrolling is a new capability for you. Even if you previously used a Windows version of AutoCAD with scroll bars, they're worth trying again, because the faster out-of-box speed of Release 14 makes the scroll bars more practical to use.

Scrolling is the same in AutoCAD as in any other Windows program; just click on the arrows in the right and bottom borders of the drawing window to pan a step at a time, or click and drag on the little square "thumbs" in those borders to pan as little or as much as you want to.

If you haven't used scroll bars much before or haven't used them much in AutoCAD, take some time to experiment with scrolling. With practice, it may become your main method of panning, reducing the need to spend time getting used to some of the more complex methods.

Real real-time panning

Real-time panning is a new approach to panning in Release 14 that mirrors panning in many other programs. In keeping with the intuitive viewing and editing approach that AutoCAD is adopting more and more, real-time panning is as simple as clicking and dragging. Just follow these steps to pan real-time in AutoCAD Release 14:

1. **Start the PAN command, with the Realtime option, by using one of the following methods:**

   • Type **Pan** at the command prompt and press Enter.

   • Click the Pan Realtime button (the one that looks like a hand) in the standard toolbar.

   The cursor changes to a hand.

2. **Pan by clicking at any point on your drawing and dragging.**

Clicking in the right spot can save you time. The farther to the left you click, for example, the farther to the right you can pan on a single drag of the mouse. Practice panning in your more complicated drawings until you are proficient.

3. **Repeat until you reach the part of your drawing that you want to reach.**

4. **To end the PANREALTIME command, use one of the following methods:**

   • Press Enter or the spacebar or the Escape key to terminate the command.

   • Right-click to activate a pop-up menu that enables you to switch to zooming.

Displaced panning

Another important approach to panning in AutoCAD is to pan by a certain distance, called a *displacement*. This method was the only kind of panning until Release 14 appeared. It is more work to make panning happen, but it provides high-performance panning, even in complex drawings. You don't pan by a specific number of units left, right, up, or down, and you don't specify the center point of your new view of things. Rather, you enter a displacement, which is the X and Y (horizontal and then vertical) distance to move the on-screen view. Or you can enter two points: a starting point and then a second point. AutoCAD figures out the distance between the two points and then pans that amount. Because the points represent a displacement, not a location, neither the starting nor finishing point actually has to appear on-screen at any point during the pan.

The following steps show you how to pan by using displacements:

1. **Start the old-style PAN command by using one of the following methods:**

   • Type **_PAN** at the command prompt and press Enter.

   • Choose <u>V</u>iew⇨Pan⇨Point from the menu bar.

2. **Type either a displacement or the first point and press Enter.**

   The displacement is the amount you want your viewpoint to move. For example, typing -3,-4 and pressing Enter shifts your viewpoint three units to the left and four units down.

   If you use a displacement, your drawing is ready to pan; just press Enter again. If you enter the first point, continue with Step 3.

3. **Press Enter (to pan by the amount of the displacement you just entered) or type the coordinates of a second point (to specify the second point of a displacement vector) and press Enter.**

   If you entered one point, the view will pan by that amount. If you entered two points, the view will pan by the difference between the second point and the first one.

   The following example shows the command line with the commands for a displacement pan:

```
Command: PAN
Displacement: -3,2 <Enter>
Second point: <Enter>
```

You can also enter the first and second point of the displacement by selecting points on-screen. Although inexact, this process can become intuitive for you with experience.

The ZOOMDYNAMIC command supports both panning and zooming; see the following section on zooming.

Time to zoom

Zooming is simply a necessity for working in AutoCAD, so take some time to find out how to zoom around, in, and out of your drawing.

The Zoom command has different options. The most important of these options are:

- ✔ **All/Extents.** ZOOMALL zooms out to the current limits of the drawing; it zooms out farther (if needed) to include objects outside the drawing limits in the zoom. ZOOMEXTENTS zooms out just far enough to show all the objects in the current drawing.

  In Release 14, ZOOMEXTENTS usually doesn't cause a REGEN, and it centers the drawing.

- ✔ **Dynamic.** This option supports both panning and zooming with a view box that you position. It's the next best thing to the aerial view (described later in this chapter), and it doesn't take up screen space, either.

- ✔ **Window.** Great for zooming in — zooms to a section of your drawing that you specify by placing a window around the area you want to look at. You can also use this option to zoom out, but then you have to enter the point coordinates at the command line.

- ✔ **Scale (X/XP).** Scales the drawing; values less than one cause you to zoom in, values greater than one cause you to zoom out. You can also think of the value as a scaling factor: 0.5X causes the screen image to shrink to half its apparent size, and 2X causes the screen image to double in apparent size. (Use XP after a number to scale relative to paper space; see Chapter 13.)

- ✔ **Real-time.** Real-time zooming enables you to zoom in and out simply by starting a real-time zoom and then moving the cursor up to zoom in or down to zoom out. This method is natural and gives a great deal of control, but performance may be slow in complicated drawings.

The zoom options take some getting used to. Experiment with all the options and the aerial view to find the approach that works best for you. (Occasionally, too, your drawing may seem to disappear. Know how to use zoom, and you can always discover where it went!)

Unfortunately, zooming to extents doesn't leave a margin of white space around the objects in the drawing. Follow a ZOOMEXTENTS command by typing **ZOOM 0.9X** at the command line (and pressing Enter) to get AutoCAD to zoom out just a little bit more.

Real real-time zooming

Real-time zooming is a new approach to zooming in Release 14, and one that's expected to largely replace other methods except for especially complex drawings. Just follow these steps to zoom real-time in AutoCAD Release 14:

1. **Start the ZOOMREALTIME command by using one of the following methods:**

   - Type **Zoom** at the command prompt and press Enter and then press Enter again to select the Realtime option, which is the default.

   - Click the Zoom Realtime button that looks like a magnifying glass with a plus/minus symbol next to it near the right end of the standard toolbar.

   The cursor changes to a magnifying glass.

2. **Zoom in or out by clicking at any point on your drawing and dragging up to zoom in, down to zoom out.**

   Clicking in the right spot initially can save you time. The farther up you click, for example, the farther in you can zoom on a single downward drag of the mouse.

3. **Repeat until you have zoomed as far as you want to.**

4. **To end the ZOOMREALTIME command, use one of the following methods:**

   - Press Enter or the spacebar to terminate the command.

   - Right-click to activate a pop-up menu that enables you to switch to panning or other zooming methods.

Getting dynamic with your zooming

The following steps show you how to use dynamic zoom to handle both panning and zooming. Until you get used to it, however, ZOOMDYNAMIC is confusing to use. After you master this method, though, it's easy and fast, even in complex drawings. Consider also using real-time zooming, described in the preceding section, and the aerial view, described in the following section.

Dynamic zooming is difficult at first, but it becomes a valuable tool after you get used to it. Follow the steps below a few times in one of your own drawings until you become proficient:

1. **Start ZOOMDYNAMIC by using one of the following methods:**

   - Type **ZOOMDYNAMIC** at the command prompt and press Enter.

   - Choose <u>V</u>iew⇨<u>Z</u>oom⇨<u>D</u>ynamic from the menu bar.

The drawing window automatically zooms out beyond its limits or extents, whichever is larger, as indicated by a dashed blue box. A dashed green box indicates the original view; a movable box with an X in it indicates a view you can pan and zoom; and a box around the edges of your drawing indicates its extents.

2. **To pan the drawing, use the mouse to move the box around on-screen and click after you finish.**

   Clicking anchors the left edge of the box and starts the zoom part of the command. Figure 8-1 shows several overlapping rectangles during execution of the ZOOMDYNAMIC command.

3. **To zoom, move the mouse left or right.**

   This action establishes the size of the new view.

X is center of dynamic zoom

Dynamic zoom window

Original view

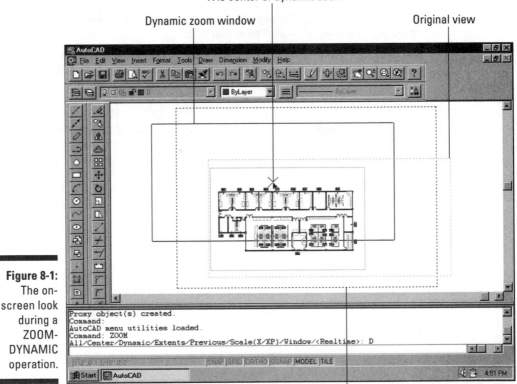

Figure 8-1:
The on-screen look during a ZOOM-DYNAMIC operation.

Limits or extents (whichever is larger)

4. **To pan while zooming, move the mouse up or down.**

   You can also combine up/down and left/right motions to pan and zoom simultaneously.

   This action establishes the up and down orientation of the new view. The left edge is anchored, but the right edge changes as you move the mouse left or right.

5. **Click to return to pan mode.**

   Now that you've set the size of the view (by zooming), you get another chance to pan.

6. **Repeat Steps 3 through 6 until the new view is the right size and in the right location.**

   At first, this procedure takes several tries, moving between panning and zooming. With practice, you're able to do this sequence quickly.

7. **Press Enter, or click the right mouse button, to establish the new view.**

The View from Above: Aerial View

The aerial view feature offers a quick way to navigate around your drawing as well as a way to magnify parts of the drawing. Although the magnification part is occasionally useful, think of the aerial view primarily as a way to control zooming and panning around your drawing. Real-time pan and zoom should be all you need most of the time, but for complex drawings, the aerial view can be very useful.

Much of the "sizzle" of the aerial view is gone in Release 14 due to the new real-time pan and zoom options; the aerial view is no longer always the easiest way to pan and zoom. However, it is still worth knowing for use in complex drawings with many levels of detail.

To open the Aerial View window, click the Aerial View icon on the standard toolbar. Figure 8-2 shows the location of the Aerial View icon and the Aerial View window. Unlike in Release 13, the button is no longer a flyout; the Aerial View icon, with the little airplane, is the default choice.

Aerial View icon   Aerial View window

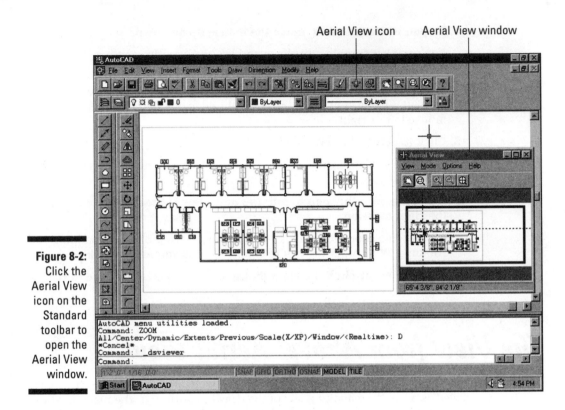

Figure 8-2:
Click the
Aerial View
icon on the
Standard
toolbar to
open the
Aerial View
window.

Zooming and panning with aerial view requires a little bit of finesse, because the actual proportions of your drawing window are fixed. If you want to both pan and zoom, it's best to zoom first, to define how big an area you want to see, and then pan. Follow these steps to zoom and pan with aerial view:

1. **Click the Aerial View icon on the standard toolbar to open the Aerial View window.**

2. **Click the Zoom icon in the Aerial View window.**

   The Zoom icon is the second button from the left, next to the hand, showing a magnifying glass with a rectangle in it.

3. **Click and drag on part of the image in the Aerial View window to create the zoom window.**

   AutoCAD updates the display in both the Aerial View window and the drawing area to show the result of the zoom. Keep clicking and dragging until you've set the zoom correctly, and then go on to Step 4 to pan.

   Figure 8-3 shows the Aerial View window and the drawing area behind it during a zoom. The dashed box is the zoom window.

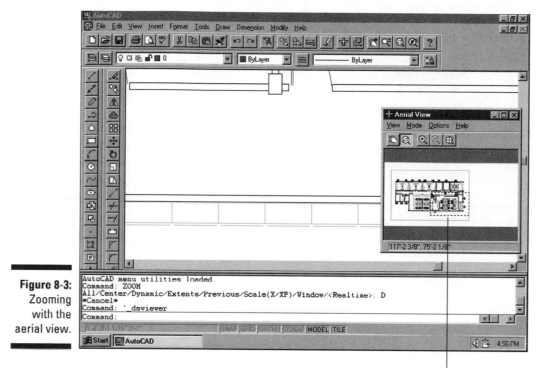

Figure 8-3:
Zooming
with the
aerial view.

Zoom in aerial view

Where you draw the zoom window determines where you pan the view
as well. The left edge of the zoom window that you create by dragging
becomes the left edge of the drawing window. If you drag correctly, you
don't need to pan.

4. To pan, click the Pan icon in the Aerial View window.

The Pan icon is the first button from the left, the one with the hand
on it. As you move the cursor into the middle part of the Aerial View
window, the cursor controls a box; this box is the panning window.

5. To pan, move the panning window around.

6. Click to establish the new view.

7. Repeat Steps 3 through 6 until the drawing area has the correct view.

**8. Click the Aerial View icon on the standard toolbar to close the Aerial
View window.**

Aerial view has other controls that you may want to experiment with, although the controls are most useful if you leave aerial view on-screen.

If aerial view is present but doesn't work, turn on Fast Zoom mode by typing **VIEWRES Yes** at the command prompt and pressing Enter.

Part III

Make Your Drawing Beautiful

The 5th Wave   By Rich Tennant

WITH DAD'S AUTOCAD RENDERING OF FOREST TROLLS, HIS CAMPSIDE STORIES ACHIEVE A NEW HEIGHT IN REALISM.

In this part . . .

Text, dimensions, and hatch patterns — mysterious embellishments to the uninitiated — have long been important elements in drawing and drafting. In AutoCAD, these elements are flexible, and you can instantly edit and update them as you change the geometry beneath them. After you get everything working, AutoCAD is definitely much better for almost all drawing purposes than pencil and paper ever could be — and far more versatile in enabling you to create a drawing that's truly beautiful. The purpose of such additions to your drawing as text or hatching is to prepare it for printing — or as CAD users say, for a *plot*. AutoCAD printing and plotting is flexible, powerful, and a little harder to use than you may think, so pay attention. In this part, you can pull all the pieces together and create a drawing that you can be truly proud of.

Chapter 9

Text with Character

Text can be one of the most important parts of an AutoCAD drawing. Text can be an intrinsic part of the drawing, integrated with other drawing elements. Text in a drawing is most commonly used for brief descriptions and notes, but it can also consist of long paragraphs that describe, annotate, or otherwise add to the drawing.

Dimensions — text that displays the measurements of objects — is a kind of text that AutoCAD handles especially well (although with a staggering number of options). Dimensions also include leaders with text. You can find more about dimensions in Chapter 10.

Text is one of the most-improved areas in Release 14. If you're upgrading from Release 13, you'll find text significantly improved. If you're upgrading from Release 12, the change will seem nearly total. The major changes you can expect are

 ✔ **Performance:** AutoCAD began using TrueType fonts in Release 13; support for TrueType fonts continues in Release 14, but now they display faster and take up less memory. (The old SHX, or "shape," fonts display faster still, but are AutoCAD-specific and limited in the number available.)

 ✔ **Quality:** Because Release 14 uses the TrueType fonts that have become standard in Windows (a big step in this version's improved Windows-compliance, which I mention in Chapter 1), it can look better.

✔ **Flexibility:** You have access to the huge library of TrueType fonts and all the sizes and styles available for those fonts. Autodesk has even created TrueType versions of the existing AutoCAD SHX fonts so that you don't lose access to those fonts.

✔ **Editability:** The built-in MTEXT editing dialog box, new in Release 14, gives you word processor-like text-editing capabilities for multiple-line blocks of text within AutoCAD.

✔ **Spell checking:** (First introduced in Release 13 for Windows.) You can now spell-check text within AutoCAD to help prevent embearassing misteaks.

✔ **Linkability:** (First introduced in Release 13 for Windows.) Because Windows supports Object Linking and Embedding, more commonly known as OLE, you can link to outside text from a database or word processor.

If you're going to pass your drawings back and forth between AutoCAD Release 14 and earlier versions, restrict yourself to the SHX fonts that come with AutoCAD; Release 13 sometimes has trouble finding TrueType fonts that have been installed on the user's system, and earlier versions of AutoCAD can't use TrueType fonts at all. Before using TrueType fonts, be sure that anyone else who will be working on your DWG file has or can get the same fonts you used. If you use TrueType fonts that are not available on another user's computer, either because they are using an earlier version of AutoCAD or because they don't have access to the fonts, your text will be preserved, but the font information will be lost.

Getting the Right Height

Both text and dimensions require that you specify a *height* for characters; text height is an important and difficult parameter to set correctly. Because it's a different kind of animal — and one that can bite you in an uncomfortable spot if you treat it badly — take a careful look at how to handle text height.

Text that looks good on-screen is no guarantee of text that looks good on your printout because the screen and the printout use text so differently. Most text in a drawing is not part of the drawing per se, but rather an attempt to communicate something about the drawing to the person using the printout. The text must be a height that the reader is used to. And physical and psychological factors have a big effect; for example, a reader tends to hold a small printout closer to his face than he does a large blueprint. Yet the larger blueprint may have more need for detail in text than the smaller drawing does.

Take note of the following tips for help in getting the height of your text right:

✔ Find out what the standard plotted text height is for your discipline, your office, and/or your current project. If several heights are standard, use the one that works best in your drawing.

✔ Divide the plotted height by the drawing scale factor given in Appendix B and use this number for the text height in AutoCAD.

The drawing scale factor is the number you multiply the right side of a drawing scale by to equal the left side. For instance, if you are using a drawing scale of $^1/_8$" = 1', the drawing scale factor is 96, because $^1/_8$" x 96 = 1'.

If you don't have a figure for plotted text height handy, use $^3/_{32}$" or 0.1", a little less than half the height of the lines in this book.

Using the Same Old Line

The DTEXT command is the simplest form of text entry and editing. This command enables you to enter single lines of text, one at a time; it's fast and easy to use for these single lines. Unlike more complex text-entry options, the text appears on-screen in the drawing area as you type it, not after you finish typing.

You can also use DTEXT for multiple lines of text; just keep pressing Enter after each line of text, and DTEXT puts the new line below the previous one. The problem is that, almost inevitably, you want to edit the text. If you cut a word or two in one line, the DTEXT command doesn't automatically adjust subsequent lines to make all lines the same width. Instead, you must go in and move words from one line to another so that all lines remain equal in width.

DTEXT creates each line of text as a separate object, which is why it can't adjust line lengths in a paragraph as you make changes; DTEXT only "knows" about one line of text at a time.

The DTEXT command also doesn't let you choose fonts; for that option, use MTEXT, described in the next section. DTEXT does enable you to select a previously created text style.

Despite its difficulties, the DTEXT command is useful. The following steps show you how to enter text by using the AutoCAD DTEXT command:

1. **Start the DTEXT command by using one of the following methods:**

   • Type **DText** at the command prompt and press Enter.

   • Choose <u>D</u>raw⇨<u>T</u>ext⇨<u>S</u>ingle Line Text from the menu bar.

2. **Specify the insertion point for the first text character.**

   You can enter the point's coordinates from the command line, use the mouse to click a point on-screen, or press Enter to locate new text immediately following a previous text object.

3. **Specify the height for the text.**

   This prompt doesn't appear if you're using a text style that already has a defined height. You can find more details about text styles in the section "Creating text styles," later in this chapter.

4. **Specify the text rotation angle by entering the rotation angle from the command line and pressing Enter or by rotating the line on-screen by using the mouse.**

5. **Type the first line of text and press Enter.**

6. **Type additional lines of text, pressing Enter at the end of each line.**

   Figure 9-1 shows text appearing on-screen as you type it, following the DTEXT command.

7. **To complete the command, press Enter at the start of a blank line.**

To align lines of text correctly, make sure that you type in all the lines just as you want them to appear, pressing Enter after each line to make the next line appear just after it. Otherwise, aligning different lines of text precisely is harder to do (unless you set your snap and grid just right and use the OSNAP command). If you're entering one and only one line of text, the TEXT command enables you to enter one line and then exit after you press Enter. The TEXT command is different from the DTEXT command, which keeps prompting you for additional lines of text. For many people, however, DTEXT is easier to use because you see the text on-screen as you type it.

To edit text, enter the DDEDIT command or choose <u>M</u>odify⇨<u>O</u>bject⇨<u>T</u>ext from the menus. The Edit Text dialog appears, enabling you to edit the text.

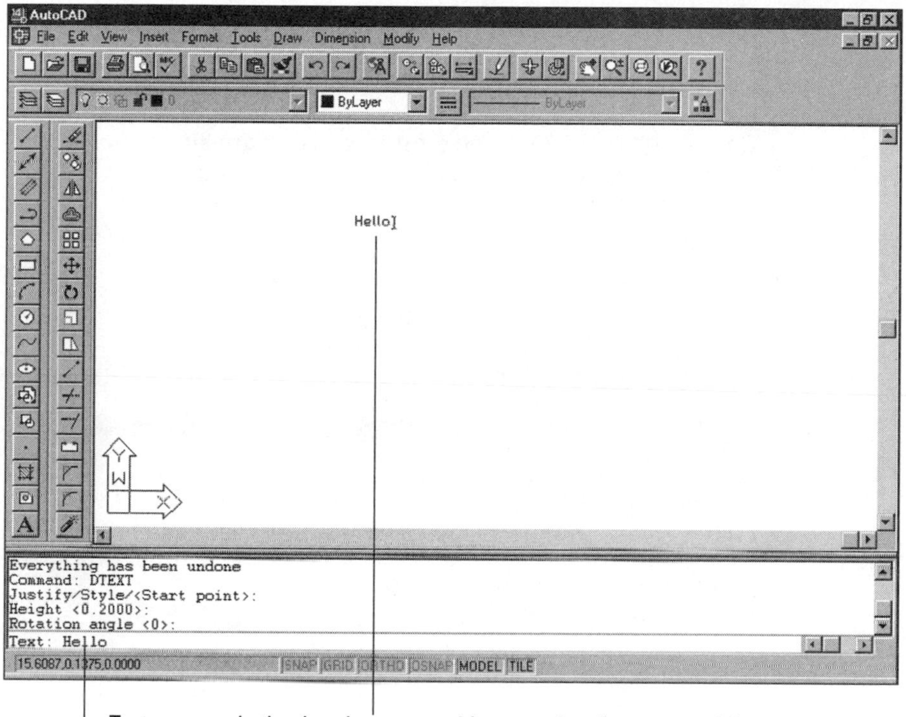

Figure 9-1:
The DTEXT
command
puts the
text directly
onto the
AutoCAD
screen as
you type it.

└─ Text appears in the drawing area as it's entered at the command line

Entering and Editing Paragraph Text

Release 14 features a much-improved Multiline Text Editor. Finally, AutoCAD has a text editor that can meet the needs of most of the users, most of the time. The text editor has a few unusual features in its interface, but it's easy to use after you master it.

In the next section, I describe the options of the Multiline Text Editor so that you can get acquainted with them, but you may just want to try the editor, especially if you have experience with other Windows word processing programs. Either read all about it here or try it in AutoCAD, and then work through the steps in the section "Using the paragraph editor," later in this chapter, to make sure that you really know how to use multiline text.

Learning multiline text character-istics

Using the Multiline Text Editor is much like using a mini-word processor, such as the WordPad that comes with Windows. The editor's three tabs — Character, Properties, and Find/Replace — are shown in Figure 9-2. All the numerous options are already familiar to most computer users and well-documented in the AutoCAD Help, so here are some key highlights of using the editor:

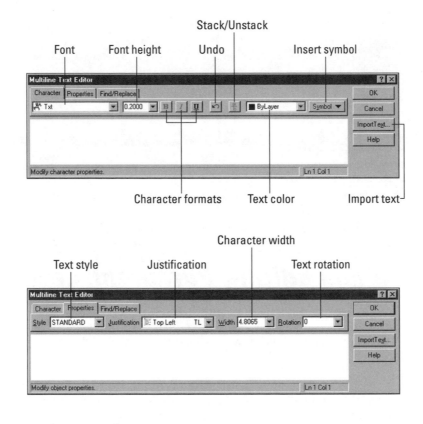

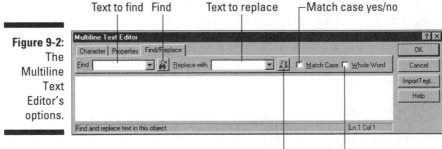

Figure 9-2: The Multiline Text Editor's options.

✔ **How to open the Multiline Text Editor:** Choose the Multiline Text icon in the Draw menu, which looks like a capital A, or use Draw⇨Text⇨ Multiline Text. The Multiline Text Editor dialog box appears, with the Character tab at the front.

To start the Multiline Text Editor dialog box from the command line, enter **mText.**

✔ **The text box:** Before you can type your text, you have to define a box to hold it. Don't worry about the height of the box; the text goes as far down the screen as it needs to. The important thing to get right is the width, which stays the same regardless of how much or little text you enter. (Though you can change the width later.)

✔ **Create text styles first:** Unlike Microsoft Word, the Multiline Text Editor doesn't enable you to make changes to your text and then name the changed text as a style. You have to create the style and define it completely before you can use it. Use the Text Style dialog box to create a style.

✔ **How to create text styles:** Use Format⇨Text Style to open the Text Style dialog box, shown in Figure 9-3. You can specify the text style's font name, style (bold, italic, and so on), and effects, such as upside down, backward, and vertical text. Use the detailed instructions later in this chapter on how to create a text style or experiment to find out how to create text styles that work well for you.

To start the Text Style dialog box from the command line, enter **STyle.**

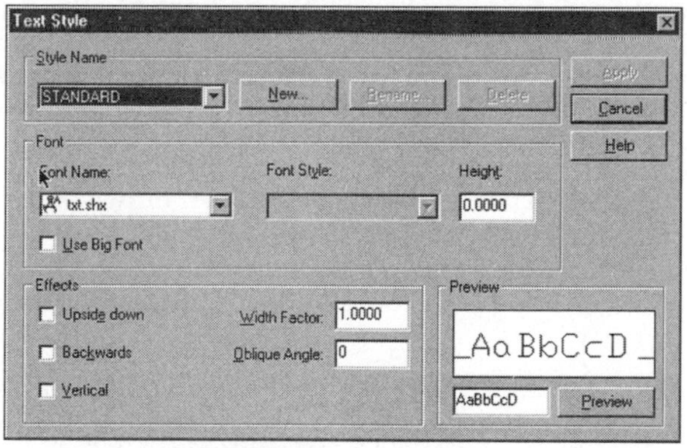

Figure 9-3:
Create your own text styles.

✔ **Specify style before character:** When you start the Multiline Text Editor, the Character tab comes up first. But if you use text styles, start by clicking the Properties tab and choosing the style you want to use. Then go to the Character tab and make any changes that you want to make.

✔ **Use a word processor:** For large blocks of text, a word processor is still the best bet; it has more functions, and you're likely to already know how to use it. Create text in a word processor, save it as RTF (Rich Text Format) text, and then use the Import Text button in the Multiline Text Editor to bring in the text.

The Multiline Text Editor window is tall enough to display only a few lines of text at a time. If you find yourself doing complicated operations (such as Find and Replace) often, you should probably use a word processor instead.

✔ **How to edit text:** To edit existing text, choose Modify⇨Object⇨Text. Then choose a text object. The Multiline Text Editor appears, with the selected object ready to be edited.

To start the Multiline Text Editor for existing text from the command line, enter **ddEDit**.

The DDEDIT command is a good example of the fact that command-first editing is buried deep inside AutoCAD. The "Windows way" to do things here would be to click on the text object and then choose a command; or better yet, just double-click on the text object. But AutoCAD requires you to enter the command first, whether from a menu or from the command line.

There is a roundabout way to use DDEDIT in the Windows manner: click on the text object and then click on one of its grips. Right-click to make the context-sensitive menu appear. Choose Properties, which will run the AutoCAD command DDMODIFY. You can then edit the text in the Contents edit box, or click the Full Editor button to bring up the Multiline Text Editor.

✔ **Cheat on width:** You can get more text into a limited space by reducing the text width by 20 percent or so, without changing legibility much.

✔ **Don't overdo it:** You can spend a great deal of time improving the content or the look of the text in your AutoCAD drawing, but the text is almost always secondary to the drawing geometry — and has to be changed anytime the geometry is changed. In other words, text is the tail, and the drawing is the dog, so don't put too much work into making text pretty.

✔ **Have someone else do it:** It's probably not a good idea for everyone on a project to be mastering the fine points of text styles and font choices. Have one person on the project be responsible for deciding what fonts to use and managing the styles for that project.

Release 14 continues a Release 13 problem of not handling stacked fractions well. If you try stacked fractions and they don't look good, it's not you — it's the program. Consider avoiding the use of stacked fractions; put the numerator and denominator of the fraction next to each other with a slash mark between them instead.

Using the paragraph editor

Here's a brief how-to on using the Multiline Text Editor. Use this section to get acquainted with the basic functions for editing blocks of text in AutoCAD. The following steps show you how to enter and edit text by using the Multiline Text Editor dialog box:

1. **Start the Multiline Text Editor by using one of the following methods:**

   • Type **mText** at the command prompt and press Enter.

   • Click the Text icon on the Draw toolbar or choose
   <u>D</u>raw⇨Text⇨<u>M</u>ultiline Text.

2. **Specify the insertion point for the first character.**

   You can either enter the coordinates of the point on the command line or use the mouse to select a point on-screen.

3. **Specify the other corner of the text box.**

   Enter the coordinates of the point on the command line or use the mouse to select a point on-screen.

   Ignore the other options that appear after you start the command; you can access all of them more easily in the paragraph editor.

   You aren't really specifying a box here, because the text just keeps spilling out of the bottom of the box if you type too much. You're really specifying the width of the text.

   After you specify the other corner, the Multiline Text Editor dialog box appears (refer to Figure 9-2).

4. **Type the text you need in the Multiline Text Editor's text box.**

5. **Modify the text's properties by using the dialog box's options.**

   The Multiline Text Editor dialog box includes a number of options, which are described in the following section. You can probably figure most of them out by experimentation.

6. **To complete the text, click OK.**

Creating text styles

A text style is a description of the properties used in creating text. A text style gives you a running start on getting all the various text settings right and helps maintain consistency of text appearance within and across drawings.

Fonts and performance

A *text font* actually consists of dozens, hundreds, or thousands of tiny lines. Drawing these lines is not a fast process, especially with the many characters that may exist in a really complicated font.

Imagine a drawing of an entire floor of a large building, with labels for each of the major parts of the floor. If you work on the whole drawing at once, AutoCAD may need to update thousands of characters each time you pan or zoom. The complexity of the task, and the time you must wait to complete the task, is greatly affected by the simplicity or complexity of the font you use.

AutoCAD includes a number of fonts. For the most effective performance, consider using the simpler fonts, such as TXT or ROMANS. ROMANS is a good compromise between appearance and performance.

You can also use more elaborate and attractive TrueType fonts for the very best appearance, but you'll pay a performance penalty. And performance is not the only concern in using these fonts; if a font is not one of the standard Windows or AutoCAD TrueType fonts, you must also load the fonts on each machine on which you intend to view or print the drawing.

When you use the Multiline Text Editor, you can change anything in the style; however, the change is not then embedded in a style for re-use by yourself or others. Also, the single-line text entry command, DTEXT, only uses existing styles; the only way to change text options for DTEXT is to set up a style with the options set as you want them.

AutoCAD comes with only a single text style: *STANDARD*. To create a new text style or to modify an existing one, follow these steps:

1. **To start the STYLE command, type STyle at the command prompt and press Enter (or choose Format⇨Text Style).**

   The Text Style dialog box appears.

2. **To modify an existing style, choose it from the pull-down menu; to create a new style, click the New button and then enter the style's name.**

3. **Select the font name from the pull-down menu.**

   The Preview box shows what the font looks like and is updated as you specify other text style options. Click Preview to make sure that the preview is up-to-date.

4. **Select the font style from the pull-down menu.**

   For fonts that have multiple styles, such as bold, italic, and so on, choose the style that you want from the pull-down menu.

5. Enter the text height in the text entry box and then press Enter.

If you enter **0**, the style definition does not determine the height of text; instead, AutoCAD prompts you for a text height each time you use this style. If you enter a value for the text height, that value is used each time you use the style.

You may want to create two or more versions of each style — one style for each of the fixed heights you expect to need, and one with no fixed height for flexibility.

6. Specify whether to use a Big Font.

To use a Big Font with an SHX font, just check the Use Big Font check box. This option is grayed out if you choose a non-SHX font.

Big Fonts are used for fonts that require additional storage space for each character. Big Fonts are used for Asian-language character sets, fractions, specialized drafting symbols, and other characters.

7. Specify effects: Upside down, Backward, Vertical, Width Factor, Oblique Angle.

Check the check boxes and enter values as needed.

For the Oblique Angle option, the angle range you can enter is from -80 degrees (tilted backward, almost horizontal) to 80 degrees (tilted forward, like normal italics, but also almost horizontal). An angle between 15 and 30 degrees looks like normal italics.

8. Click Apply when you're finished.

The new style is created.

It's easy to spend a great deal of time experimenting with text style options; set a time limit for yourself or choose a time when you're not under deadline pressure.

Checking It Out

AutoCAD Release 14 continues a feature first introduced in Release 13: a spell checker. If you're upgrading from Release 12, this feature is new to you; if you're upgrading from Release 13, the spell checker is unchanged. Although the spell checker may seem like a small deal, given that most drawings contain relatively few words, even one misspelling in a drawing for a $10 million proposal can be a major problem. So the spell checker is a welcome addition to AutoCAD. Use it!

Because most computer users are, by now, pretty familiar with the general concept of a spell checker and because the one in AutoCAD is relatively simple, the following steps should be enough to get you started on checking your spelling in AutoCAD:

1. **Start the spell checker by using one of the following methods:**

   - Type **SPell** at the command prompt and press Enter.
   - Choose Tools➪Spelling from the menu bar.

2. **Select the objects you want to check by clicking them in the drawing area.**

   Entering ALL in the command line selects all text objects. Press Enter to initiate the check.

   If AutoCAD finds no misspellings, it displays an alert box, and the command terminates. If the program finds a misspelling, the Check Spelling dialog box appears with the misspelled or unrecognized word. See Figure 9-4 for an example.

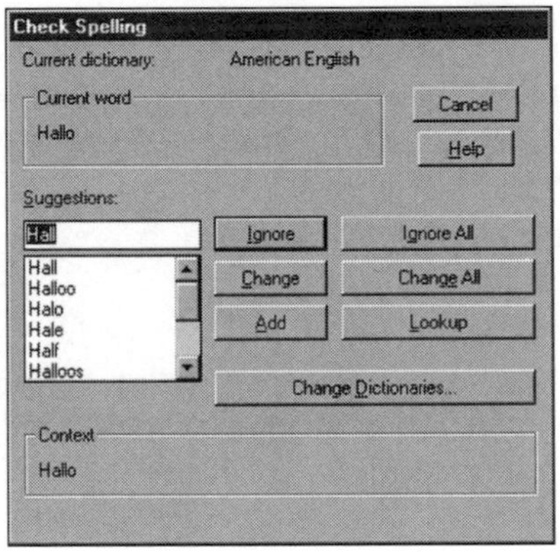

Figure 9-4:
Checking
for the
correct
speeling.

3. **Use the following options to tell AutoCAD how to handle a misspelling:**

   - **Suggestions:** AutoCAD puts its #1 suggestion here. Click another suggestion in the list to use that suggestion instead, or type the correct spelling yourself.

   - **Ignore/Ignore All:** Ignores the current word and continues checking, or ignores the current word and any future instances of it as well.

- **Change/Change All:** Changes the current word to the highlighted word and continues checking, or changes the current word and all other instances of it as well.

- **Add:** Adds the misspelled word to the custom dictionary.

- **Lookup:** Looks up the new word entered in the text-entry area under Suggestions.

- **Change Dictionaries:** Changes to a different dictionary.

- **Context:** Displays the words among which AutoCAD found the misspelled word.

AutoCAD continues with spell checking until it has checked all the selected text objects. If it finds no more misspellings, the dialog box disappears and the "all clear" alert appears.

Using the spell checker can save you a great deal of trouble and embarrassment. As ads for spell-checking products have long pointed out, a boss or client who finds an error in your spelling is likely to be suspicious of the correctness of the rest of your drawing as well. So always spell-check your document before you make a final plot of it.

Chapter 10

Entering New Dimensions

● ●

In This Chapter

▶ Delving into dimension basics

▶ Exploring linear, radial, angular, ordinate, and other dimension types

▶ Creating dimensions

▶ Using dimension styles

● ●

*F*irst, let me assure you that you have not actually entered the Twilight Zone in this chapter (although sometimes, when working with dimensions in AutoCAD, it may *seem* as though you have). *Dimensions* are labels that you put on an object to show the object's length, width, diameter, and other important numbers. AutoCAD dimensions automatically update themselves as you change the objects they are associated with. If you have a dimension that shows the length of a gun barrel, for example, and you drag the barrel to lengthen it, AutoCAD automatically updates the dimension that shows the barrel length. Sounds easy, right? (Oh, you wish!)

Unfortunately, dimensioning is one of the most complicated features of AutoCAD. Marking dimensions with pencil and paper is so flexible that drafters have developed an enormous number of ways to show dimensions. And with the cramped nature of most drawings, both traditional and CAD drafters want many ways to force dimensions into small spaces in the drawing. Myriad ways exist to depict dimensions, therefore, and AutoCAD offers dozens of dimensioning variables to support as many dimension styles as possible.

Dimensioning has improved a great deal in the last few versions of AutoCAD, including many changes in Release 13. If you're upgrading to Release 14 from Release 12, you see many changes. If you're a Release 13 user, you see just about no changes in Release 14.

AutoCAD now groups dimension variables into dialog boxes, reorganized in Release 13, that enable you to easily change the variables by clicking an image of the dimension. Dialog boxes also remind you what your options are and show you how related variables may affect each other.

Dimension styles enable you to group options together and apply them as a group, and dimension style families make handling minor variations within a style easier than the task would otherwise be.

But even with all these changes, complexity abounds. Dimensioning in AutoCAD is just so powerful that getting to know it all takes time. To avoid being overwhelming (and very lengthy), this chapter covers only the basics of dimensioning. The chapter is very useful to the novice who wants to get a feel for dimensioning, as well as to the more advanced user who wants a quick look at the dialog boxes introduced in Release 13. For more information on the advanced features of dimensioning, however, you need to go to the AutoCAD documentation — and be ready to do a great deal of experimenting as well.

Among the important concerns in dimensioning is getting the size of dimensions right. Make sure to use the Geometry subdialog box of the Dimension Styles dialog box to set the Scale of the dimensions to the drawing scale factor, which is explained in Chapter 4 and Appendix B. See the section on the Geometry subdialog box later in this chapter for more information.

New Dimensions of Sight and Sound . . . and CAD

(Okay, so maybe we *have* entered the Twilight Zone. Rod Serling, where are you?) Although you may have drawn or at least have seen dimensions in your past work, you may not realize that a dimension actually consists of many parts. Figure 10-1 displays the following important parts of a dimension:

- ✔ **Dimension text:** Dimension text is the set of numbers that indicate the actual dimension. In AutoCAD, you can specify prefixes to appear before the dimension text, suffixes to appear after it, and tolerances to indicate the precision of the measurement.

- ✔ **Dimension line and arrowhead:** The dimension line goes from the dimension text outward, to indicate the size of the dimension. The arrowhead shows where the dimension line terminates. You can also use another kind of line ending, such as a tick mark, to indicate the end of the line.

- ✔ **Extension line:** The extension line extends from the end of the dimension line to the object that the dimension measures.

Imagine that you have to specify to a very young child — who is, of course, excellent at drafting — every aspect of every part of a dimension and how it fits into a drawing; only then can you start to realize the potential complexity of dimensioning in AutoCAD. To get the most out of the limited attention span that most people have for dimensions, this section explains dimensions in general via the Dimension Styles dialog box and then describes specific types of dimensions only to the extent that they differ from linear dimensions.

Setting up dimensions

To create even a simple dimension, you must do some setup work and then make an informed choice from many different options. This section includes what you need to know to start using dimensions.

Release 14 combines the new dimensioning features found in Release 13 and all methods of accessing them: the menu bar, a special toolbar, and the command line. (In Release 13, the menu options were only available in the DOS version, and toolbar access only in Windows.) The actual features of dimensioning are familiar to Release 13 users and new to those folks upgrading from Release 12.

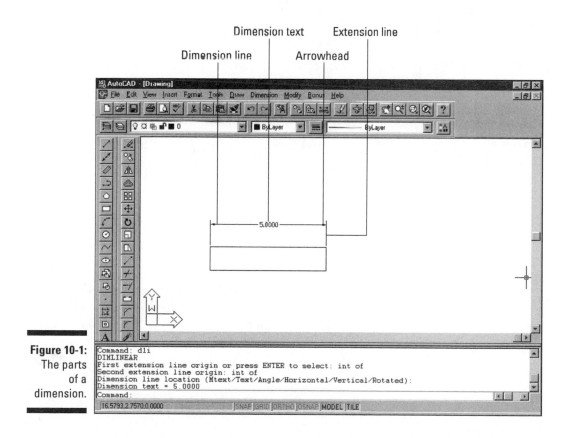

Figure 10-1:
The parts
of a
dimension.

The fastest way to access dimensioning commands is from the Dimension toolbar. The only trouble is that you want to put this toolbar away much of the time because it takes up so much screen space. So train yourself to bring the toolbar up and put it away quickly; for extra productivity, memorize the command line commands for the dimensioning that you use most.

The following steps show you how to make the Dimension toolbar appear and disappear on-screen:

1. **Choose View➪Toolbars from the menu bar to bring up the Toolbars dialog box and then click the Dimension check box to turn on the Dimension toolbar.**

   The Dimension toolbar appears on-screen, as shown in Figure 10-2.

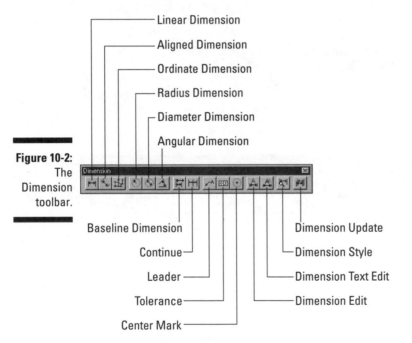

Figure 10-2:
The Dimension toolbar.

The keyboard shortcut for turning on the Toolbars dialog box is Alt+V, O.

2. **Use the mouse to click and drag the Dimension toolbar to where you want it on-screen.**

   You can dock the toolbar on any side of the screen or leave it floating.

3. **After you finish using the Dimension toolbar, close it by clicking the close box in the upper-right corner of the toolbar.**

The Dimension toolbar vanishes from your screen — poof! (Almost as though it disappeared into . . . another dimension!)

What all these crazy dimensions mean

The options in the Dimension toolbar are almost the same as in the Dimensioning toolbar in Release 13 for Windows, but the order is a little different. Also, Release 14 has a separate Dimension menu.

Take a few seconds to start the Dimension toolbar when you need it and hide it when you don't; the productivity improvement over using the menu is likely to be worthwhile.

Several different types of dimensions are available from the Dimension toolbar. Not all the options are equally important to everyone, but knowing in general what these options are certainly helps you get to the actual work of creating a dimension sooner rather than later. (The Dimension menu is similar to the Dimension toolbar; only some of the last few items on the menu are different.) The following options are represented by the icons, from left to right, on the Dimension Toolbar:

- ✔ **Linear Dimension** (also accessed by using the DIMLINEAR command, keyboard shortcut DLI): A *linear dimension* is a horizontal or vertical dimension with extension lines going vertically (for a horizontal linear dimension) or horizontally (for a vertical linear dimension) to the origins of the extension lines, which define the endpoint of the dimension.

- ✔ **Aligned Dimension** (also accessed by using the DIMALIGNED command, keyboard shortcut DAL): An *aligned dimension* is a linear dimension tilted to the same angle as a line drawn through the endpoints of its extension lines.

- ✔ **Ordinate Dimension** (also accessed by using the DIMORDINATE command, keyboard shortcut DOR): An *ordinate dimension* is a leader (defined later in this section), followed by the X or Y coordinate of the point.

- ✔ **Radius Dimension** (also accessed by using the DIMRADIUS command, keyboard shortcut DRA): A *radius dimension* is a dimension from the center of an arc or circle, with one end of the dimension line at the center and an arrowhead at the curve.

✔ **Diameter Dimension** (also accessed by using the DIMDIAMETER command, keyboard shortcut DDI): A *diameter dimension* is a dimension through the center of an arc or circle, with each end of the dimension line at an opposite point on the curve.

✔ **Angular Dimension** (also accessed by using the DIMANGULAR command, keyboard shortcut DAN): An *angular dimension* is a dimension drawn inside an angle; the dimension line curves along an arc inside the measured angle.

✔ **Baseline Dimension** (also accessed by using the DIMBASELINE command, keyboard shortcut DBA): A *baseline dimension* is actually a series of related dimensions drawn from a single baseline. Each dimension is incremented from the previous one by a value that you enter. Baseline dimensions can be angular, linear, or ordinate, depending on the type of the previous dimension. If the previous dimension isn't one of these three types, AutoCAD prompts you for a dimension of one of the types.

✔ **Continue** (also accessed by using the DIMCONTINUE command, keyboard shortcut DCO): This option *continues* a dimension from its second extension line.

✔ **Leader** (also accessed by using the LEADER command, keyboard shortcut LE): A *leader* is a pointer that connects an annotation to a drawing feature. (So if you're asked by a spacey-looking stranger to "take me to your leader," just turn on AutoCAD. . . .)

✔ **Tolerance** (also accessed by using the TOLERANCE command, keyboard shortcut TOL): A *tolerance* is a specifically formatted description of the maximum allowable variation in a measurement. The TOLERANCE command enables you to specify the symbol and other aspects of the tolerance.

✔ **Center Mark** (also accessed by using the DIMCENTER command, keyboard shortcut DCE): The *center mark* indicates the central point of a diameter or radial dimension. It can have several different aspects that you specify. The Center Mark icon gives you direct access to this feature.

✔ **Dimension Edit** (also accessed by using the DIMEDIT command, keyboard shortcut DED): This icon lets you edit dimension characteristics, one or several dimensions at a time.

✔ **Dimension Text Edit** (also accessed by using the DIMTEDIT command): This icon gives you direct access to text location and rotation angle.

✔ **Dimension Style** (also accessed by using the DDIM command, keyboard shortcut D): This icon enables you to specify the *dimension style,* a set of dimension options that are grouped together and given a name, and modify the style's characteristics by using the Dimension Styles dialog box.

 ✔ **Dimension Update** (also accessed by using the DIMSTYLE command): Runs the old DIM Update subcommand, which applies the current dimension style, plus any style overrides that are currently in effect, to the dimension or dimensions you select.

AutoCAD does not require you to specify objects to dimension; it draws a dimension between any points you specify. Usually, however, the points for which you want to indicate a dimension are part of an object. To keep things general, though, the points that you attach the dimension to are referred to as the *origins* of the dimension's extension lines, and they can be any points that you want to create a dimension between.

Creating a dimension

Although many types of dimensions exist, most dimensioning concerns the three most common types you encounter: *linear dimensions, radial dimensions,* and *angular dimensions.* This section describes how to create dimensions and about how easy dimensioning can be if you can use an existing dimension style. Look for more about the detailed options for different kinds of dimensions in the section "Doing Dimensions with Style(s)," later in this chapter.

The following steps show you how to create linear dimensions for both sides of a rectangle:

1. **Draw a rectangle by typing** RECtangle **at the command prompt and pressing Enter.**

   If you already have a rectangle in your drawing, you can use that instead. (If you want to apply dimensioning to another shape, use these steps as a general guideline, filling in the appropriate commands and data as applicable to your drawing.)

2. **Start the DIMLINEAR command by using one of the following methods:**

   • Type **DimLInear** at the command prompt and press Enter.

   • Click the Linear Dimension icon (the left-most icon) on the Dimension toolbar.

3. **To specify the origin of the first extension line, snap to a corner on the left side of the rectangle by using the intersection snap.**

   Type **INT** and then click the corner you want. Or right-click to use the Cursor menu.

4. **To specify the origin of the second extension line, snap to the other corner on the left side of the rectangle by using the intersection snap.**

   Type **INT** and then click the corner you want. Or, right-click to use the cursor menu.

   AutoCAD automatically draws a *vertical* dimension — that is, it displays the length of the object in the up-and-down direction.

5. **Click anywhere on-screen to indicate where you want to place the dimension line, or type a location for the dimension on the command line and press Enter.**

6. **Repeat Steps 2 through 5 to create a horizontal linear dimension.**

   This time, AutoCAD automatically draws a *horizontal* dimension — that is, it displays the length of the object in the crossways, or left-to-right, direction.

Doing Dimensions with Style(s)

Using the Dimension Styles dialog box is probably the best way to begin to understand dimensions thoroughly. The Dimension Styles dialog box enables you to change just about any dimension variable and almost automatically groups the variables into a style you can use later. Though still no picnic, understanding dimensioning variables in terms of the Dimension Styles dialog box is probably not a bad idea, because the dialog box is likely to be the main way you interact with dimensions.

The Dimension Styles dialog box

Except for a crisper, Windows-standard look, the Dimension Styles dialog box and its subdialog boxes are exactly the same in Release 14 as in Release 13. If you've already mastered this dialog box, you can just skim this section to refresh your knowledge; but if it's new to you and you do much modification of dimension options, take the time to read this section carefully, experiment, and get to know the Dimension Styles dialog box well.

Figure 10-3 shows the Dimension Styles dialog box, which is really the doorway to a number of related dialog boxes. The following sections explain the parts of this initial dialog box; descriptions of other, related dialog boxes follow. Type **Ddim** at the command line and press Enter to open the Dimension Styles dialog box.

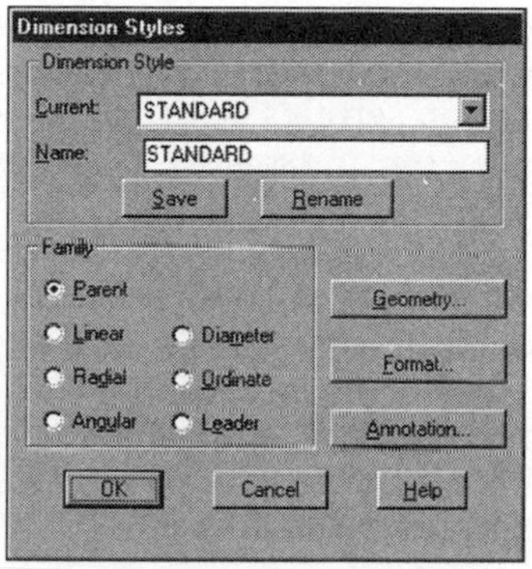

Figure 10-3:
The
Dimension
Styles
dialog box.

The Dimension Style area

The Dimension Style area of the Dimension Styles dialog box dictates what style is currently in use. I suggest that you leave the STANDARD style unchanged, so that you have a base from which to work, and then create at least one style of your own for your dimensions. The name you create can be up to 31 characters long, so calling your version MYSTANDARD may be a good choice.

To create a new style, first use the Current drop-down list to select the existing style you want to use as a starting point and then type the name of the new style in the Name text box. Click Save to save the original definition of the style, and then you can modify options as described in the following sections. Click Save again to save your modifications.

If you don't click Save to save your modifications, your changes are not saved in the dimension style. Instead, they temporarily override settings in the current dimension style.

Family area

If you assume that you use the Family area to specify what type of dimension the style applies to, you're wrong; this area doesn't work as you think. A dimension style applies to any kind of dimension. The Family area of the dialog box enables you to specify a family of dimensions — Linear, Radial, Angular, and so on — to which a given dimension style option applies. (The Parent family enables you to make certain settings global for all families; you can then override Parent settings within other families where it makes sense.) For example, although the overall style for different types of dimensions may use a certain font, a radial dimension within the style may use an entirely different one. This differentiation enables you to build up complex styles with many variations.

Complicated styles may be hard to maintain. If you're planning to have several of them, consider documenting the choices — a one-page description of each style you create and its option settings is sufficient. Also consider centralizing the work — making one person the keeper of dimension styles for your department or company.

The Family area affects the options available in the Geometry, Format, and Annotation dialog boxes, which are described in the following sections. If a given option doesn't make sense for the dimension family that's currently in force, AutoCAD dims the option in the dialog box, making it unavailable for use. If you choose a different family for which the option is pertinent, the option becomes available again.

The Geometry, Format, and Annotation buttons

The Geometry, Format, and Annotation buttons lead to dialog boxes that enable you to specify the major options for the dimension style.

One or more system variables control each aspect of dimensions. In general, memorizing which of the dozens of dimensioning-related system variables control which aspect isn't worth your valuable time; just use dimension styles to control each parameter. If you frequently find yourself changing one or two specific aspects of a dimension, however, finding out the name of the appropriate variable so that you can set it directly may actually be worth the effort. Check your AutoCAD documentation for information about which system variable controls which parameter.

The Geometry dialog box

Figure 10-4 shows the Geometry dialog box, which you can open from the Dimension Styles dialog box (by clicking the Geometry button, of course). The Geometry dialog box enables you to specify options that relate to the look of the dimension.

The following sections briefly explain the major areas of the Geometry dialog box.

The Windows dialog box hot keys that take you directly to that option are underlined. To use Windows menu hot keys to open the Geometry dialog box, press Alt+O, D, G (that's for Format⇨Dimension Style⇨Geometry) and then the hot key for the specific option.

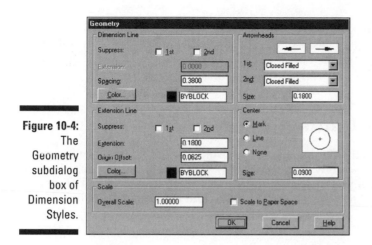

Figure 10-4:
The
Geometry
subdialog
box of
Dimension
Styles.

Dimension Line

The Dimension Line area enables you to control the suppression of either the 1st or 2nd dimension line that you pick. Extension specifies the length that the dimension line gets extended outside of the extension lines; it is only available for certain kinds of arrowheads, such as tick marks. You can also set the Spacing between dimension lines of a baseline dimension and the Color of the dimension line.

Extension Line

The Extension Line area enables you to control the suppression of the 1st or 2nd extension line. You can also set the Extension distance beyond the dimension line for the extension lines, specify the gap by which the extension line is offset from its origin (Origin Offset), and choose the Color of the extension line.

Arrowheads

You can specify the look of 1st and 2nd arrowheads and the arrowhead Size in this area.

Center

You can specify the appearance of the Center Mark used in a radial dimension — as a small cross inside the circle (Mark), a small cross plus cross hairs (Line), or no mark at all (None) — as well as its Size.

Scale

You can set the Overall Scale of the dimension here, either as an absolute scale or as a Scale to Paper Space, discussed in Chapter 13. See Chapter 3 and Appendix B for more information on dimension scales.

The Format dialog box

Figure 10-5 shows the Format dialog box, which you open from the Dimension Styles dialog box (by clicking — yes — the Format button). The Format dialog box enables you to specify options that relate to where you place a dimension, the origins of its extension lines, and how the dimension is aligned.

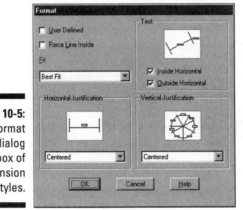

Figure 10-5:
The Format subdialog box of Dimension Styles.

The following sections describe the major areas of this dialog box.

The Windows dialog box hot keys that take you directly to that option are underlined. To use Windows menu hot keys to open the Geometry dialog box, press Alt+O, D, F (that's for Format⇨Dimension Style⇨Format) and then the hot key for the specific option.

Fit

In this area, you can tell AutoCAD to prompt you as to where to put dimension text in a new dimension (User Defined); you can instruct the program to add a line inside the dimension, even if the arrowheads are outside the extension lines (Force Line Inside); and you can specify how to Fit different parts of the dimension, even if the space between extension lines is too narrow for everything.

This is an important option that takes practice to get right. Experiment with different Fit options to see how each affects the way dimensions work.

Text

You can indicate here how to align your dimension text: horizontally (Inside Horizontal) or aligned with the dimension line (Outside Horizontal).

Horizontal Justification and Vertical Justification

You can choose from a number of options for the horizontal and vertical justification of text, including centered, justified to the first or second extension line, and over the first or second extension line.

The Annotation dialog box

Figure 10-6 shows the Annotation dialog box, which you open from the Dimension Styles dialog box (by clicking — that's right, you guessed it — the Annotation button!). The Annotation dialog box enables you to specify options that relate to the look of the text that displays the value of the dimension.

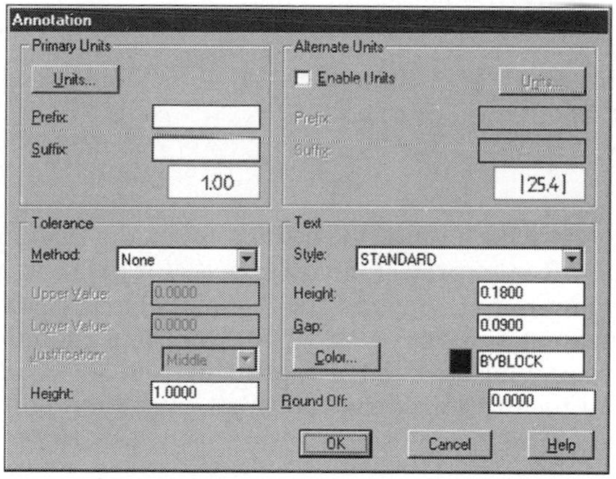

Figure 10-6: The Annotation subdialog box of Dimension Styles.

The following sections describe the major areas of this dialog box. (Is that an echo I hear?)

The Windows dialog box hot keys that take you directly to that option are underlined. To use Windows menu hot keys to open the Geometry dialog box, press Alt+O, D, A (that's for Format⇨Dimension Style⇨Annotation) and then the hot key for the specific option.

Primary Units

Clicking Units opens a secondary — sorry, tertiary — dialog box, where you can specify a great number of things about the primary units used in your dimensions, including the type of units, type of angular units, precision and zero suppression for measurements, precision and zero suppression for tolerances, and scaling factor. You can also specify in the Primary Units area a Prefix or a Suffix for your units (such as "inches").

Alternate Units

You can use the options in this area to display alternative units in square brackets after your dimension text. If your primary units are decimal, for example, you may also want to display the measurements in fractions. All the options available for primary units are available for alternative units as well, through that secondary — oops, I mean tertiary again — Units dialog box. Select Enable Units and then click the Units button to choose the type of units you want.

Tolerance

You can specify in this area a vast number of Methods for displaying tolerances as well as the Upper Value, Lower Value, Justification, and Height for a dimension.

Text

You can specify in this area a text Style (including font), plotted text Height, the Gap around text, and the Color of text.

Round Off

Round Off is the value to which AutoCAD rounds off all dimension distances. Coordinate this value with the precision you specify for primary and alternate units. Displaying four digits beyond the decimal of precision and then rounding off to the nearest unit, for example, may not make much sense. (By now, of course, you may think that all too many things in AutoCAD don't make much sense; but having your displayed digits and round off precision different really doesn't. Trust me!)

Chapter 11
Hatch . . . Hatch . . . Hatchoo!

A *hatch* is a pattern that fills in an area of a drawing. Hatching is often used to convey the type of material represented by an object, such as insulation, metal, and so on. A hatch is similar to a linetype in that it conveys information about part of the drawing. But unlike with a linetype, you don't connect a hatch to an object. Instead, you connect a hatch to an empty space, surrounded by objects. (In many fields, showing empty space is important, such as when an architect depicts a wall or a grassy open space or an engineer shows a cutout.)

These details help explain why *hatch* is actually a short name for a longer idea. A hatch is a pattern that fills an area that you define by using points. But the more useful, and common, kind of hatch is a *boundary hatch* — that is, a hatch pattern filling an area within an existing boundary. (A *boundary* is the edge of an object.) If you apply a boundary hatch to an area, AutoCAD must engage in some guesswork about the exact nature of the boundary, as well as what areas within the boundary you do and don't want hatched. If AutoCAD guesses wrong, you must tell it what to do.

Even *boundary hatch* is short for a longer term. The default type of boundary hatch is called an *associative boundary hatch*. This kind of hatch was introduced in Release 13. An associative boundary hatch remains associated — clever, huh? — with the objects that make up its boundary. If you modify the objects that make up the boundary, AutoCAD tries to adjust the hatch to fit. Of course, if the changes open up a hole in the boundary, AutoCAD may just have a hard time adjusting the hatch correctly.

If you use only simple hatches, you may not need to worry about modifying the objects of the hatch or whether AutoCAD can make the correct adjustments. You should, however, at least know what to do if you run into a situation that requires modification or adjustment. With this knowledge, you can avoid problems with the hatch and have some idea of how to go about making the hatch right if you do experience problems.

A good way to avoid problems related to a hatch is to avoid hatching until late in the drawing process. Creating the hatch near the end of your project benefits performance and can even help you avoid the need to rework your drawing.

Not much about hatches has changed in Release 14, except for one obvious and one hidden — but pleasing — difference. *Solid fills* are a new hatch pattern. Assuming that your printer or plotter and its device driver support this new pattern, you now have a whole new way to hatch areas. (Yes, AutoCAD neophytes, solid fills are a new feature in AutoCAD. I know you've had them in CorelDRAW for a decade or so, but it's hard for a pen plotter — the traditional way of printing out CAD drawings — to do a solid fill. Nevertheless, solid fills are finally here!)

The hidden difference is that AutoCAD now stores hatches differently. Within a drawing, AutoCAD Release 14 stores the hatch's boundary and a pointer to a hatch pattern definition. The hatch pattern is stored separately within the drawing. In previous versions of AutoCAD, a hatch was stored in the drawing as a large, or even huge, number of little lines. With the old way, hatches added measurably to the file size and display time of a drawing. With the new way, things are smaller and faster.

If you don't want to worry about hatch pattern files, just select the hatched areas of your drawing and use the EXPLODE command to explode the hatch into its constituent lines. Your file size grows, and the drawing displays more slowly, but you don't have to worry about those annoying little hatch pattern files anymore.

If you're experienced with early releases or if you make many changes in hatch options, and you want to speed things up by using the keyboard, use the HATCH command. You are prompted for the key hatch options; Figure 11-1 shows a simple hatch created with the HATCH command so that you can see what the options are. Use the dialog box to gain an understanding of what the options mean and then use the keyboard as an accelerator for the changes that you make most frequently.

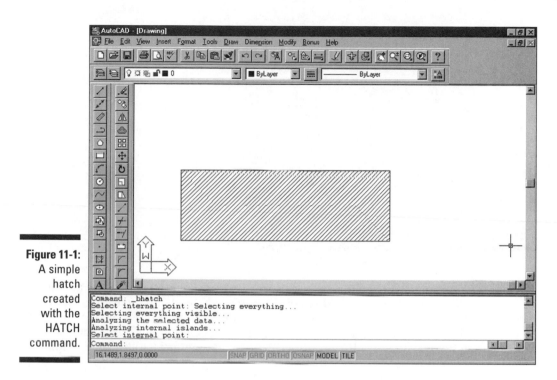

Figure 11-1:
A simple hatch created with the HATCH command.

Using the Boundary Hatch Dialog Box

If you want a flexible hatch that's defined by its boundaries — that is, a hatch that updates if you update its boundaries — use boundary hatching. You can control boundary hatching by using the Boundary Hatch dialog box (see Figure 11-2), which you access by any of the following methods:

- ✔ Choose Draw⇨Hatch from the menus.
- ✔ Click the Hatch icon (the bottom-most icon) on the Draw toolbar.
- ✔ Type **BHatch** at the command prompt and press Enter.

Either H or BH will work as a shortcut for the BHATCH command, but you might as well learn the shorter one. Use H as the keyboard shortcut for the BHATCH command.

The Boundary Hatch dialog box enables you to do two main tasks: specify the hatch pattern to use and define the boundary of the hatch area. Just about every option in the dialog box relates to one of these two tasks.

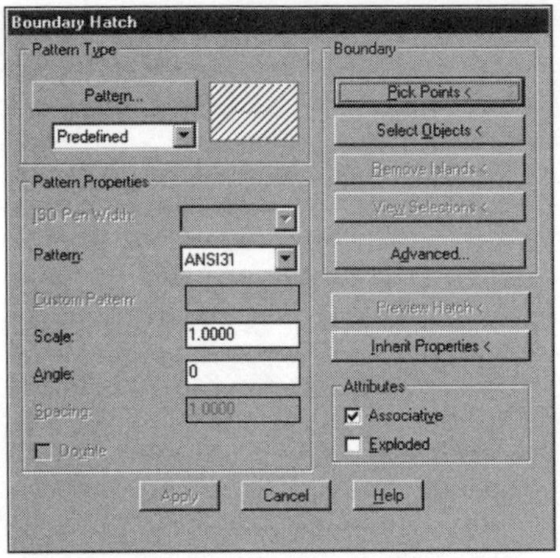

Figure 11-2:
The
Boundary
Hatch
dialog box.

You can use predefined, user-defined, or custom hatch patterns. Most of the time, you're likely to find yourself using predefined hatch patterns, but the other hatch pattern options are nice to have. The next three sections describe the basics of specifying a hatch pattern. You can find out how to create a boundary hatch in the section, "Creating a boundary hatch," later in this chapter.

Accessing predefined hatch patterns

To use *predefined* hatch patterns that exist in all copies of AutoCAD, select Predefined from the drop-down list box in the Pattern Type area of the Boundary Hatch dialog box. This selection sets the stage for choosing the hatch pattern.

You can scan through the hatch patterns in one of three ways:

✔ By selecting the name from the Pattern drop-down list box in the Pattern Properties area; this action changes the hatch pattern shown in the preview square in the Pattern Type area.

✔ By clicking the Pattern button; this brings up a pattern preview that shows twenty patterns at a time.

✔ By clicking the preview square; this action changes the hatch pattern shown and the Pattern name in the list box as well.

AutoCAD has about 70 predefined hatch patterns from which to choose, which is quite a long list. The list includes ANSI (American National Standards Institute) and ISO (International Standards Organization) standard hatch patterns. Figure 11-3 shows the ANSI hatch patterns to give you an idea of the kinds of hatch patterns available.

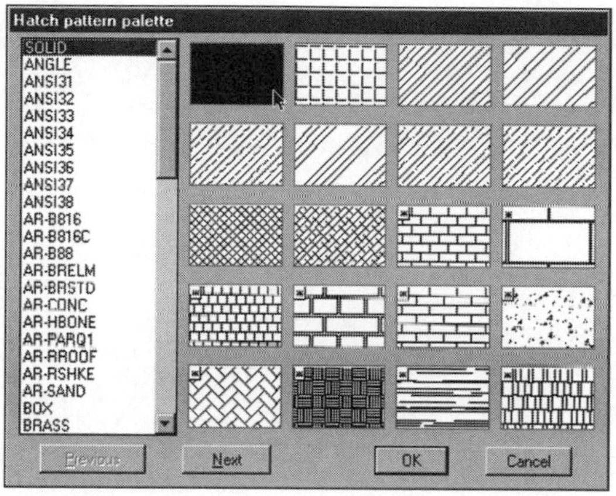

Figure 11-3:
The first 20
of the 68
predefined
hatch
patterns
available in
AutoCAD.

A good idea is to print out a small cheat sheet of hatch patterns that you commonly use and a larger one of all the hatch patterns available to you (whether predefined, user-defined, or custom) and then share them with others in your organization. These cheat sheets can save time and help you choose the right hatch pattern for your drawings instead of settling for one of the first hatch patterns you stumble on while clicking through the hatch patterns list.

Using user-defined and custom hatch patterns

In addition to the predefined hatch patterns, you can use *user-defined* hatch patterns and *custom* hatch patterns. These two kinds of hatch patterns meet two different needs.

A *user-defined* hatch pattern makes a hatch pattern out of the currently selected linetype. Start by going into your drawing and specifying the linetype you want to use. Then go back into the Boundary Hatch dialog box and specify User-defined hatch pattern in the Pattern Type area. You can specify the Angle and Spacing of the lines in the Pattern Properties area. Figure 11-4 shows four user-defined hatch patterns with spacing increasing from one to four units and angles increasing from 20 degrees through 80 degrees. All the shapes are squares, aligned at right angles; the apparent tilt in the third and fourth squares is an optical illusion. Use it to confuse any nearby children! (If no kids are handy, a boss will suffice.)

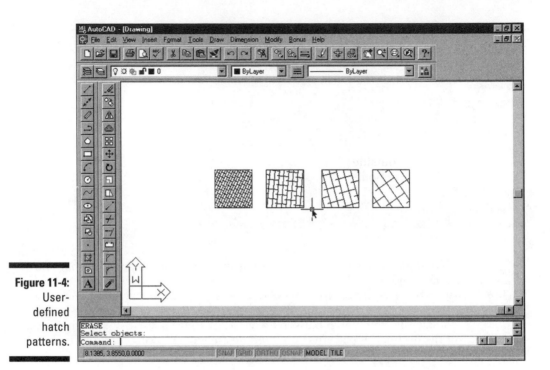

Experiment with different options to determine what works well for you. Unfortunately, even after you find a hatch pattern that works well for a particular purpose, you can't save it. But you can write down how you created that pattern so you can re-create it.

A *custom* hatch pattern is a hatch pattern that you can define and save in a file with a file extension of PAT. (No, football fans, I'm sorry. PAT doesn't stand for "point after touchdown"; it stands for *pat*tern.) This type of hatch pattern, however, falls out of the scope of a book such as *AutoCAD Release 14 For Dummies,* but you can find out more about creating custom hatch patterns in your AutoCAD documentation.

Defining basic boundaries

After you define your hatch, you define the boundary in the Boundary section of the Boundary Hatch dialog box. (Makes sense to me!) You can define the boundaries of a hatch in two ways: by picking points in the area(s) you want hatched or by selecting objects that AutoCAD hatches for you. The actual operation involved in using either of these options is confusing to most people, and you'll probably need a little practice before you get used to it. (Not that you're simply "most people" — after all, you *did* buy this book. . . .)

The idea behind either definition option is simple, if applied to simple areas — that is, closed objects with no additional objects inside them. To hatch such a simple area, you enter the BHATCH command on the command line and then either pick points on the inside of the object or select the object or objects surrounding the area. AutoCAD then applies the hatch for you — and you're done.

This simple hatching gets a little more complicated if you have one closed object inside another. If you pick points inside the *enclosing* (outermost) object but outside the *enclosed* (inner) object, you hatch only the area between the boundaries of the two objects. If you pick some points inside each object, you hatch the entire area within the outermost surrounding boundary, including the area within the inner boundary.

The results are somewhat reversed if you select objects instead of picking points. If you pick the outermost enclosing object(s) as well as the enclosed one(s), AutoCAD uses both boundaries and only hatches the area between them. Pick only the outermost object to hatch everything within it. In any event, after you finish picking or selecting, press Enter to return to the dialog box.

Creating a boundary hatch

To demonstrate the workings of boundary hatches, the following steps show you how to hatch an object, such as the wheels of a (very) simple drawing of a car, by using the "picking-points" method of selecting the hatch area:

1. **Draw any object for use in creating a boundary hatch (or use an existing object that you want hatched).**

   You can, for example, draw an object such as a car. If you want to hatch an existing object in a drawing, you can do so, too, using these steps as a guideline.

2. **Open the Boundary Hatch dialog box by using one of the following methods:**

   • Type **Hatch** at the command prompt and press Enter.

   • Click the Hatch icon on the Draw toolbar.

   • Choose <u>D</u>raw⇨<u>H</u>atch from the menu bar.

   The Boundary Hatch dialog box appears.

3. **Choose any predefined hatch by selecting a hatch from the Pattern list box.**

   You can cycle through the 68 available predefined hatch patterns by clicking the pattern preview rectangle in the Pattern Type area of the dialog box. (Whether you want to is another matter, of course. . . .)

The new Solid hatch pattern is the first option among the predefined hatch patterns. Like any other object, a solid hatch takes on whatever color you assign it.

4. **Click the Pick Points button.**

   The Boundary Hatch dialog box (temporarily) disappears, and your drawing reappears.

5. **Select a point inside the object you want to hatch by clicking it with the mouse.**

   On a simple drawing of a car, for example, you select a point inside the left tire — that is, between the outermost and innermost circles and below the side of the car.

   AutoCAD analyzes the drawing and decides what boundaries to use. On a larger drawing, this analysis can take quite a while.

6. **Press Enter to indicate that you have no more points you want to select.**

   The Boundary Hatch dialog box reappears.

7. **Click the Apply button.**

   AutoCAD hatches the part of the object you selected. (If you're using the tire example, it hatches only the part of the tire below the car; the central axle area is not hatched.) If you want to hatch another object in the drawing with the same hatch pattern (such as the other tire in the car example), you can continue on with Step 8. If you have only one object to hatch, you're finished.

8. **Open the Boundary Hatch dialog box again if you want to hatch another object by using the same hatch pattern, and repeat Steps 3 through 7.**

   In the car wheels example, you repeat these steps for the second tire. Figure 11-5 shows how this drawing appears midway through the hatching process for the second tire.

Inheriting properties

A neat option that can change the entire way you hatch objects is the Inherit Properties button on the Boundary Hatch dialog box. Despite its position in the Boundary Hatch dialog box (underneath the Boundary area), this feature works only with the Pattern Type and Pattern Properties areas and doesn't affect how boundaries are handled.

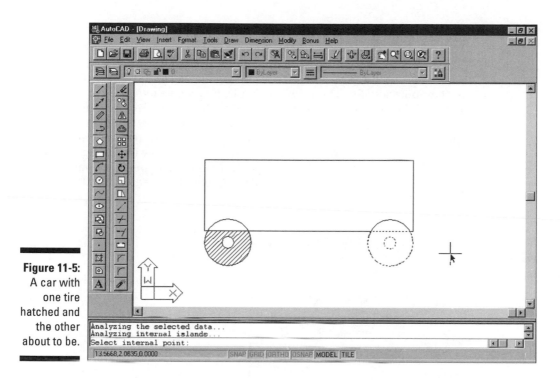

Inherit Properties simply updates the pattern characteristics in the dialog box to make them the same as a hatch pattern you pick from the screen; so you can clone an existing hatch pattern simply by clicking Inherit Properties and then choosing the existing hatch pattern from the screen. You can use the copied hatch pattern as is or modify it by making changes in the Boundary Hatch dialog box.

Advanced Hatching Options

AutoCAD has a number of advanced options for hatching, most of which you can ignore. This section covers two worthwhile options, however: defining boundary sets and styling. Figure 11-6 shows the Advanced Options subdialog box, which you can open by clicking the Advanced button in the Boundary Hatch dialog box. The Advanced Options subdialog box contains the Define Boundary Set and Style areas that the following two sections describe.

Boundary sets

If an area is bounded by several different objects and is part of a complex drawing, for AutoCAD to determine the boundaries of the area to hatch can be "computationally expensive" — that is, it can take a *long* time! A *boundary set* limits the area that AutoCAD considers when it determines where to hatch, thus saving you time. If you choose the Make New Boundary Set option in the Advanced Options subdialog box, you temporarily return to your drawing, where you can create a bounding window (dragging left to right) or crossing window (dragging right to left) that specifies some of the objects on-screen. AutoCAD then considers only the areas within the objects you selected as it decides what to hatch.

Figure 11-6:
The
Advanced
Options
subdialog
box for
hatching.

To return to using the entire screen, click the From Everything on Screen radio button in the dialog box. All objects on-screen are again available for boundary selection.

Styling

If you have several objects enclosing each other, knowing exactly which objects you hatch and which ones you don't can be very important. AutoCAD offers three style options in the Style drop-down list box of the Advanced Options subdialog box to help you determine the hatch object: Normal, Outer, and Ignore. Each is described briefly in the following list.

✔ **Normal:** This option may seem strange to users with no AutoCAD experience. The Normal option hatches the outermost ring between boundaries, skips the next ring in, hatches the next one, and so on, until alternating enclosed areas are hatched. This style is the default.

- ✔ **Outer:** This easy-to-understand option simply hatches the outermost area of an object and ignores all enclosed objects.

- ✔ **Ignore:** This option is also easy to understand. It ignores the boundaries of enclosed objects and hatches everything within the outermost boundary of the object.

After you design your hatch and pick points or select objects to hatch, click the Apply button to close the Boundary Hatch dialog box and reveal your newly hatched drawing.

Chapter 12

The Plot Thickens

*P*lotting and printing are nothing new in AutoCAD, although these tasks weren't always easy to get right in older versions of the program. (*Plotting* originally meant printing to a different kind of printer device that uses pens instead of other, more common types of print technologies. Because more and more AutoCAD output is printed rather than plotted, this book uses the term *printing* to refer to both printing and plotting.)

In Release 14, AutoCAD uses the term "print" in some places and "plot" in others to mean basically the same thing. For example, to print (or plot) in AutoCAD, you either choose Print from the File menu or type Plot on the command line! Whichever method you use, the Print/Plot Configuration dialog box appears. Besides using the word "print" more often in the program, not all that much has changed in printing since way back in Release 12. The main changes that are specific to Release 14 are better integration with Windows printing and, as a result, the capability to *batch plot* a group of drawings to a disk file that then prints in the background while you do other work.

Back in Release 12, AutoCAD added several features that make printing much easier, including two of particular importance: the Plot Configuration dialog box (now called Print/Plot Configuration) and the Plot Preview feature (still called Plot Preview). This chapter discusses all the many printing options in AutoCAD to help you get the most out of them. You can then spend less time trying to figure out printing and more time getting work done.

AutoCAD printing is a big deal. Just the task of printing a drawing can be time-consuming and expensive. A *pen plotter,* still frequently used for large-format plots and high-quality output, is a device that actually uses mechanical arms to run different-colored pens around a sheet of paper until the drawing is complete. (If you've never been present when a pen plotter is at work, you have to see this process happen to believe it.) A pen plotter costs a great deal of money to buy or lease and additional money to maintain. Pens jam and run out of ink, and the control software and hardware are vulnerable to bugs and problems.

If everything does work, the resulting plot is expensive and time-consuming to produce. Even a small error forces a replot, which means more time and money. Luckily, ink-jet and laser printing have fewer difficulties, but these methods can also be slow, time-consuming, and expensive. These concerns are the main reasons why setup is so important for AutoCAD printing; the cycle of print, find problem, fix problem, reprint is so costly and such a waste of time that you want to avoid it whenever possible.

Until Release 12, AutoCAD was part of the problem rather than part of the solution. Printing controls were hard to find and use, and AutoCAD didn't show you in advance what the result of a plot would be. But starting with Release 12 and continuing into Release 14, AutoCAD printing has improved greatly. The Print/Plot Configuration dialog box may appear to include too many functions, but it does enable you to control everything about printing from one dialog box. (Though I must admit that it is just a tiny bit more complicated than your typical Windows Print dialog box!) The most valuable feature in the Print/Plot Configuration dialog box is Plot Preview, which basically enables you to check a plot on-screen. You can detect obvious problems quickly and easily, and you can even find problems in the details if you take the time to inspect the plot preview carefully.

This chapter covers the two most frequently used aspects of printing: plot previews and actual printing. You can also find more detailed information on printer/plotter configuration and performance concerns.

Simple Plotting

Actually, creating a *printout,* also known as a *plot,* is easy, if you don't want to use any of the options. Just make sure that you have a drawing open on-screen and then follow these steps:

1. **Open the Print/Plot Configuration dialog box by using one of the following methods:**

   • Type **PRINT** at the command prompt and press Enter.

- Click the Print icon on the standard toolbar.
- Choose File⇨Print from the menu bar.

The Print/Plot Configuration dialog box appears, as shown in Figure 12-1.

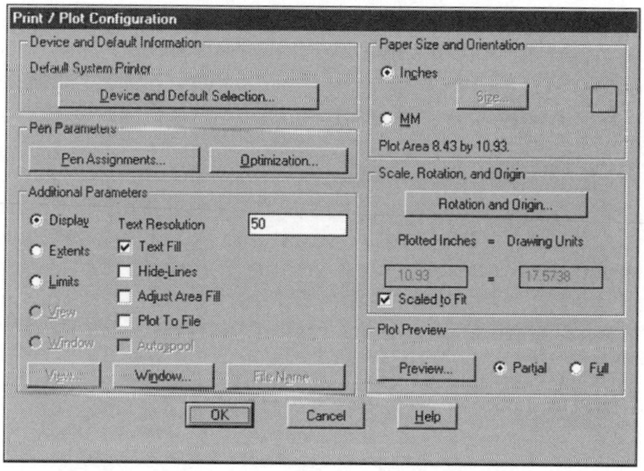

Figure 12-1:
The Print/
Plot Con-
figuration
dialog box.

[Print / Plot Configuration dialog box showing Device and Default Information, Pen Parameters, Additional Parameters, Paper Size and Orientation, Scale, Rotation, and Origin, and Plot Preview sections]

2. **To specify what to print, click the Extents radio button in the Additional Parameters area.**

3. **Click OK.**

   AutoCAD prints your drawing.

If you haven't set up your drawing's scale correctly, it may not fit on the paper. If so, repeat the printing process above, but click the Scaled to Fit checkbox to scale the drawing to the paper.

You should usually do a plot preview before actually printing your drawing so that you don't waste your time and money on a bad printout or plot.

In Release 14, AutoCAD includes a Visual Basic application, EBATCHP.EXE, that lets you print multiple drawings at once (also known as *spooling*). You can select multiple drawings to print and assign a configuration file to each drawing individually. It's part of the AutoCAD Release 14 Bonus Tools. For more information about it, see the online documentation for the bonus tools.

Although ADI (Application Device Interface) drivers no longer work for screen display in Release 14, they still work for printing and plotting. Update to ADI 4.3 drivers to get spooling capability and to support the new Release 14 capability to output raster objects, as described in Chapter 14.

I suggest that you continue using ADI drivers until Windows-system printer and plotter drivers get better AutoCAD support in general and Release 14 support in particular. Keep your eye out for printers and plotters with fast, effective, solid drivers, and support them with your buying dollars. See Chapter 18 for resources to use in keeping your eye on the printing and plotting scene.

The following sections discuss the areas of the Print/Plot Configuration dialog box in a different order than you may expect. The order matches the frequency with which you're likely to use and need information about the areas of the dialog box, rather than the order in which the areas appear in the dialog box. Use the figures as a visual guide to find the section of the dialog box that you want quickly.

Plot Preview

For every final plot you do, you should make several *check prints*. So what's a check print? A check print simply involves printing your drawing to a smaller, faster, cheaper device than the big, expensive, slow plotter on which many drawings are plotted. Because they're cheap and fast, laser printers are being used more and more for check prints. The only problem is that a laser print is small and monochrome, so not all problems are visible in the check print. But in terms of time and money, a check print is nearly free of charge compared to a plot, so detecting even an occasional problem this way makes check prints more than worthwhile.

And before every check print you do, you should do at least one *plot preview*. The on-screen plot preview is a nearly perfect complement to a check print. The plot preview is in color, which eliminates the biggest drawback of a check print. And although the plot preview is small, you can use it to zoom in on likely trouble spots, possibly spotting — and eliminating — potential problems in your final plot.

Plot previews are also valuable early in the drawing process, just after you set up your drawing. Draw a few rectangles to represent roughly the objects you'll be drawing and then do a plot preview. The results may surprise you; if they do, you get a chance to fix problems early, saving hours of work and rework.

Doing a partial plot preview

A *partial plot preview* shows only a rectangle that represents the boundaries of the area you're plotting, overlaid on a rectangle that represents the usable area of the paper you're plotting on. The following steps show you how to do a partial plot preview:

1. **Open the Print/Plot Configuration dialog box by using one of the following methods:**

   • Type **PRINT** at the command prompt and press Enter.

   • Click the Print icon on the standard toolbar.

   • Choose File➪Print from the menu bar.

   The Print/Plot Configuration dialog box appears.

2. **Click the Partial radio button.**

3. **Click the Preview button.**

   The Preview Effective Plotting Area dialog box appears, as shown in Figure 12-2. This dialog box appears only if you do a partial plot preview. Its only function is to show what the plotting area looks like.

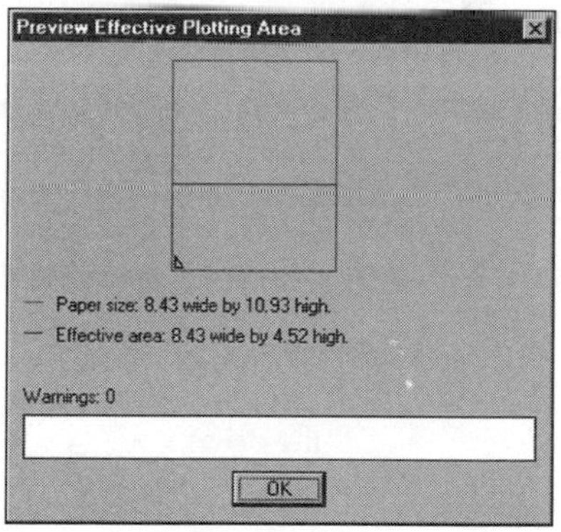

Figure 12-2:
The Preview Effective Plotting Area dialog box.

4. **Click OK to close the Preview Effective Plotting Area dialog box and then click OK again to close the Print/Plot Configuration dialog box.**

So now you've done a partial plot preview. What good did it do you? Well. . .

An ineffective preview?

The Preview Effective Plotting Area dialog box leaves a little to be desired in terms of helping you preview your drawing. The image of the drawing at the top of the dialog box is a little hard to figure out. The image shows only the paper and the boundary of the drawing; none of the objects in the drawing appear in the image.

The *effective area* — that is, the boundary of the drawing area that you're plotting — appears with a little triangle in one corner. This blue triangle, the *Rotation icon,* represents the rotation of the drawing that you specify elsewhere in the Print/Plot Configuration dialog box. (See the section "Scale, Rotation, and

Origin," later in this chapter, for more information on your drawing's rotation.)

The paper size appears as a red rectangle. The paper size dimensions are the part of the paper that you can print on, not the actual paper size. (See the section "Paper Size and Orientation," later in this chapter, for more information on paper size.)

If the blue rectangle doesn't fit within the red rectangle, or is much smaller than the red rectangle, or is not aligned with the red rectangle (both taller than wide, or both wider than tall), you may have some problems with your plot. Correct the problems as described in this chapter, then rerun the preview.

Doing a full plot preview

A *full preview* shows the entire plot on-screen. It takes more time than a partial plot preview but shows the actual objects that you plot and is quite a bit more useful. The following steps show you how to do a full plot preview:

1. **Open the Print/Plot Configuration dialog box, as described in Step 1 of the preceding section.**

2. **Click the F<u>u</u>ll radio button.**

3. **Click the P<u>r</u>eview button.**

   A preview of your drawing appears. If you're working on a complex drawing, AutoCAD may take some time to create the preview. A rectangle indicates the boundaries of the printable area. Figure 12-3 shows a full plot preview with the button menu showing.

   The Plot Preview opens in real-time Zoom mode, which is new in Release 14. To zoom in and out, drag the cursor up to zoom in and down to zoom out. (Keep in mind that *drag* means that you hold the mouse button down while moving the mouse.) To shift to panning, right-click to get the button menu and choose Pan.

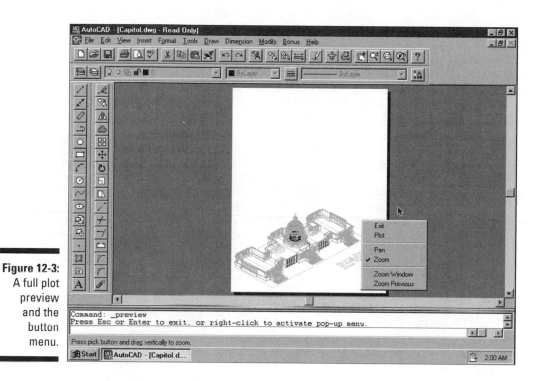

Figure 12-3:
A full plot
preview
and the
button
menu.

4. Inspect the drawing.

Use pan and zoom to inspect the drawing for problems. If you find more than one or two problems, write them all down; otherwise you're likely to forget and end up with an avoidable error in your next plot preview or even your final printout.

5. Press the Escape key or the Enter key to end the preview; or right-click to bring up the cursor menu and choose Exit.

After you end the preview, you return to the Print/Plot Configuration dialog box.

6. Click on the Cancel button to exit the Print/Plot Configuration dialog box.

Choosing Cancel abandons any changes you've made in the Print/Plot Configuration dialog box. You must click OK to retain changes — which, unfortunately in many cases, starts the print job! On some systems, you may be able to press the Escape key to abort printing; on others, the print job will run to completion almost no matter what you do.

Configuring the Plot

You have many options to choose from when configuring your plot with the Print/Plot Configuration dialog box. Because there are so many options, you need to be careful to avoid the temptation of not looking at all of them closely and therefore doing too little configuration.

Because you can rescale and reorient your drawing to fit it onto the paper you've chosen, you may be tempted to ignore the task of setting up your drawing and just fix the scale problems at plotting time. This temptation has two potential problems: First, linetype spacing needs to look right, and text must be readable in the final drawing. If you're rescaling your drawing image arbitrarily, linetypes or, especially, text are unlikely to come out right. Second, the geometry parts of your drawing need to fit a recognizable scale, such as 1 inch = 1 foot. Your scale is not likely to be recognizable if, at the last minute, you shrink your drawing by 37.46 percent to force-fit it onto the paper.

The options in the Print/Plot Configuration dialog box are so numerous that you really must experiment with them to get a feel for how to use them well. This section discusses the general areas of the dialog box so that you can quickly head to the settings that you need to change.

You can do a preview of the plotting changes you make "free of charge" by using the Plot Preview option. In other words, don't waste time or paper on an incorrect plot — use plot preview.

Paper Size and Orientation

The Paper Size and Orientation area of the Print/Plot Configuration dialog box, as shown in Figure 12-4, is where you start the process of telling your drawing how to print itself.

Start by specifying inches or millimeters (MM) as the plotting units, whichever is natural for the paper and drawing scale you're using. This specification affects how you set up the plot scale in the Scale, Rotation, and Origin area of the Print/Plot Configuration dialog box and whether the Pen Width values displayed in Pen Assignments are in inches or millimeters.

Pen Parameters　　　　　　Paper Size and Orientation

Device and Default Information

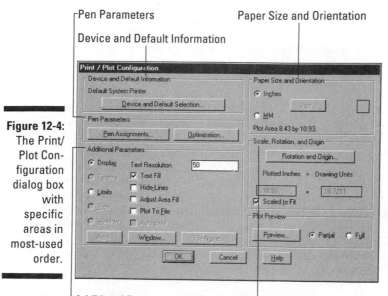

Figure 12-4:
The Print/
Plot Con-
figuration
dialog box
with
specific
areas in
most-used
order.

Additional Parameters　　Scale, Rotation, and Origin

Next to the Size button is a designation of the currently selected paper size.
(You can find a review of some of the more common paper sizes in the
sidebar "A few thoughts on paper," in Chapter 4.) You can change the paper
size by clicking the Size button. The Paper Size dialog box appears, containing a list of all the standard paper sizes your printer or plotter can handle.
You can also specify up to five user-defined paper sizes to appear in this list.
(To add to the list, just enter a new width and height in one of the USER size
areas.) Finish by selecting the paper size you want from the list and clicking
OK. The Print/Plot Configuration dialog box reappears.

The Size button isn't available if you're using the AutoCAD System Printer
driver. In that case, use the Change option in the Device and Default Information area to change the size.

Also next to the Size button is a small pictorial representation of the plotter
orientation. (You may have to look twice; this item is easy to miss.) *Orientation* means that your plot can be either *landscape* (sideways, long axis on
the horizontal) or *portrait* (upright, long axis on the vertical).

Scale, Rotation, and Origin

The Scale, Rotation, and Origin area of the Print/Plot Configuration dialog box (refer to Figure 12-4) enables you to adjust the appearance of your drawing on the final plot. You can specify the scale you want your drawing plotted at, effectively zooming in or out; change the location of the drawing's origin (usually the lower-left corner of your drawing), which has the same effect as panning the drawing on the sheet of paper; and change the rotation of the drawing so that the drawing is plotted at different orientations (portrait or landscape) on the paper.

If turned on, the Scaled to Fit option forces the plot area to fit the available paper size. This option also displays the ratio of plotted inches to units in the drawing. Each plotted inch, for example, may represent 20 drawing units; each drawing unit may be a foot, a kilometer, or any other measure, depending on how you set up and use your drawing. One of the great things about CAD is that your drawing can be huge or small, and you can plot it at any scale you want.

The Scaled to Fit option is especially valuable if you're printing on a different kind of paper than the paper you set up your drawing for, such as in making a check print. If the paper you're making the check print on is the same proportion and orientation as the paper you're using for the final plot, the relationship of the drawing to the paper should be the same in both cases; only the scale differs.

If Scaled to Fit is turned off, the Plotted Inches = Drawing Units text boxes take on a new meaning, representing the scale you've created for your drawing. You can enter values in the text boxes to force a different plotting scale for your drawing.

The Rotation and Origin button opens the Plot Rotation and Origin dialog box. This feature enables you to rotate your drawing on the plot and set the origin of the plot on the paper. You can specify where on the paper you want your drawing's lower-left corner to be. (Some plotters can accept negative numbers so that the origin point is off the paper, and some of the drawing is effectively cropped by the paper's edges.) If you use this dialog box, do a full plot preview to make sure that everything in your plot will come out the way you want it to.

Additional Parameters

The Additional Parameters area of the Print/Plot Configuration dialog box contains a number of loosely related options that you can set (refer to Figure 12-4). Not all the options are available all the time; for example, the View parameter appears only if you've set up a view. The major purpose of this area, however, is to help describe which rectangular area of the drawing you're plotting. The radio buttons down the left edge of the Additional Parameters area control this function.

The Display, Extents, and Limits radio buttons are just about always available. Display plots the displayed portion of the current viewport. (If you divide the drawing area into multiple viewports, as described in Chapter 13, the current viewport is simply the one you're working on right now.) Limits plots everything within the drawing limits, which you set by using the LIMITS command, as described in Chapter 4. Extents is the rectangle that includes all objects in the drawing. You can update the extents only by using a ZOOM ALL or ZOOM EXTENTS command. So enter one of these commands before clicking the Extents radio button.

To use the View radio button, first click the View button at the bottom of the area. (Keep in mind that this button is available only if you've saved at least one view, as described in Chapter 13.) The View button (as opposed to the View radio button!) opens the View Name dialog box, which enables you to select any named view. After you select a view, the View radio button becomes available in the Additional Parameters area of the Print/Plot Configuration dialog box.

To use the Window radio button, first click the Window button at the bottom of the area. This button opens the Window Selection dialog box, which enables you to specify any rectangular area on-screen that you want to plot. You can use the Pick button to pick the corners if the area is completely visible on-screen; otherwise, you can enter the coordinates of the corners. After you specify a window, the Window radio button becomes available in the Print/Plot Configuration dialog box.

Other options in the Additional Parameters area of the Print/Plot Configuration dialog box include Text Fill, which causes text characters to be filled in (if checked) or just outlined; Hide-Lines, which removes hidden lines in 3D drawings before plotting; Adjust Area Fill, which reduces boundaries of filled areas by one-half the pen width (to improve accuracy); and Plot To File, which enables you to plot to a disk file.

After you click the Plot To File check box, the File Name button becomes available to open a dialog box, in which you can enter a filename to plot to. If you don't enter a filename, the filename used is the current drawing name plus the extension PLT. Then you can copy the PLT file to the plotter or use it as a file to send to another AutoCAD user. AutoCAD PLT files are usually much smaller than AutoCAD DWG files. (To copy a file to the plotter, choose the DOS prompt option in the Windows start menu, get to a DOS prompt, and type **copy /b filename.plt prn**. Then press Enter.)

Any time you are printing or plotting (plotting a drawing, that is, not the relocation or reassignment of your management chain), you should save frequently. Though it's not supposed to happen, printing and running a complex program like AutoCAD can strain your system's memory, available hard disk space, or other resources to the extent that system crashes become more likely.

Configuring the Plotter

Configuring the plotter (or *device,* as it's called in several areas of the Print/ Plot Configuration dialog box) simply means, in this case, selecting the name of the plotter or printer available to you from the list that AutoCAD supplies and then setting up any pen-related options that are available. You actually *configure* a printer or plotter during AutoCAD configuration, using the Printer tab of the Preferences dialog box; see the AutoCAD documentation for more information.

The Device and Default Information area of the Print/Plot Configuration dialog box (refer to Figure 12-4) contains a single button: Device and Default Selection. This button opens, naturally enough, the Device and Default Selection dialog box. This dialog box enables you to save to and retrieve printer defaults from a file, as well as show and change the device requirements of your plotter. Although the options available vary greatly from one plotter or printer to another, this dialog box gives you considerable flexibility in managing them.

The Device and Default Selection dialog box allows you to save the print settings and any device-specific settings in a file called a PC2 file. A PC2 file is a superset of the R12 and R13 print settings file called a PCP file. To load a PC2 file, use the Replace option; to use a PCP file as a starting point for your print settings, use the Merge option.

The Pen Parameters area of the Print/Plot Configuration dialog box (refer to Figure 12-4) contains two buttons: Pen Assignments and Optimization.

The Pen Assignments button is available only if a pen plotter is configured or if the output device supports different plotted line widths, and it opens the Pen Assignments dialog box. You can use this dialog box to specify the pen number assigned to each AutoCAD color, the linetype, the speed, and the pen width. (You can't edit all features on all plotters.) The Feature Legend button in the Pen Assignments dialog box displays information specific to the selected plotter. In the case of a specific Hewlett-Packard plotter, for example, the Feature Legend button opens a display of available linetypes.

Some printer or plotter drivers use the Pen Width setting to control the plotted line width; others use the Pen No. setting. You may need to experiment to see which one works with your printer or plotter.

During System Printer configuration, AutoCAD displays a dialog box, AutoCAD System Printer Configuration, with two check box settings that need explanation. The first, "Default to control panel settings," is confusingly named; it determines whether the printer should be set to Windows printer settings. The second, "Allow dithered output," allows monochrome printers to approximate colored lines with grayscale patterns; the result looks odd, so you should turn this setting off.

Which driver to use?

You often have a choice of two print drivers to use with AutoCAD: the Windows System Printer driver, or a device-specific ADI driver. Follow the printer manufacturer's instructions for installing an ADI driver if one is offered for your printer. Then choose the driver to use from the Printer tab of the Preferences dialog box, described in Chapter 3.

The System Printer driver gives you access to the Windows printing system. This driver is easy to set up initially and relatively certain to work — if you can print from other applications, you're likely to be able to print from

AutoCAD, also, if you use the System Printer driver. To make changes in printer setup if you use this driver, click Device and Default Selection, then choose Device Requirements. This is where you choose Portrait or Landscape mode and other settings.

A device-specific ADI driver may give you more features and faster performance. Try using the System Printer driver first; after you have that working, try an ADI driver if you have one. That way you know you can fall back on the System Printer driver if the ADI driver gives you problems.

Plotting and Performance

You can optimize plotting performance in AutoCAD a number of ways. Some of these optimizations are printer- or plotter-specific, and other users of the same device, or even the device's manufacturer, can be welcome sources of information about them.

You can also save time with a few general tips. Obviously, plotting less stuff results in a faster plot. So turn off any layers that you don't need for the current plot before you start it. This tip is especially useful if you have a border or a title block around your drawing. If you turn off the border, AutoCAD can plot the next line much more quickly than if it must always draw a border line on the far right edge of the paper. You may even want to design your drawing so that areas along the right edge of the paper are empty whenever possible, enabling AutoCAD to do a carriage return that much more quickly.

Do be sure to turn *on* any layers that you *do* need before plotting; forgetting to do so is an easy mistake to make and, at best, can cause you to have to do an extra check plot with the right layers turned on. At worst, it can cause you to send an incomplete plot out as part of a job proposal or contract.

You can also optimize pen motion by using the Optimizing Pen Motion dialog box. You open this dialog box by clicking the Optimization button in the Print/Plot Configuration dialog box. However, this is a setting that is best left alone.

Part IV
Having It Your Way

The 5th Wave — By Rich Tennant

"Is this what they mean when they say AutoCAD uses the third dimension?"

In this part . . .

Once you get the lines and text right, you might be justified in thinking that your work in AutoCAD is done. But AutoCAD enables you to do so much more! Paper space turns AutoCAD into a kind of homegrown desktop publishing program for graphics, and in Release 14, you can pan and zoom smoothly in paper space. Blocks and external references help you manage data within drawings, between drawings, and even across a network. Release 14 makes it much easier to manage your blocks and external references. It also adds the ability to include scanned photos and other raster images in your AutoCAD drawing. 3D commands enable you to do a whole new kind of work in AutoCAD, without buying any add-on packages or a different program. Together, these options extend AutoCAD's capabilities beyond anything possible without a computer — and even beyond those of just about any other drawing/drafting program in existence.

Chapter 13

The Paper Space Chase

*O*ne of the biggest conceptual leaps in the development of AutoCAD was the addition of paper space in Release 11. Before I launch into an explanation of paper space, however, I need to introduce some terms. A *model* is the main thing that you create through your work in AutoCAD; a model is a representation of a real-world object or place. *Model space* is your normal working mode in AutoCAD, in which you create one or more models that represent objects or places.

Paper space is a different working mode that enables you to treat the screen as one or several views on a model. You don't actually create or change models in paper space; instead, you create views on existing models. For example, you can show a car engine from the top, the side, from a perspective view (above and at an angle), and in a cross-section. Each view can be at a different scale, with different layers showing, and so on; but for each view the underlying model is the same.

Paper space enables you to rework the appearance of your printed drawing without changing the underlying geometry. Although much of CAD is an attempt to reproduce, or incrementally improve on, the pencil-and-paper work environment, paper space can be a leap forward toward getting more out of the computer.

On the other hand, paper space is not strictly necessary for most work. Paper space is an "extra" that gives you a way to create many plotted views of your drawing efficiently.

Note that I mention a cross-section earlier. Paper space is most useful for models that are rendered in three dimensions. If you aren't rendering your models in 3D, think about staying in model space.

In Release 14, paper space becomes much more useful because of the real-time pan and zoom feature of AutoCAD. Now, getting your paper space views right is much easier. Many people who had avoided paper space in the past because using it caused so many *regens* (time-consuming updates of the computer screen image) can now be expected to make it part of their AutoCAD tool kit.

Real-time panning and zooming does cause the computer to do a great deal of work, and the more views you have open in paper space, the more work AutoCAD has to do to keep them all updated. Experiment with simple and complex models from your own work to see at what point your computer starts begging for mercy, and don't expect to work efficiently in paper space on models big enough to slow down your computer significantly.

Why Paper Space?

Before moving forward, defining paper space in more depth is important; many experienced AutoCAD users don't do much with paper space, and it's conceptually difficult for most novices to grasp.

Paper space is the opposite of model space. In model space, which is the only space discussed so far in this book, you draw objects, combine them into models — a circle is an object; a steering wheel is a model — and then print the result. Model space can print only one view at a time.

In paper space, by contrast, you can use previously drawn objects, combine different ways of looking at them, and then print the result. Paper space can print multiple views at a time. Figure 13-1 shows some work in progress in paper space.

In model space, an "X-Y" icon called the *UCS* (User Coordinate System) icon appears in the lower left corner to indicate the current X (horizontal) and Y (vertical) directions. In paper space, the icon changes to a triangular shape.

The icons in the status bar are confusing, so read this carefully: The word TILE appears solid to indicate that paper space is in effect (when model space is in effect, TILE is grayed out). When AutoCAD is set to paper space and the cursor is also in paper space, the word PAPER appears in the status bar. When the cursor is in model space, the word MODEL appears in the status bar.

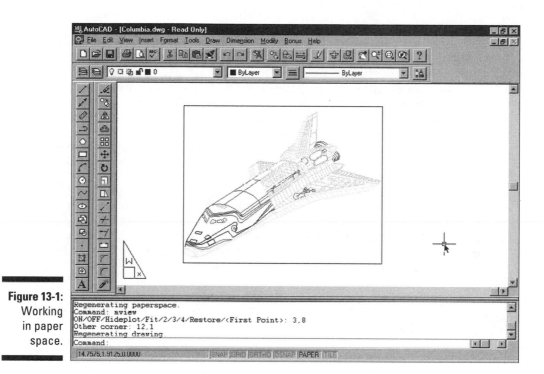

Figure 13-1:
Working
in paper
space.

Using paper space is like creating a page in a magazine. You arrange text and graphics as needed to best communicate information to the person who receives the printed output (though AutoCAD work tends to have more graphics and fewer words than most magazine pages). You move around and resize each element freely to get the overall effect you want. And you don't need to choose from just one image of something that you want to show; you can take almost any view on it that you want.

In AutoCAD, the graphics come from views on your drawing. Each view is displayed in a rectangular area called a *viewport.* You can mix and match different sizes of viewports and different kinds of views within the viewports to achieve the desired overall effect. And you can make all these adjustments without changing anything in the underlying drawing.

Your paper space work is much less trouble if you come up with one or two standard setups for paper space layouts. A typical use is to have a paper space blueprint with a border and title block and four equal-sized viewports, often a plan view (from directly overhead), an orthographic view (from the side), a detail view of part of the drawing, and a perspective view (from about a 45-degree angle above the horizon). This set of views is easy for users to understand, because they're accustomed to seeing these views, and is easy to create the same way for many different models.

Paper space adds some additional maintenance and work to your drawing and has some performance concerns that limit its general usefulness, though real-time pan and zoom improve performance. Paper space is easy to misunderstand as a place to fix things that aren't right with the underlying model instead of fixing the model itself. Fixing problems in paper space is usually harder than fixing them in the underlying drawing and much harder than doing it right in the first place — which is why this book contains so much setup information. So use paper space sparingly, and when you do use it, take a gradual approach; otherwise, you may end up starting over again with a new paper space setup or even with a new model a couple of hours before a deadline.

The main time you need paper space is when you want to place different views of the same objects on one sheet of paper. Without paper space, you would need to redraw the objects from every point of view you want to show; with paper space, you can simply create multiple views of the same objects and combine them on the same sheet.

Think twice before using paper space, however, unless your needs are similar to those described in one of the following situations:

- **Different layers:** You want to show different groups of layers of a model so that different views of the model appear in different areas of the printout.

- **Different zooms:** You want to show different zoom resolutions of a model on the same printed sheet — for example, an overall plan and a zoomed-in detail of part of the plan.

- **Different areas:** You want to show different parts of a drawing at the same scale. This is common in large building plans, where the building won't fit on one sheet at a usable scale.

- **See in 3D:** To show what a 3D (three-dimensional) object looks like, you usually need to show multiple views of the object from different points of view on the same printed sheet. Paper space is ideal for this kind of work.

To see paper space in action, pull up one of the sample drawings that comes with Release 14. They all have paper space on, but use one big viewport.

Why Not Paper Space?

Paper space creates a whole 'nother level of things to worry about, over and above the problems you encounter in model space. In AutoCAD, getting yourself into situations where you spend more time figuring out than you do drawing is easy enough to do in model space; with paper space, these situations can multiply. So if paper space is new to you, consider staying in model space as long as you can, especially if you're still on the steep part of the learning curve for AutoCAD as a whole.

If that's not enough reason to avoid paper space, consider the following factors:

- **Slow performance:** Repeatedly rerendering multiple views can really slow down your computer. Yes, you can turn off all the viewports but the current one, and you can creatively turn layers on and off to help, but then you're spending valuable time managing your viewports and layers. Because you're more likely to use paper space for complex 2D or 3D models, this kind of overhead can be a daunting prospect.

- **Time sink:** Just as in any other program where appearances are the focus of your task, working in paper space can be a real time drain. Trying to get the viewports set up just right, changing the angle in the view, and other tasks can literally take hours. (Fortunately, after you get to know the right settings, you can more quickly reapply them to other drawings you do.)

- **Other ways to do it:** Many times you can get a paper-space-like effect without going into paper space. To combine views of pieces from several drawings, for example, you can create a new drawing in model space and then use external references (as described in Chapter 14) to pull in views of different pieces.

Setting Up Paper Space

You can set up paper space by using individual commands or through MVSETUP, a program that gives a structured way to get into using paper space. Because MVSETUP takes you through the process in steps, use it at least the first few times you try paper space. You can then try individual commands on your later paper space efforts.

Using MVSETUP

The following steps are long, but they help you get paper space going effectively. (Imagine how many different things you'd need to remember if not for these steps!) From a high-level point of view, the parts of the process are as follows:

✔ Create a *title block* — an area of the drawing in which you enter the drawing name, the drafter's name, and any other relevant descriptive information you want to include.

✔ Create viewports.

✔ Get the model into the viewports.

The following 13 steps (Yikes! Thirteen steps? Isn't there a "light" version?) show you how to set up paper space by using the MVSETUP program:

1. **Turn on paper space by double-clicking the TILE button on the status bar to change it from grayed-out to solid.**

   The UCS icon switches from its usual "X-Y" configuration to a triangular shape to indicate that paper space is on.

2. **Start MVSETUP by typing** MVSETUP **at the command prompt and pressing Enter.**

   Note: If you start MVSETUP with paper space off, the program asks whether you want to turn on paper space. If you answer yes, MVSETUP works as described in these steps. But if you say no, MVSETUP works as a model space setup program, although you still need to complete some steps after it's finished.

3. **Type** Options **at the command line and press Enter.**

   When working at the AutoCAD command line, you can enter an option more quickly by just typing the first letter or first few letters of the option's name. AutoCAD shows you how many letters you need to type for each option by making the needed letters uppercase capital letters. For example, typing **O** is enough to choose options; but in Step 5 you need to type **LI** to choose limits. So AutoCAD displays the word options as Options, indicating *O* is the shortcut for options; the word limits is displayed LImits, to indicate that *LI* is the shortcut for limits.

4. **Create a layer for the title block by typing** LAyer **at the command line, followed by the name of the layer, and pressing Enter.**

   The layer name can be either an existing or a new layer name.

   Put the paper space stuff — title block, viewports, and so on — on a separate layer or on a group of layers with names that start with the same character or two. You can create layers PSTITLE and PSVIEWS, for example, as described in Chapter 5, to hold the title block and viewports, respectively.

5. **To reset the drawing limits so that they enclose the paper space border, type** LImits **at the command line, press Enter, and then type** Yes **and press Enter again.**

6. **To specify how you want paper space units expressed, type** -UNits **and press Enter, and then enter** Feet, Inches, MEters, **or** Millimeters **at the command prompt.**

You can use the Xref option to attach or insert an external reference as a title block at this point. (Xrefs are explained in Chapter 14.)

7. **Press Enter to return to the original prompt that lists the overall options for MVSETUP.**

8. **Type** Title **(for Title block) at the original command prompt and press Enter.**

AutoCAD opens a text window that lists the options for paper size. Figure 13-2 shows this text window.

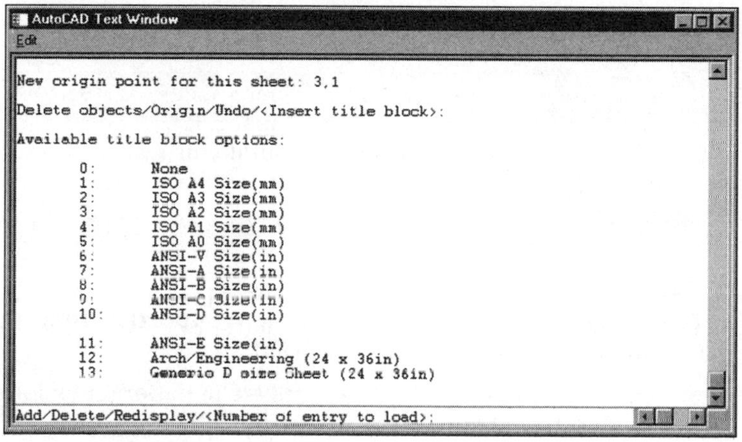

Figure 13-2:
A text window displays the options for paper sizes.

```
AutoCAD Text Window                                              _ □ ✕
Edit

New origin point for this sheet: 3,1

Delete objects/Origin/Undo/<Insert title block>:

Available title block options:

        0:      None
        1:      ISO A4 Size(mm)
        2:      ISO A3 Size(mm)
        3:      ISO A2 Size(mm)
        4:      ISO A1 Size(mm)
        5:      ISO A0 Size(mm)
        6:      ANSI-V Size(in)
        7:      ANSI-A Size(in)
        8:      ANSI-B Size(in)
        9:      ANSI-C Size(in)
        10:     ANSI-D Size(in)

        11:     ANSI-E Size(in)
        12:     Arch/Engineering (24 x 36in)
        13:     Generic D size Sheet (24 x 36in)

Add/Delete/Redisplay/<Number of entry to load>:
```

Be careful what you enter when choosing paper size; typing **B** for paper size A, for example, instead of the option number that AutoCAD lists, which is 7, is all too easy an error to make.

9. **Type the number that corresponds to the paper size you want to use and press Enter.**

AutoCAD closes the text window and then inserts the title block and border. Figure 13-3 shows the screen with title block and border.

10. **Type** Create **on the command line and press Enter to start the process of creating viewports.**

11. **Type** Create **(for Create Viewports) on the command line and press Enter to create the viewports.**

AutoCAD opens a text window and lists the options for viewport creation.

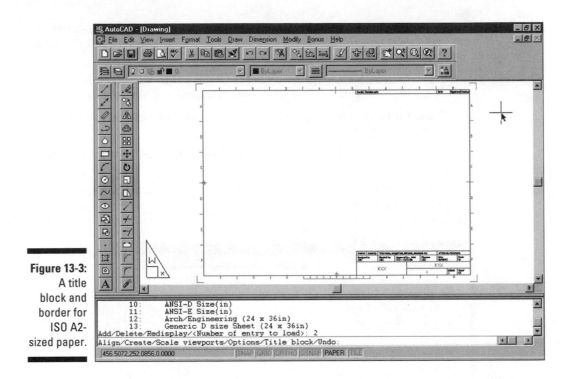

12. To specify the size and location of the viewport(s), enter the number corresponding to the option you want.

Notice that the sizes of the viewports are in paper units; for example, an 8-x-10-inch viewport fills a letter-sized sheet of paper.

Use the following list as a guide in determining the viewport(s) you want:

- **0** (None) creates no viewports.

- **1** (Single) creates one viewport. You specify size by using the mouse or by typing in the locations of the viewport's corners.

- **2** (Std. Engineering) creates a set of four equal-sized viewports. Specify the area that is to contain the four viewports and the X and Y distance between viewports.

- **3** (Array of Viewports) creates an array of as many columns and rows of viewports as you specify. Enter the number of columns of viewports (X), the number of rows of viewports (Y), the area into which you want to insert the viewports, and the X and Y distance between viewports.

13. Press Enter to leave MVSETUP.

Congratulations! You just created a title block and several paper space viewports.

Using (paper) space(y) commands

You can also set up paper space by using commands entered on the command line. The important commands are as follows:

- **TILEMODE:** Moves back and forth between showing model space (SET TILEMODE = 1) on the screen and showing paper space (SET TILEMODE = 0).

- **MVIEW:** Controls the number and layout of paper space viewports. (MVSETUP uses the MVIEW command but doesn't enable you to see it directly.)

- **MSPACE/PSPACE:** Moves the cursor back and forth between the model space "inside" paper space viewports and paper space itself.

- **VPLAYER:** (Say "V-P-LAYER", not "V-PLAYER.") Turns layer visibility on and off in a specific viewport.

- **ZOOM XP:** The XP option of the ZOOM command zooms relative to paper space units rather than model space units. To show an entire drawing, put the cursor in a paper space viewport and then use **ZOOM 1XP**; to show close-ups, use a value less than one. (To see your model correctly if it was drawn at 1/8"= 1', for example, use **ZOOM 1/96XP**.)

Using paper space viewports

After you have gone into paper space and created viewports (see the preceding set of steps), you can use the following three ways to access your drawing:

- **Paper space:** Working in paper space, you can change viewport sizes, arrange the viewport layout, add text to the title block, or add notes to the drawing. None of this activity affects the underlying model space drawing.

  Figure out in advance what text goes with the model and what text goes in paper space, and then follow the rules consistently. Otherwise, your model won't have the proper text associated with it.

- **Model space viewports in paper space:** If in paper space, use the MSPACE command to work in model space within the viewports. (For the MSPACE command, use MS for short; PS to quickly change back to paper space.) Use PAN, ZOOM XP, and VPLAYER to change the appearance of your model and the displayed layer within each viewport. Limits, snap, and grid settings are kept separately for paper space, so you can change these settings in a viewport without affecting the underlying drawing.

✔ **Paper space off:** Turning off paper space returns you to your original model space drawing; all signs of paper space disappear. The information is retained, but it doesn't show up while you're in model space. After you return to paper space, changes in the underlying model are reflected in the viewports.

To exit paper space completely, type **TILEMODE 0** on the command line and press Enter. To return to paper space, type **TILEMODE 1** and press Enter.

This information is enough for a good start, but you can discover many more things to get the most out of paper space. After you've used MVSETUP and created a drawing or two with paper space, see the AutoCAD online and printed documentation for more details.

Chapter 14

Playing Blocks and Rasteroids

A thing of beauty is a joy forever, as the old saying goes. But if you work and work on a drawing until it's a thing of beauty, you must be able to reuse it to make it a joy forever. Reusability is also a huge advantage of CAD over paper drafting. That's where the blocks and external references of AutoCAD come in.

A *block* is a collection of objects grouped together to form a single object. A block can live within a specific drawing, or you can export a block so that multiple drawings can reference it. At any time, you can *explode* the block — that is, divide it back into the objects that make it up — and edit the objects.

An *external reference* is like an industrial-strength block. An external reference is a pointer to a separate drawing outside the drawing you're working on. The referenced drawing then appears on-screen and in printouts as part of the original drawing but continues to "live" as a separate document on your hard disk. This arrangement lets you include a whole separate drawing without increasing the size of the drawing you're working on. But you can't explode the external reference; you can only change its appearance by editing the externally referenced drawing. If you do actually edit the externally referenced drawing, the appearance of the drawing changes in all the other drawings that reference it, too.

Blocks are unchanged and xrefs are little-changed in Release 14; but the changes to xrefs are very helpful for heavy users of this feature. In Release 14, you can "clip" an xref to use only part of it, and only the part you need is loaded into memory while you are working on your document. This change saves you time while working in your drawing and prevents you from having to split xrefed files into little pieces that can be loaded separately. You also have better control of what paths (Windows folders) AutoCAD looks in to find the file named in the xref.

When should you use a block or an external reference? Start with blocks; using blocks is what you do most often for individual work. Blocks save storage space within a drawing and make work more convenient. Writing out a block to a separate file by using the WBLOCK command is an intermediate step and makes the block more easily accessible to multiple drawings while preserving the capability to explode the block. An external reference is for truly serious data sharing and is used most often in a networked environment, with multiple users sharing data files. Your own preferences and work style, however, as well as the standards in your organization, ultimately determine how you use blocks and external references.

Raster image importing is a crucial new feature of Release 14. Each *raster,* or bit-mapped, image is imported as a separate object into a regular AutoCAD drawing. Raster images in AutoCAD drawings can be plotted with most new ADI (AutoCAD Device Interface) 4.3 printer/plotter drivers. (Drivers that don't support raster images have the letters NR after them.) Raster images matter a great deal to some AutoCAD users and little to others. Read about the new features here to help you decide how much you need them.

This chapter describes how to use blocks, external references, and raster image importing. (What a coincidence, considering that's what I was just talking about! Wonder of wonders. . . .) Try these features out and then use each as often as makes sense for your work.

Rock and Block

First, a little more block theory, and then you can rock right into those blocks.

A block — formally called a *block definition* — is a collection of objects stored together under a single name. You can reinsert the block repeatedly into your drawing simply by typing its name. Convenience isn't the only reason for using blocks; blocks are also great file-storage savers. Repeatedly using a block within the same drawing takes up only a little bit of storage space for each use, and AutoCAD stores only a single use of the block definition itself in each drawing.

Blocks are great for convenience and storage savings within a drawing. Blocks *aren't* great for drawing elements used in multiple drawings, however, especially in a multiuser environment. That's because blocks, after they get into multiple drawings, stay there; a later modification to the original block does not automatically modify all the drawings that use that block. So if you use a block with your company's name in a number of drawings and then you decide to use fancier lettering on the name, you must make the change within each drawing that uses the block.

External references, however, do enable you to modify multiple drawings from the original referenced drawing. You can find out more about external references in the section "Going External," later in this chapter.

Though not as flexible as external references, blocks are important and convenient; they save file space and organize your drawing better. They are also an important step on the way to using external references. So take the time to explore blocks and then use them as much as possible.

Creating and writing out blocks

To create a block, you can either use the BLOCK command to create a block for local use in the current drawing, or you can use the WBLOCK command to write the block out to its own file. (In other words, you can transform a block into a separate drawing simply by using the WBLOCK command.) The WBLOCK command enables you to access a block from other drawings but takes up more storage space and brings up maintenance concerns if, for example, you have different layer names in the main drawing and in the block. Use the BLOCK command first and the WBLOCK command if you need a block available to all your other drawings. (If, for example, you use a particular bolt in several drawings, you can write it out as a block and then reuse it elsewhere.)

To create a block for use within the current drawing, use the BMAKE, for Block MAKE, command. The following steps show you how:

1. Start the BMAKE command by using one of the following methods:

- Type **Bmake** at the command prompt and press Enter.
- Choose Draw⇨Block⇨Make from the menu bar.
- Choose the Make Block icon (the yellow circle and square) from the Draw toolbar.

The Block Definition dialog box appears (see Figure 14-1).

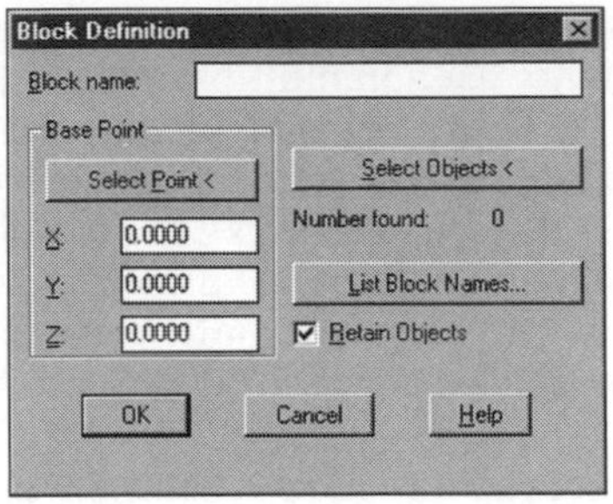

Figure 14-1:
The Block
Definition
dialog box.

Whenever you create a block, notice what AutoCAD layer is current — that is, what layer you're working on. In AutoCAD, layer 0 is known as a construction layer for blocks. If you create geometry on layer 0 and later include it in a block, the block acts as though it was part of the layer on which the block is inserted. If you create a block from geometry drawn on any other layer, it always retains the color and linetype in effect when it was created. Think of blocks created on layer 0 as chameleons. (If you don't know what a chameleon is, ask a zoology teacher, or search for the word on the Internet.)

2. Type the block name in the text entry box.

You must name the block before you create it, so have a good name thought up in advance. (Hmmm — how about "Godzilla"? Oh, been used before? . . .)

If you use the name of an existing block, AutoCAD replaces that block with the new group of objects you select. AutoCAD first warns you and then updates all instances of the block in the current drawing to match the changed block.

The AutoCAD capability to replace instantly all occurrences of a block with the new block that you create with the same name is a good reason to have all your blocks' names written down, along with a picture of what they look like. (You can store this information in a separate file — or a handwritten note.) Redefining all instances of a block just by using the same name for a new block can be a powerful feature. On the other hand, it can be an unintended mistake, too.

To see a list of the names of all the current blocks in your drawing, click the button List Block Names.

3. Specify the insertion point of the block, using either of the following methods:

- Enter the coordinates of the insertion point at the *X, Y,* and *Z* prompts.

- Click the Select Point button and then select a point on the screen.

The *insertion point* is the point on the block by which you insert it when copies of the block are used elsewhere.

Try to use a consistent point on the group of objects for the insertion point, such as the upper-left corner, so that you always know what to expect when you insert the block. (Some people mark the insertion point with a tiny cross or circle.)

4. **Click the Select Objects button and then select the objects that you want as part of the block.**

   Figure 14-2 shows a group of selected objects that are part of a block. (The dashed linetype shows which objects are selected.)

5. **To keep the objects that make up the block in place, check the check box, Retain Objects; to delete the objects, clear the check box.**

6. **Click OK to complete the selection process.**

   If you don't check the Retain Objects check box, your objects disappear! AutoCAD has stored the block, however, and the block is ready to use. If you check the Retain Objects check box, the objects remain in place.

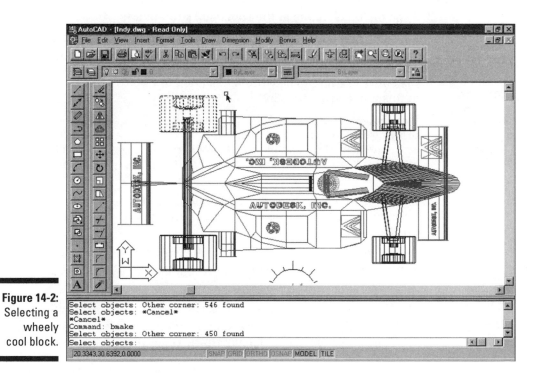

Figure 14-2:
Selecting a
wheely
cool block.

The difference between the objects that make up a block and the block itself is a little tricky. The easiest way to work with blocks is to draw a group of objects; create a block from them; then delete the objects. (AutoCAD deletes the objects by default.) Then insert the block wherever you want it. The objects that make up the block disappear as separate objects and only exist as part of the block. If you want to keep the blocks as separate objects in their original position, check the Retain Objects check box.

The Make Block command is great for use within a drawing, but what if you want the block to live independently, available for use in multiple drawings? To create a block and write it out for use with multiple drawings, use the WBLOCK command. The following steps show you how to do so:

1. **Type** Wblock **at the command prompt and press Enter to start the WBLOCK command.**

   The Create Drawing File dialog box appears.

2. **Enter the name of the file to create.**

   The dialog box closes, and AutoCAD prompts you for the name of the block to create.

3. **Type the block name at the command prompt and press Enter.**

   You can type the name of an existing block and press Enter to write that block to a file — you can just press = to specify that the existing block and the output file have the same name; or you can type * to specify the entire drawing to be written to an output file. To create a new block at this point, just press Enter.

   Managing your blocks is easier if you create the block within your drawing first, using the instructions earlier in this section, and then write the named block out to disk. If you create the block "on the fly," as occurs if you press Enter at this stage, the objects in the block are always deleted afterward, even if you don't want them to be.

4. **If you press Enter to create a new block, AutoCAD prompts you for a base point for the new block and then prompts you to select objects for the block.**

   Choose the insertion base point and then select the objects. AutoCAD writes out the block and then deletes the selected objects.

Type **OOPS** to undo the deletion; the newly created DWG file isn't deleted.

Put all the blocks you write into one subdirectory or set of subdirectories. The performance of AutoCAD then improves whenever you browse for a block because the program doesn't need to load extraneous filenames. And your performance improves because you know where to look for a block. You can store external references the same way.

Inserting blocks

AutoCAD provides you with four ways to insert a block into your drawing. The INSERT command drives the insertion process from the command line. The MINSERT, or Multiple Insert, command inserts multiple copies of a block in a rectangular array. The DDINSERT command opens a dialog box for insertion and is the method that you should use most often.

The fourth way to insert a block is to minimize AutoCAD to an icon and then drag and drop a file's icon onto the AutoCAD icon. AutoCAD then opens and continues with the prompts for a block insert. This option is so different from most AutoCAD commands that it's more like a stupid pet trick; so show it to your friends, but don't bother using it unless you're easily entertained and need some fun in your day.

To insert a block, follow these steps:

1. Open the Insert dialog box by using one of the following methods:

- Type **ddInsert** at the command prompt and press Enter.

- Choose Insert⇨Block from the menu bar.

The Insert dialog box appears, as shown in Figure 14-3.

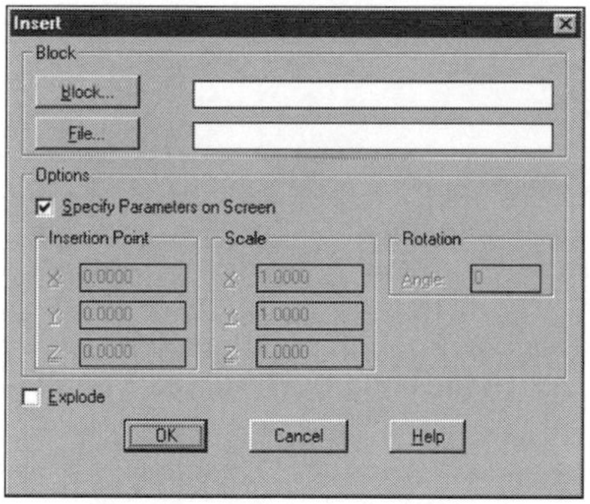

Figure 14-3:
The Insert
dialog box.

> **Insert**
>
> Block
> Block...
> File...
>
> Options
> ☑ Specify Parameters on Screen
>
> | Insertion Point | Scale | Rotation |
> | X 0.0000 | X 1.0000 | Angle 0 |
> | Y 0.0000 | Y 1.0000 | |
> | Z 0.0000 | Z 1.0000 | |
>
> ☐ Explode
>
> [OK] [Cancel] [Help]

2. Enter the block or external filename by using one of the following methods:

- Enter the name of the block defined in your current drawing in the Block text box or the filename of the block that's been written to disk in the File text box.

- Click the Block button to select from a list of blocks in the drawing.

- Click the File button to select an external drawing.

If you click the File button, you can modify the name in the Block text box so that the name of the block in your drawing is different from the filename. You might want to do this to make the block name more descriptive of the way the block is used in your drawing.

If you use the File button and enter the name of a block that's already in your drawing, AutoCAD warns you, then updates the block in your drawing with the current contents of the file.

3. **Enter the insertion point, scale, and rotation angle of the block.**

   You can either click the Specify Parameters on Screen check box, to specify the parameters on-screen, or type the values you want in the Insertion Point, Scale, and Rotation text boxes.

4. **(Optional) Click the Explode check box if you want to insert the block as several individual objects rather than as a block.**

5. **Click OK.**

The GRIPBLOCK system variable controls the number of grips shown on each block. Normally, you should set GRIPBLOCK to 0, indicating that one grip is on the block (0 = 1; got that?). If you set GRIPBLOCK to 1, multiple grips appear on the block (1 = 2 or more; got that?). Drawing all those grips on each block can slow down performance. But if you use grips to snap to objects and you want to snap to different points on a block, set GRIPBLOCK to 1 when needed.

Exploding a block

This feature is easy but important. Simply type the EXPLODE command at the command prompt and press Enter, choose Modify⇨Explode from the menu bar, or choose Explode (the firecracker icon) from the Edit toolbar. Then select the block. AutoCAD breaks down, or explodes, the block into its component objects. You can then add to the component objects to create another block or make changes to the component objects and use them to create yet another block.

Going External

In AutoCAD, an *xref,* or external reference, is not someone who used to be an official in a sporting contest. (Ex-ref — get it?) An xref is a reference to another, *external* file — one outside the current drawing — that you can make act as though it's part of your drawing. Technically, a reference is simply a pointer from one file to another. The xref is the actual pointer, but the combination of the pointer and the external file is often called the xref. Drawings that you include in other drawings by means of an external reference are "xref-ed in."

The big advantage of xrefs over blocks is that if you change an original file, AutoCAD automatically copies the change into your drawing when you reload the xref — that is, force an update — or when you save or reopen the drawing. This feature is both good and bad news.

If you improve the hatching on the screw drawing that you've xrefed in (so that it looks better) voilà, your drawing also looks better.

But if you lengthen that screw $^1/_4$ inch and then you decide that you don't want that change or you discover that your plot no longer fits on a single sheet, you have problems. To avoid any other problems, AutoCAD creates new layers in your current drawing that correspond to the layers that are xrefed in. The new layers have the form drawing name/layer name; for instance, If you xref in layers from the drawing MYSCREW.DWG that have the names GEOMETRY, TEXT, and so on, the xrefed layers will be named MYSCREW|GEOMETRY, MYSCREW|TEXT, and so on.

xref

So you need a certain amount of trust within an organization to use xrefs. If you don't have that feeling of trust (or even if you simply doubt your own abilities at remembering what you can use an xref for and how to update it correctly), don't use xrefs.

The other major advantage of xrefs over blocks is that they aren't stored in your drawing even once. The storage space taken up by the original drawing you're xrefing in isn't duplicated, no matter how many people refer to that file (probably a much more efficient way than blocks to reuse other people's drawings).

But xrefs are basically good because they enable you to leverage your own or someone else's work easily and transparently, thereby increasing productivity.

How you use xrefs, or whether you use them at all, varies greatly depending on your own tastes and needs and those of the organization you work in, if any. So this book doesn't go into great depth on how best to use and manage xrefs. If you're in an organization that uses them, find out from colleagues how they use xrefs and imitate them. If you want to initiate greater use of xrefs on your own, use the AutoCAD documentation and other in-depth AutoCAD resources to find out more.

Creating an external reference file

To create a file that you can use as an external reference, just create a drawing and save it. That's it. You can then start up a new drawing and create an external reference to the previous one. The xrefed drawing opens into your drawing as a visible but untouchable part of your drawing. You can measure or object snap the xrefed geometry, but you can't modify or delete xrefed geometry until you "own" it. (More on that later in the chapter.) This arrangement is so simple that it takes a while to figure out all the opportunities that xrefs provide. But don't worry; if you've been setting up your files carefully and following some of the other suggestions in this book, such as using blocks whenever possible, you're at least mostly ready to use xrefs.

Release 14 greatly improves the use and management of xrefs. For one thing, you can now *clip* an xref — that is, use only the layers or the area of the xrefed drawing that you need in your drawing. Also important is that external references are now managed through a dialog box interface instead of from the command line. The dialog box makes it easier to specify the options for an xref and to see how the files relate. One welcome addition is a new button that enables you to see a tree view of xref file hierarchies; if you have more than a few such files, you may see a noticeable improvement in your ability to organize and retrieve them.

Attaching an xref

Attaching an external reference is easy. Just use the following steps:

1. **To start the XREF command, use either of these methods:**

   - Type **XRef** at the command prompt.

   - Choose Insert➪External Reference from the menu bar.

   The External Reference dialog box appears (see Figure 14-4).

2. **Click on the Attach button.**

   The Select File to Attach dialog box appears.

Unfortunately, you can't copy or move files from within any of these dialog boxes. If you get a sudden urge to organize your files differently in order to better support using them as xrefs, you have to go into Windows and make the necessary changes before proceeding.

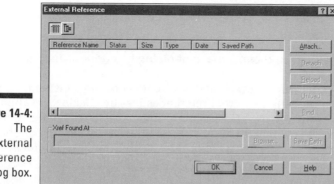

Figure 14-4:
The
External
Reference
dialog box.

3. Browse to find the file you want to attach, select it, and then click Open.

The Attach Xref dialog box appears.

If you choose a file that is already being used as an xref in your document, it is re-referenced with the parameters you specify.

4. Specify the parameters for the xref in the dialog box.

Parameters include the insertion point, scaling factors, and rotation angle. You can set these parameters in the dialog box or specify them on-screen, similar to what you can do with blocks, as described earlier in this chapter. Use the AutoCAD online help to find out more about specific options.

You can choose the Attachment or Overlay radio button to tell AutoCAD how to handle the xref. The choice only matters if you create a drawing that uses xrefs, and then your drawing is in turn used as an xref. Attachment is the default choice, and it means that the xrefed file will always be included with your drawing when someone else opens it as an xref. Overlay, the other choice, means that you see the xrefed drawing, but someone who xrefs your drawing won't see the overlaid file. By choosing Overlay you can xref in a map, for instance, to your drawing of a house, but not have the map show up when someone else xrefs your house drawing.

5. Click OK.

The externally referenced file appears in your drawing. Layers from that file also appear as layers in your file, with the name of the xrefed drawing included before the layer name.

To drive the process of attaching external references from the command line, type **-XRef** at the command line and follow the prompts.

Managing xrefs and more

The External Reference dialog box includes many more options for managing xrefs after you attach them. Important dialog box options include:

- ✔ **List of external references:** You can change between a List and a Tree view of your drawing's external references just by clicking the appropriate button at the top of the dialog box. You can also resize the columns by dragging the column dividers or resort the list by clicking on the column header names, just as in other AutoCAD Release 14 dialog boxes.
- ✔ **Detach:** Completely separates the xref from your drawing.
- ✔ **Unload/Reload:** Temporarily separates the xref from your drawing and then renews the attachment.
- ✔ **Bind:** Imports the xref into your drawing as a block.

None of these options affect the xrefed drawing itself; it continues to exist as a separate file. If you need to delete it, do so as a separate operation (quickly, before you forget!).

You can do quite a bit more with xrefs. You can clip an externally referenced file so that only part of it is used in your drawing; use the XCLIP command or choose Modify⇨Object⇨Clip from the menu bar. You can create indices to help AutoCAD load external references more efficiently. (See the Options button in the Save Drawing As dialog box to see the options, and see the AutoCAD online help for more information.) You also need to watch out for people who may move your xrefed files out from under you or change them without telling you. (This sort of situation can have very embarrassing results if you make a presentation to a client and are surprised by something you see in your own drawings!)

You also need to watch out for circular references, in which two or more files refer to one another in an overly intimate, if no doubt enjoyable, fashion. If you really have time on your hands between projects, you can even enable and monitor an Xref Log File and then use it to track your xref history. See the AutoCAD documentation if you need to know more about xrefs.

Also beyond the scope of this chapter and this book are other xref concerns to think about: standard ways of maintaining xrefed files, specifying who is in charge of changing them, and more. The information in this chapter, however, is enough to get you started and maybe enough to get you finished, too. If you start to use xrefs extensively, find out what standards exist for their use in your organization; if none exist, make some up and publish and distribute them. The people who should have done it in the first place will (hopefully) be appropriately grateful.

Master the Raster

AutoCAD Release 14 is the first version of AutoCAD to allow full support for *bit-mapped,* or *raster,* images. A raster image is an image that's defined by storing each of the points that make it up. For example, a TV screen displays a raster image. If you capture an image of your computer screen, that's a raster image, too.

Most AutoCAD drawings, by contrast, are *vector* images. A vector image is an image that's defined by storing a bunch of objects. A typical object may be a circle with its own center point and radius. Every time the object is displayed or printed, the pixels to create an image of it must be recalculated from the image's description. Vector-based images are typically smaller and more flexible than raster images, but are also less rich in visual detail and slower to display or print.

Raster images normally come into the computer from some kind of scanner that imports a blueprint, photograph, or other image. Raster images, such as company logos, can also be created in programs like Photoshop. You may end up outsourcing your scanning work or buying your own scanner — but be warned, a good scanner that can handle large-format images such as blueprints and capture the full-color depth of a photograph well is expensive. Whether you're doing your scanning yourself or having a service bureau do it for you, you need to know that AutoCAD handles most of the popular image file formats including the Windows BMP format, the popular Web graphics formats GIF and JPEG, the popular PCX and TIFF formats, as well as DIB, FLC, FLI, GP4, MIL, PNG, RLE, RST, and TGA.

Consider outsourcing scanning work until you're sure that you need a scanner of your own and have a firm grasp on what features you need.

An AutoCAD drawing that incorporates a raster image is called a *hybrid* image, because it uses both the object support built in to AutoCAD and its support of raster images.

Why is AutoCAD Release 14, which Autodesk tells us is the most object-oriented version of AutoCAD yet, also the first to support raster images? Because a large subset of AutoCAD users need to incorporate raster images in their drawings. Here are just two of the many scenarios in which raster images are important:

> ✔ **Vectorization:** Imagine that you want to convert a raster image into a vector image by tracing lines in the raster image. What simpler way to do so than by importing the raster image into AutoCAD, tracing the needed lines, and then disposing of the raster image?

> ✔ **Design visualization:** Imagine that you want to show how a new building will look in an existing location. What more effective way to do so than by importing a photograph of the location into AutoCAD and then drawing the new building *in situ* (that's "in place," if you skipped Latin), surrounded by its future environment?

Using raster images is much like using external references. The raster image isn't actually stored with your drawing file; instead, a reference to the raster image file is established from within your drawing, like an xref. You can clip the image and control its size, brightness, contrast, fade, and transparency. These controls enable you to fine-tune the appearance of the raster image both on-screen and on a printout or plot.

Don't save drawings that use raster images to Release 12 format; they lose the connection to the external image file, and you have to reestablish the connection when you bring the image back into Release 14.

Before you start using raster images in AutoCAD, make sure that you can output them. Check whether your printer or plotter has an ADI 4.3 driver that supports raster plotting. (If not, it will have NR after the name.)

Attaching an image

Follow these steps to bring a raster image into AutoCAD:

1. **Choose Insert⇨Raster Image from the menu bar or type** IMage **at the command line to start the IMAGE command.**

   The Image dialog box appears (see Figure 14-5).

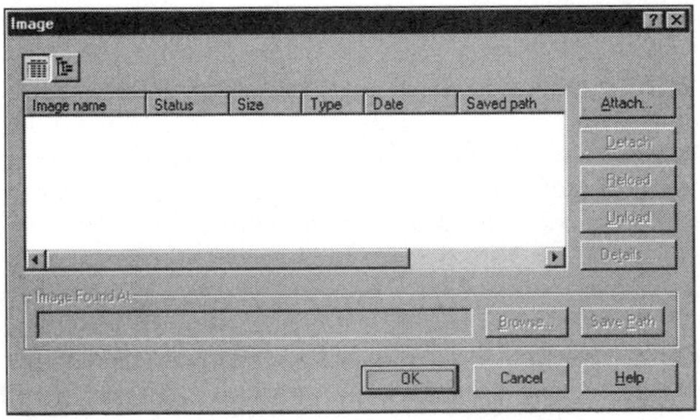

Figure 14-5:
The Image dialog box.

2. Click the Attach button.

The Attach Image dialog box appears.

3. Browse to find the file you want to attach, select it, and then click Open.

The Image Attach dialog box appears.

Get in the habit of clicking the Details button to see more information about the resolution and image size of the image you're attaching.

4. Specify the parameters for the attached image in the dialog box.

Parameters include the insertion point, scale factor, and rotation angle. You can set these parameters in the dialog box or specify them on-screen, similar to what you can do with blocks and external references, as described earlier in this chapter. Use the AutoCAD online help to find out more about specific options.

To set the scale factor, use the scale factor for your drawing as described in Chapter 4 and Appendix B.

5. Click OK.

The image appears in your drawing. Figure 14-6 shows a drawing with a raster image attached to it, with the Attach Image File dialog box in the foreground.

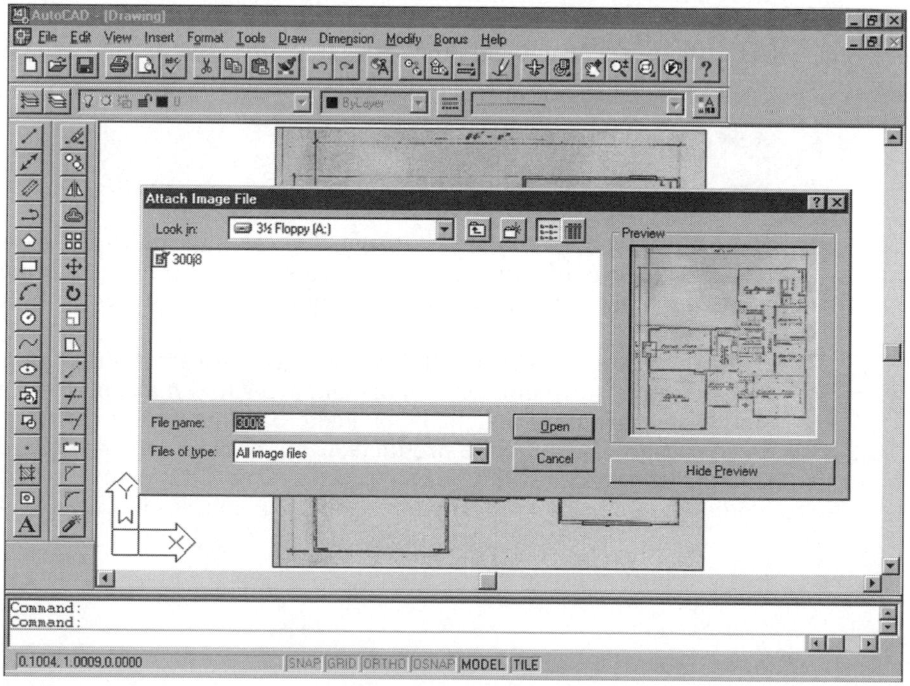

Figure 14-6:
The Attach Image File dialog box with an image in the background.

6. **If needed, set the drawing order — start the command from the menu bar or from the keyboard:**

   • **From the command line, type** DRaworder **and press Enter; select the raster image and then press Enter to select the default choice, which puts the selected object at the bottom of the drawing order.**

   The command ends.

   • **From the menu bar, start by selecting the raster image and then choose Tools⇨Display Order⇨Send to Back.**

   The raster image is put at the bottom of the drawing order.

To drive the process of attaching images from the command line, type **-IMage** at the command line and follow the prompts.

Managing images

Images in your drawing can be managed from the Image dialog box, which includes virtually the same options as the External References dialog box. Important dialog box options include a list of image references; the capability to detach (remove) image references; and the capability to unload images to save memory and then to reload them when needed. You can't bind an image to your drawing; it always remains an external file.

As with xrefs, you can clip images so that only part of the image is displayed in your drawing. Use either of the following methods:

✔ Choose Modify⇨Object⇨Image Clip.

✔ Enter **ImageCLip** on the command line.

Follow the prompts to clip the image. You can have multiple overlapping or distinct "pieces" of any number of images in your drawing, and only the parts you need are loaded into memory when you have your drawing open.

The new raster image capabilities in Release 14 were defined by Autodesk in consultation with a consortium of companies that make plotters, scanners, and other imaging products. If you need to do more with raster images, look for hardware and software products, from these and related companies, that can greatly extend what you can do with raster images in AutoCAD. Start your search for more information with the resources in Chapter 18.

Chapter 15

3D for Me, See?

● ●

In This Chapter

▶ Deciding when to use 3D

▶ Using viewports and viewpoints

▶ Extruding 2D objects into 3D objects

▶ Shading 3D objects

● ●

*T*hree-dimensional (3D) drafting and design capabilities — that is, adding height as well as length and width to your drawing — were once a high-end, extra-cost add-on to AutoCAD. Users who wanted to tackle 3D bought high-end machines and underwent additional training to be able to work in this new environment. Now 3D is part of the base AutoCAD package, but it has not suddenly become fast, easy-to-use, or trouble-free. This chapter offers a gentle introduction to the power and promise of 3D work in AutoCAD.

The 3D capabilities of AutoCAD are largely unchanged in Release 14. The main 3D-specific change is improved rendering of 3D models, which is not described in detail in this book; the process of defining points and shapes in 3D space is basically unchanged. However, overall Release 14 improvements such as increased performance and reduced memory footprint are of special interest to 3D users, because 3D needs plenty of speed and plenty of RAM. Real-time pan and zoom and the resulting improved usability of plot preview and paper space are also of special interest to 3D users, who are likely to need the multiple views that paper space makes possible. And xref clipping includes front and back clipping planes, so xrefs are now more useful to 3D users.

VRML, or Virtual Reality Modeling Language, is rapidly becoming the leading standard for 3D files on the Web. Unfortunately, AutoCAD Release 14 doesn't include "save as VRML" capability; instead, AutoCAD uses its own propri-etary format for Web publishing, as described in Chapter 17. However, I expect to see third-party translators that create VRML files from AutoCAD files fairly soon. Check Chapter 16 for possible leads if you need to find a program to perform this function for you.

3D thumbs up

Using 3D is more work and it slows down your computer, so why bother using it? Here are four key reasons why anyone in his right mind would bother with 3D:

Wave of the future. As CAD pursues greater and greater realism, 3D becomes important in more and more areas. So any CAD user who wants to be competent a few years down the road needs to become familiar with 3D now.

Sometimes it's nice. Drawing in 3D is useful for a number of tasks, including creating shaded renderings to help sell a design to a client and fit-and-finish testing to find potential problems before a design is actually put into construction or manufacturing.

Sometimes it's needed. Drawing in 3D is required for a small but growing number of tasks. Many mechanical designs are converted into 3D at some point in the design process. And the shaded renderings used for both designing and selling are becoming a practical necessity in some fields.

Sometimes it's faster. The fastest way to create a single view of something is to draw it in the needed size and perspective in 2D. But if you need multiple views, it may be faster to create a 3D model, then slice and render it as needed for the views you want to create.

3D for Me? . . .

The concept of 3D hardly seems to need introduction. We live in a three-dimensional world, and all the objects you can model in AutoCAD are actually three-dimensional.

But at a basic level, the way in which people see things is actually a two-dimensional (2D) representation of the three-dimensional world. The image that your eyes project onto the inside rear of your eyeballs is, after all, just as two-dimensional as a TV picture. (It's upside-down, too, but that's another problem.)

Your mind uses a number of clues to generate a moving, three-dimensional model from this two-dimensional image. These clues include depth cues from combining left-eye and right-eye images and inferences from the motion of objects, sounds, and previous experience. The mind puts all this information together to help you perceive the world in 3D.

Similarly, drafting provides clues to help the mind construct a 3D model from the 2D image on paper. The use of multiple views and the experience of the viewer are probably the two most important clues to making 3D sense of 2D drawings. Design and drafting have succeeded pretty well for a long time by using 2D representations as the guide to creating 3D objects. But at some point, nothing can replace a true 3D model, such as in helping someone understand how a building will look when constructed or how two parts fit together.

TIP

3D thumbs down

Why not use 3D all the time? For several reasons, which you should take into account before you decide how much to use 3D on any given project:

2D input and editing. The mouse, keyboard, and drawing tablet are all 2D devices; the more complex the 3D object you're trying to model, the more unsuitable these input devices are.

2D output. Almost all the output methods available to you, notably paper and the computer screen, are 2D; the full beauty of your 3D model may only be known to you!

Performance. Today's personal computers are just now becoming adequate for the task of storing complex 2D models and rendering them on-screen and on the plotter; if the model is 3D, the difficulty increases geometrically, and performance seems to slow geometrically as well.

So what does using 3D in CAD mean? Basically, it means creating models instead of views. Instead of creating cross-sections of objects, or views of objects from certain perspectives, the designer or draftsperson creates a complete, accurate, 3D model of each object. This description or depiction of each object includes all the necessary information for AutoCAD to create a view from any perspective. With a properly constructed 3D model, AutoCAD can even output commands to machines to create actual 3D objects, whether plastic prototypes carved from a tank of Jelly by lasers or an actual bolt, valve, or piston created by numerically controlled machine tools.

You can do some experimentation with 3D on any computer system that can run AutoCAD. But if you want to pursue serious work in 3D AutoCAD, pay attention to the following prerequisites:

- ✔ **Know AutoCAD well.** You need to know the ins and outs of AutoCAD as a 2D tool thoroughly before doing much with 3D. Otherwise, the time you waste may be your own! If you're making avoidable errors at the 2D level at the same time that you're trying to get to know and use 3D, accomplishing anything is slow going.

- ✔ **Get a fast computer.** For serious work with 3D models, you need the fastest computer you can get. One or two Pentium Pro microprocessors running Windows NT with 128MB of RAM and a two-gigabyte hard disk is in the ballpark. The additional processor won't help AutoCAD directly, but it will help some 3D programs you may run along with AutoCAD, and will also help you multitask with AutoCAD and another program simultaneously. (Now you know why "real" 3D work is done on high-end workstations!)

✔ **Get and master additional software.** In addition to AutoCAD, you need other programs — either AutoCAD add-ons or separate packages — to do work that AutoCAD isn't as good at. Illustration packages, for example, can really help jazz up the appearance of your drawing.

✔ **Do a real project.** Real work is the best motivation of all for discovering 3D. If you don't have an actual work assignment, create a task for yourself. Something as "simple" as creating a 3D model of your living room and its furniture can make the difference between really finding out something useful about 3D and just reading about it in the manuals.

The Mechanical Desktop product from Autodesk has advanced 3D features, including a fast display driver specifically for 3D. Contact Autodesk for more information.

Starting with 3D

The best way to get started with 3D is to take an existing 2D drawing in good shape and extending it into the third dimension. This process usually means taking something flat, such as a floor plan, and extending it straight up. This modification gives you exposure to a number of 3D commands without having to go into all the details; it can also deliver some immediate benefit by helping you get more information out of a drawing you've already done.

Don't let this approach give you a false sense of security, though. To use 3D effectively, you basically must relearn how to enter coordinates, create and manipulate objects, and more. The rest of this chapter skips all that relearning in favor of getting a quick 3D bang for your buck with AutoCAD features most users already know. For a more thorough approach to using 3D with AutoCAD, see the AutoCAD documentation and check out the reliable AutoCAD resources in Chapter 16.

To demonstrate 3D, this chapter uses a simple 2D drawing extended into the third dimension — that of the living room mentioned in the preceding section.

Figure 15-1 shows a simple floor plan for a living room. In 3D, you can extrude the walls upward and shade them to help visualize the final appearance of objects created from 2D drawings. Create a similar drawing or use a 2D drawing you already have as the base for your experiments with 3D.

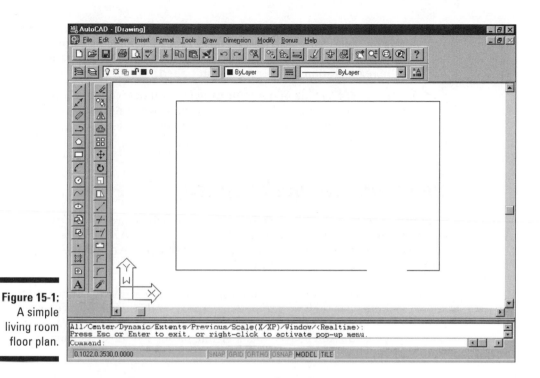

Figure 15-1:
A simple
living room
floor plan.

Cleaning up your drawing

Unnecessary complexity or simple mistakes in your 2D drawing can cost you many minutes of manipulation, redrawing, and rendering time when you take your drawing into the third dimension. Make use of the following suggestions to clean up your drawing before you start:

- ✔ **Make needed fixes.** You can put off many tasks until late in the process of creating a drawing. You should, however, complete all tasks and fix any problems before starting to work in 3D. Adjust for that quarter-inch discrepancy in the meeting of two walls. Change the layer names to your company's standard set. Generally, finish any task that you've been putting off.

- ✔ **Xrefs and blocks.** Preparing for 3D work is a good time to implement some of the suggestions from Chapter 14 about subdividing your drawings into blocks and xrefs. Building a 3D model out of parts is much easier than dealing with an entire scene at once. Consider dividing your drawing into blocks and xrefs as much as possible. Then take each piece into 3D one at a time.

✔ **Freeze layers.** Freeze any and all layers that contain text, dimensions, plumbing, and other drawing elements that don't need to show up in the 3D version of your drawing. No sense in taking a performance hit for the regeneration of layers you don't need.

✔ **Anything else?** Think about your drawing and determine whether it has any other loose ends that you can tidy up. Consider creating a drawing that's just a subset of the data to experiment on before going to 3D with the entire drawing.

Viewports in model space

Chapter 14 discusses viewports in paper space, which are useful for laying out plots and presentations in both 2D and 3D. *Model space viewports,* cousins of paper viewports, are less powerful but simpler, and they impose less of a performance hit on AutoCAD.

Unlike paper space viewports, model space viewports divide the screen into separate rectangles with no gap between them, and you can't move or stretch them. You can't plot multiple model space viewports; that's what paper space is for. And a layer that's visible in one model space viewport is visible in all of them.

Model space viewports enable you to see several views of your model at once, each from a different angle. Although the different views subdivide the screen, using them can have performance advantages. Shading a small viewport, for example, is much quicker than shading a full-screen image. After you get everything the way you really want it, you can change your drawing back to full-screen and shade the whole thing. Model space viewports are also very helpful when working in 3D. If you have different viewpoints in three or four viewports, creating 3D models is much easier. An object that looks correct in one viewport can be "double-checked" in another viewport for accuracy.

To set up model space viewports, use the Tiled Viewport Layout dialog box. Start it by choosing View⇨Tiled Viewports⇨Layout from the menu bar. Figure 15-2 shows the dialog box, which makes choosing the viewport setup you want very easy.

AutoCAD inserts a UCS (User Coordinate System) icon into the lower-left corner of each viewport — the little X-Y icon that you usually see in the same position in the drawing area. This icon helps you know what angle you're viewing the viewport from.

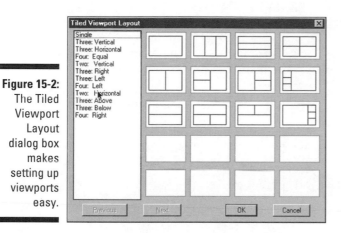

Figure 15-2:
The Tiled
Viewport
Layout
dialog box
makes
setting up
viewports
easy.

Start your viewport explorations with the menus, as described above. For speed, you can set up model space viewports from the menu bar by using the VPORTS command, which enables you to create, save, and restore viewport layouts. To use VPORTS, you tell AutoCAD how many viewports to create and then specify the style. Experiment to find out how it works.

Watch out; AutoCAD continues to subdivide the screen each time you use the VPORTS command. You can have up to 16 viewports open at a time. Of course, at that point they're too small to see much of anything in them.

Expect delays when you first start using 3D as AutoCAD loads into memory the needed code to support different 3D operations. (Not loading this code is how AutoCAD stays "lean and mean" while you work with 2D drawings.) Of course, loading this code uses up RAM that you would just as soon have for your model. Gotten more RAM yet?

Changing the viewpoint in your viewports

AutoCAD initializes all your viewports with the same point of view. You can change the viewpoints of your various viewports so that your viewports all have different points of view — or else, what good are they?

To change the viewpoint in a viewport, choose View⇨3D Viewpoint⇨Select from the menu bar to open the Viewpoint Presets dialog box, as shown in Figure 15-3. Unfortunately, this dialog box is one of those things that you must ponder for a while before it makes sense.

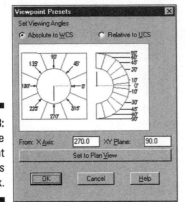

Figure 15-3:
The
Viewpoint
Presets
dialog box.

To set viewpoint options with the keyboard, type **VPOINT** at the command prompt and press Enter. Prompts appear to take you through the steps to set viewpoint options. However, I recommend using the Viewpoint Presets dialog box; it's easier and more powerful because the options are right there in front of you, increasing your freedom to experiment.

To help you make sense of the Viewpoint Presets dialog box, review the following description of its parts:

✔ **Set Viewing Angles.** This option tells the dialog box whether to set the viewing angle Absolute to WCS, in relation to the World Coordinate System (WCS), or Relative to UCS, in relation to the current User Coordinate System. (*Note:* The WCS is the standard XYZ coordinate system, where X is horizontal, Y is vertical, and Z extends out into the third dimension.)

✔ **From X Axis.** This text box and the square area above it set the viewing angle relative to the horizontal, or X, axis.

Changing this angle on a typical house plan, for example, is similar to strolling around the house to look at the house from different horizontal vantage points. To set the exact angle to within a fraction of a degree, enter the value in the text entry box or click a spot on the circumference of the circle. To set the angle to a 45-degree increment, click inside the square but outside the circle, near to the angle that you want.

✔ **XY Plane.** This text box and the curved area above it set the viewing angle relative to the flat, 2D XY plane — the "floor" of the living room for a model of a house.

Changing this angle from 90 degrees to –90 degrees on a typical house plan, for example, is similar to floating from directly above a house, down one side of it, and then down into the ground until you're looking up at the house from directly beneath it. You can consider the half circle shown in the dialog box to be an arched catwalk, with its endpoints directly above and directly under the house. As with the X Axis choice, you can set the exact viewing angle by entering a value in the text entry box or by clicking a spot on the circumference of the inner semicircle. You can set the viewing angle in larger increments by clicking one of the numbers at various increments around the semicircle.

✔ **Set to Plan View.** This option resets the X axis and XY plane views to 270 degrees from the X axis and 90 degrees from the XY plane, which is the AutoCAD default, top-down plan view.

By using the Viewpoint Presets dialog box, you can change the viewpoint in a viewport. (Say "viewpoint in a viewport" three times fast and notice the funny looks you get.) This dialog box even works on a single 2D viewport.

The results of using the Viewpoint Presets dialog box can be surprising at first. Carefully compare the current settings indicated in the dialog box to the new settings — you want to make sure that you're doing the right thing. Accidentally changing the XY plane angle so that you're looking at your plan from underground, for example, is all too easy to do. You may not even notice what you've done until you use a HIDE or SHADE command; get in the habit of checking yourself by using the HIDE command whenever you use 3D objects.

Going to the Third Dimension

AutoCAD doesn't do a good job of handling some conversions of 2D objects to 3D. In fact, the way in which AutoCAD handles these conversions is often counterintuitive. So this section takes some extra steps to try to relate the 2D world to the 3D world as much as possible.

After you have your drawing set up in model space viewports and angled correctly, you can start extending it into the third dimension. (You can extend it anyway, but this way you can see the result.) This section presents some simple changes to make so that you can add the third dimension to a 2D drawing.

The methods used in this section are very introductory and are not suitable for "true" 3D work, such as that used in presentations, for checking fit between objects, and so on. But these methods, which some call "2.5D" (ha, ha!), are a good start to getting some value out of the 3D capabilities of AutoCAD, short of getting a master's degree in the subject.

Extruding

Extruding just means pushing something into the third dimension. Remember that scene in the movie *Fantasia* where the mountains and volcanoes push up through the earth? That's extrusion.

Unfortunately, extruding doesn't work well on objects that have no enclosed area, such as a typical line. If a line does enclose an area, AutoCAD extrudes the area, not the line. If you were to extrude a floor plan, for example, the extrusion either doesn't do anything (if the area isn't completely enclosed) or it creates a solid block the size and height of the building. Pretty hard to rearrange furniture within a solid block.

What extruding does work well for is "massing studies." If you wanted to see how a new building or building wing would look in the real world, you might represent the current and proposed buildings in the area with simple blocks. This is called a massing study, since it compares the mass of the buildings rather than the details. Extruding works well for this.

So to extrude, you need to start with closed areas such as circles and polylines. This example starts with a simple floor plan made of polylines instead of lines. (AutoCAD used to have a DLINE command that was great for this stuff, but it was dropped in Release 13.)

The process starts by using the VPORTS and DDVPOINT commands to set up a group of model space views that show the drawing in plan view, from ground level, and from an offset view above. Just getting this setup takes a great deal of panning and zooming.

Use the following steps to extrude the walls of the living room plan to a height of eight feet:

1. **Type EXTrude at the command prompt and press Enter to start the EXTRUDE command.**

2. **Select the objects that you want to extrude by using a bounding or crossing window; in this case, select all the walls.**

   The objects must define closed areas for the EXTRUDE command to work. If the areas are not currently closed, you may want to create a separate layer, then add geometry on the new layer to close the shapes. (You can freeze or delete the added layer later.)

3. **Press Enter after you finish selecting objects.**

4. Type 8' **for the height of the extrusion and then press Enter.**

Make sure that you specify feet, not inches.

You can also specify an extrusion path, but for now, just use the default path, which is to extrude at right angles to the plane the object is in.

5. Press Enter to specify the default (0) as the extrusion taper angle.

AutoCAD extrudes the walls. Figure 15-4 shows the living room with its walls extruded to a height of eight feet. Notice that the plan view is unchanged, and the ground-level view is incomprehensible; only the offset view from above shows what the room really looks like.

Shading

Shading a figure is a quick way to make the figure's "3D-ness" apparent. Shading has fewer complications than *rendering,* a feature not covered in this book, but it does help make a drawing look solid. (Rendering creates a more realistically shaded image.) The SHADE command obscures hidden lines and then "paints" surfaces. The SHADE command also has a simple lighting scheme that doesn't do much but is simple to use. Notice that you can't print the shaded image, so shading is really useful only for quick on-screen views and presentations.

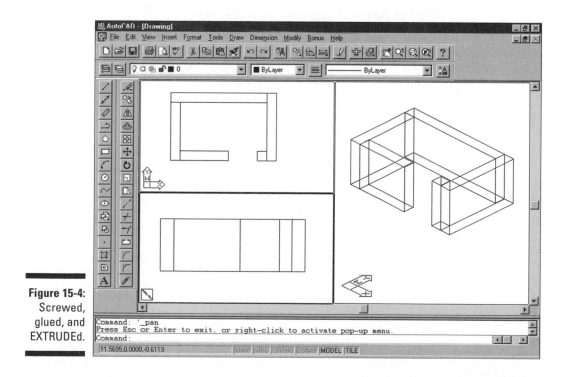

Figure 15-4:
Screwed,
glued, and
EXTRUDEd.

Before shading, you may want to adjust the SHADEDGE and SHADEDIF system variables. The SHADEDGE system variable has four values: 0 uses a simple light source but doesn't highlight the edges of your objects; 1, the most useful setting, uses a simple light source and highlights edges; 2 simply performs a simulated hidden line removal; and 3 doesn't use lighting effects but does highlight edges. You may want to experiment with all these settings, but 1 is the setting that you're likely to use most.

The SHADEDIF system variable controls the kind of lighting that AutoCAD uses. The higher the value, from the low of 0 to a high of 100, the "sharper" and more contrasted the light. However, a high value makes the entire drawing appear dark. A value of 50 is a good compromise in many cases.

Unfortunately, the SHADEDGE and SHADEDIF system variables are command-line entries that you must set before you shade, so experimenting with them is a bit of work. The following steps show you how to change the drawing's color, set the shading variables to new values, and then shade the drawing:

1. **Type** SHADEDGE 1 **at the command prompt and then press Enter.**

   This command sets the shading to use lighting effects and highlighted edges.

2. **Type** SHADEDIF 50 **at the command prompt and then press Enter.**

   This command sets an equal balance between ambient and direct light.

3. **Click the viewport you want to shade.**

4. **Type** SHAde **and then press Enter.**

5. **Repeat Steps 3 and 4 for any other viewports you want to shade.**

More 3D Stuff

This chapter only touches on what 3D can do — and on what you need to find out to use it effectively. To shade the tops of the walls, you need to use the 3DFACE command to stretch a "skin" over them. Or you can use the BOX command to create the walls as solid objects in the first place. And rendering the walls produces a much better result than shading — and you can print it, too! Rendering is much improved in Release 14. But these topics are worth a book of their own.

If you want to continue to experiment with 3D, take a course or two and buy one or more books on the topic. Your reading and training time will be quickly repaid in fewer mistakes and REDRAW commands — and better results.

Part V
The Part of Tens

The 5th Wave   By Rich Tennant

"What is it, Lassie? Is it Gramps? Is it his hard disk? Is he stuck somewhere, girl? Is there trouble with his system variables? What, girl, what?"

In this part . . .

"Tens" sounds a lot like "tense," and tense is how AutoCAD may make you feel sometimes. But never fear — help is on the way! Checklists are always a big help in getting things right and fixing things that are wrong. And a Top Ten list is a good way to quickly spot the best (or the worst) of almost anything — AutoCAD included. This Part of Tens features several lists — not all of which have exactly ten items (but, hey, who's counting?) — designed to help you get right into AutoCAD, get right out of trouble, and maybe have a chuckle or two in the meantime.

Chapter 16

Ten Great AutoCAD Resources (Plus One)

· ·

In This Chapter

▶ Going online for help

▶ Checking out resources on the World Wide Web

▶ Hanging out on CompuServe — GO ACAD!

▶ Thumbing through *CADALYST* and *CADENCE* magazines

▶ Exploring the AutoCAD Resource Guide

▶ Getting involved with local users' groups

▶ Joining AUGI

▶ Training at the AutoCAD Training Centers

▶ Calling Autodesk

▶ Keeping in touch with your dealer

▶ Plus one: bonus files

· ·

*1*f you don't have time to read this entire chapter, I recommend the following resources as the minimum survival kit for an AutoCAD user:

✔ **A registered copy of AutoCAD:** AutoCAD may be expensive, but it's worth it; otherwise, it wouldn't have more than 1.6 million paid users. If you've been using a pirated copy, contact Autodesk now to get a paid-up copy.

✔ **A CompuServe account with Web access:** CompuServe is the *PC Magazine* Editors' Choice for best online service, and it's also the #1 service for AutoCAD information and support. And it includes Web access. (Web resources are described in Chapter 17.)

✔ **Subscriptions to *CADENCE* and *CADALYST* magazines:** Get both magazines for a year, and then you can cut down to the one you like better if you want to save a few bucks.

✔ **Membership in a local users' group:** The AutoCAD world really is a community, and local users' groups are the town halls. They're also sometimes the hiring halls! Go to at least a few users' group meetings to make some contacts and find out whether you like it.

✔ **Your dealer's phone number:** The dealer who sold you AutoCAD is your main contact point for sales and support. Keep your dealer's contact information handy.

A short list of great AutoCAD resources, with contact information, can be found right here in Table 16-1. You can find much more detail on Web-based resources in Chapter 17.

Table 16-1	The AutoCAD Resources Short List	
Resource	*Web Address*	*Phone Number*
AutoCAD Resource Guide with local users' groups, Autodesk Training Centers	`www.autodesk.com`	415-332-2344 or 800-964-6432
CompuServe	`www.compuserve.com`	Customer Service, 800-848-8990
CADENCE magazine	`www.cadence-mag.com`	800-486-4995
CADALYST magazine	`www.cadonline.com`	800-949-6525
AutoCAD User Group International (AUGI)	`www.augi.com`	415-507-6565

Be sure to bookmark the Web addresses for *CADENCE* and *CADALYST* magazines in your browser; neither of them is particularly easy to remember. (The obvious URL for *CADALYST* magazine, `www.cadalyst.com`, is not in use by anyone; the obvious URL for *CADENCE* magazine, `www.cadence.com`, is already in use by Cadence Design Systems, Inc.)

Now here, in no particular order, are ten great AutoCAD resources for you to use.

Online Help

The most-overlooked resource for help with your AutoCAD questions is the online help and documentation. Hundreds and hundreds of pages of AutoCAD help and information are right on the AutoCAD CD-ROM. Look there first!

You can get printed versions of the online documentation from Autodesk. I recommend getting the printed versions as well as using the online version, because you're more likely to browse printed documentation in your spare time than online documentation. Paging through the documentation in a relatively free-form way is usually how you pick up or figure out that one key tip or insight that saves you dozens of hours while you're using AutoCAD. So although you should start with the online documentation, get the printed documentation, too.

The World Wide Web

 The World Wide Web is a hot topic of conversation, well, worldwide, and it's becoming a great resource for CAD use (catching up fast to CompuServe, which has long been the top stop online for AutoCAD users). You really need both CompuServe access and Web access to be an effective CAD user going forward. Luckily, you can get both from CompuServe.

Use the URLs in the table of AutoCAD resources, earlier in this chapter, as your first stop for Web access to AutoCAD information. Then see Chapter 17 for detailed info.

GO ACAD

CompuServe is the #1 hangout on the Information Superhighway for AutoCAD users. After you're on CompuServe, GO ACAD is the command you use to get to the AutoCAD forum. You can find out more about how to use AutoCAD here than in any one class or book (except this book, of course). And CompuServe is interactive; if you post a question, whether a detailed technical question or a more general one, you're likely to get an answer within a day. (Remember I mention in the Introduction those expert users for whom this book wasn't written? Most of them hang out on CompuServe.)

CompuServe also has dozens of data libraries with information about setting up plotters or networks or configuring your system. Most often you can "browse" on a keyword or topic and find several pieces of information available. Then you can read a brief description of the information and decide whether you want to download the whole piece.

 Introductory CompuServe memberships are included with many hardware and software purchases, and you can purchase a CompuServe starter kit in many stores. You can also order a kit by calling CompuServe's customer service at 800-848-8990. Or download the software from CompuServe's Web page at www.compuserve.com. You can also call this number to find out about membership fees, log-in numbers, and more.

I hate to tell anyone who's trying to get a handle on AutoCAD that they need to add to their troubles, and getting online is not an easy task if you haven't done it before. You need to set up a modem to your computer's serial port and run a phone line to the modem. You can then install your access software and connect to CompuServe. (Whew!) But for AutoCAD users, CompuServe is worth it.

Other online services are great for many different things, and some even offer AutoCAD-specific forums. You can also hook up to forums for PC, printer, plotter, and graphics card support, often from the manufacturers themselves, via many such services. Unless you're already on CompuServe and looking for more online action, however, forget about it; CompuServe is the first and foremost online place for AutoCAD users to be.

CADALYST and CADENCE Magazines

Although AutoCAD is no doubt responsible for billions of dollars in sales of PC hardware and related software, most of the computer press tends to ignore AutoCAD. *CADALYST* and *CADENCE* are the leading magazines devoted exclusively to AutoCAD. Both magazines provide tips and tricks, tutorials, technical columns, and hardware and software reviews, all specifically for CAD users. They have very similar circulation figures, approaching 100,000 each, and somewhat different layouts and editorial focus. Get them both for a year while you're on the AutoCAD learning curve, and then, when renewal time comes, drop the one you like the least.

To subscribe to *CADALYST,* call 800-949-6525. To subscribe to *CADENCE,* call 800-486-4995.

 If you'd rather not subscribe yourself, your copy of AutoCAD may come with a free trial subscription to one or both of the magazines, and you can often find free copies at AutoCAD Training Centers and dealers. Or see whether you can get your company to pay for a subscription. But if you can't get either magazine free, shell out the bucks for at least one; they're worth it.

AutoCAD Resource Guide

This handy little manual includes an overview of the different AutoCAD versions and supporting computer platforms, third-party add-on applications and their developers, peripheral devices, books and training products, a directory of users' groups, and a directory of Autodesk Training Centers (ATCs). The book also contains a CD-ROM version with additional product information, device drivers, and more. To get the AutoCAD Resource Guide, call Autodesk customer information at 800-964-6432.

Local Users' Groups

Local users' groups are the heart and soul of the AutoCAD community. The biggest, most exciting users' group meeting of any sort that I've ever attended is the Silicon Valley AutoCAD Power Users group, in San Jose, California. Find out where the users' group nearest you meets and go to a few meetings. Call Autodesk at 800-964-6432 or look in the AutoCAD Resource Guide to locate the group nearest you.

AUGI

No, "AUGI" isn't what you yell after a basketball hits you in the wrong spot. The Autodesk Users' Group International is administered by Autodesk, but it's a real users' group made up of real users, dealers, and other concerned individuals. AUGI sponsors an annual learning conference (Autodesk University), a newsletter, software, and more. To join, see their Web site at www.augi.com or call the User Group Hotline at 415-507-6565. You can also find information about how to join AUGI on the AutoCAD CD-ROM in the Bonus folder; look for the text file AUGI.

AutoCAD Training Centers

AutoCAD Training Centers, or ATCs, are the only authorized deliverers of AutoCAD training. Courses are expensive, so try to figure out the basics on your own and then take courses at the local ATC only to fill in gaps where you need more knowledge. Check the AutoCAD Resource Guide, call Autodesk, or check out the Autodesk home page on the Web for the number of the ATC nearest you.

Autodesk

In my experience, Autodesk is much more accessible than most big companies. Their main numbers are 415-507-6000 or 800-964-6432. Call and tell them what you're looking for; you're pretty likely to reach a friendly and helpful reception person who connects you to another friendly and helpful person who gives you the information you need or tells you where to find it.

The big exception to Autodesk's accessibility is technical support. AutoCAD depends on its dealers to provide technical support, so don't call Autodesk with technical questions.

Your Dealer

The first and foremost line of support for AutoCAD users is the dealer from whom you bought AutoCAD. Dealer support policies and areas of expertise differ, but the dealer is your starting point for AutoCAD support and information.

If you're using AutoCAD within a multiuser, networked setup, though, find out whether someone in your company has been designated as the first line of defense for technical support and other information. Contact that person first with your questions.

Plus One: Bonus Files

Number 11 in your list of ten great AutoCAD resources is the set of Bonus files on the AutoCAD CD-ROM. You can have literally hours of fun exploring the tools, fonts, and utilities in the Bonus folder. And you can have the AutoCAD installer include them in your AutoCAD Release 14 setup; you get a Bonus menu in AutoCAD, and several additional toolbars become available for using Bonus tools. See Chapter 2 for more information.

Even if you install the bonus routines as part of AutoCAD Release 14, some stuff still lives on the AutoCAD CD-ROM and doesn't make it to your hard disk. This stuff includes Asian fonts and sample drawings, including classic drawings used as example files in earlier versions of AutoCAD. Try installing and using the Bonus files, and explore the remaining stuff that is only on the CD-ROM; it can increase both your productivity and your knowledge of how AutoCAD really works.

Chapter 17

Ten Ways to Use the Web with AutoCAD

· ·

· ·

*T*he World Wide Web is the biggest thing to hit computing since possibly the PC itself. AutoCAD Release 14 includes enough Web features to let you go as far as you'd like in integrating the Web into your daily work.

Get on the Web

The World Wide Web is the hottest topic in computing, but that doesn't mean that everyone is on the Web yet. If you aren't yet on the World Wide Web, now is the time to "get wired"; Release 14 is very Web-aware, and you need Internet and Web access to get key information that is increasingly available only from the Web. Because this level of Internet access is a new thing for AutoCAD, this whole Part of Tens chapter is Release 14-specific.

The easiest way to get started with the Internet is by joining CompuServe (see Chapter 16 for details and contact information). CompuServe offers relatively fast and highly reliable connections. Though you have to pay for your CompuServe access by the hour, unlike other providers who charge a flat rate per month, CompuServe is worth the money, both for the reliability of connections and the great support you can get online. CompuServe and its users are a rich source of help and insights for getting connected and for using the Web well. If you run up a big access bill, consider moving to a flat-rate provider after you know your way around on your own.

The "browser wars" between Microsoft and Netscape are a big topic of conversation, right up there with the Web itself. However, as an AutoCAD user, you probably need to choose the latest version of Internet Explorer. Autodesk is committed to working with Microsoft and with Internet Explorer-friendly technologies, such as Visual Basic; CompuServe offers Internet Explorer as the browser bundled in the CompuServe access software package. That means that most of your AutoCAD-using and CompuServe-using colleagues are using, and programming for, Internet Explorer. Though Netscape makes a great browser suite, and I hope that they can replace Apple as the biggest thorn in Microsoft's side for the next decade or more, you (as an AutoCAD user) are best off with Internet Explorer.

If you want to find out the basics, check out *The Internet For Dummies,* 4th Edition (by John R. Levine, Carol Baroudi, and Margaret Levine Young), from IDG Books Worldwide, Inc. But if you're in a hurry, just get that CompuServe access kit and get started.

Get the Right System

Any computer system capable of running AutoCAD Release 14 is capable of running Web access software; as a Release 14 user, you have the right kind of computer (100 MHz Pentium or better), the right amount of RAM (32MB or more), the right amount of hard disk space free for swap and cache files (50MB or more), and the right-size screen (800 x 600 resolution or better).

However, if you want to run a Web browser and AutoCAD *at the same time,* which of course you do want to do, the price of admission goes up a bit. The main problems are free RAM and screen space. Your Web browser (see the next suggestion) is really going to want at least 8MB of RAM for itself while loading graphics-rich pages; to prevent a great deal of swapping, then, you need at least 8MB more RAM free than AutoCAD is using. Because RAM is cheaper in 32MB chunks, look at a 64MB system to accommodate simultaneous AutoCAD use and Web surfing.

The other Web-specific concern is your modem. I strongly recommend a 56K or X2 modem, the fastest regular modems now available. 56K and X2 are tradenames for two different kinds of new modems that run at up to 53 Kbps, almost double what a 28.8 Kbps modem offers, but you and your service provider have to use the same kind of modem or you don't get the speed increase. Check with your service provider to see which way they're leaning at the time you read this book.

I don't recommend ISDN or other fast access methods for most individual users. (The exception is business users working at home who need fast access to the company network; if this is you, see your company's information systems people for more info.) ISDN is expensive, buggy, and at best "only" twice as fast as the new regular modems. Usually, you don't see the full speed increase, because crowding on the Internet or bottlenecks at the Web server keep you from getting full speed from your access method. Start with a fast regular modem and consider ISDN or other technologies — and, shameless plug, the IDG Books publication *ISDN For Dummies* by David Angell — if your Web-surfing habit, and your Web knowledge, really do turn out to be that much greater than most people's.

Surf Defensively

A quick but vital tip: Save your drawings before you start running any Internet access program or Web browser, including CompuServe. The race between Microsoft and Netscape to lead Web browser development, and the simultaneous race among online services to provide the latest and greatest features, mean that plenty of buggy and crash-prone software is getting sent out there right now. So save early and often if you're going to be running AutoCAD and any kind of Internet connection at the same time.

Autodesk and others are encouraging you to use the Internet as a kind of slow but extremely large hard drive, so that your drawings could include xrefs, for example, from an intranet or the open Internet. But for intranets, be careful: If your drawing ever goes outside the network of computers connected to your company's servers, the xref is lost. And as for the open Internet, I think that the Net itself, as well as the browser and other connection software, is too unreliable to count on for production work. Do use the Internet for exchanging drawings and other information; don't use it in a way that it's not ready for by including Internet-based data in production drawings.

Open Your Web Browser from AutoCAD

With Release 14, AutoCAD now includes a button for opening your browser from within AutoCAD. Although doing so is something of a stupid pet trick — there's no reason you can't take an extra step and launch your browser from Windows — it does make things a little easier and underscores Autodesk's desire to make Web access seamless from within its programs.

The first time you click on the Launch Web Browser button, the button with the globe icon located in the middle of the standard toolbar, it either finds the browser identified in your system registry or asks you to locate the browser you want to use. Identify the browser on your hard disk, and that's it. From now on, you can quickly launch your browser from within AutoCAD. Save early and often, and have fun — but don't let all those fun sites out there stop you from getting your work done.

If AutoCAD can't find what it needs when you click on the Launch Web Browser button, it may crash. If this happens, try launching your Web browser first and then starting AutoCAD and clicking the Launch Web Browser button. And always save your drawings frequently.

Put URLs in Your Drawings

You can put URLs in your AutoCAD drawings. You usually do so as a preparatory step before putting your drawing on the Web. Just use the Release 14 Internet Utilities toolbar to create and manage the Web links, which are stored on a separate layer from the rest of your drawing. (Storing them on a separate layer makes turning them on and off as needed easy, without messing up anything else.) The last command on the Internet Utilities toolbar, INETHLP, brings up online help for Release 14's Internet-related capabilities.

To turn the Internet Utilities toolbar on and off takes an extra step compared to other toolbars. Bring up the Toolbars dialog box, either by typing **TOOLBAR** at the command line or by choosing View⊃Toolbar from the menus. You won't see the Internet Utilities toolbar in the scrolling list of toolbars just yet, though. Go down to the Menu Group area and choose inet from the scrolling list. Then the Internet Utilities toolbar will appear in the toolbar list. Use the check box next to it to turn the toolbar on and off.

I encourage you to put URLs in drawings that are published on the Internet or an intranet and are viewed through a Web browser and the WHIP! plug-in, described later in this chapter. I don't encourage you to put URLs in ordinary drawings that are viewed and modified by using AutoCAD. For example, some people will no doubt put the Web address of a part's manufacturer into a drawing that includes that part, but I discourage this practice. Why? It's still early in this Web thing. Not everyone who uses your drawing is likely to have Web access, and even those who do may have problems with the wait for a Web browser to start up, the possibility of the browser crashing, the problem of knowing exactly what on the Web you intend for them to see, and so on.

Share AutoCAD Drawings on the Web

You can share your AutoCAD drawings on an intranet or the open Internet. Start by putting one or two URLs into a drawing; you probably want to test this capability even if you don't really need it yet. Then use the File⇨Save As command to save your file as a Drawing Web Format, or DWF, file.

Then you can include the DWF file in your Web page, just as you would any other Web graphic. Any Websurfer with the WHIP! plug-in installed is able to view it.

However, that's the problem: Only a minority of Web users are going to have the WHIP! plug-in installed. Only a few of the most popular plug-ins have been installed by more than a tiny percentage of Web users. However, a pretty good percentage of AutoCAD users may well take the plunge. If you do publish a DWF file on the Web, include detailed instructions on how the user can get and install the WHIP! plug-in (see the section "Get AutoCAD Information on the Web," later in this chapter, for the URL).

Install the WHIP! ActiveX Control

To see AutoCAD DWF files from within your browser, you need the WHIP! plug-in (for Netscape Navigator) or ActiveX control (for Microsoft Internet Explorer). If you follow my recommendation in Chapter 16 to use Internet Explorer, you're in luck; the needed version of the ActiveX control is automatically downloaded to and installed on your machine the first time you access a page with a DWF file in it. From then on, the ActiveX control lives on your machine and executes whenever needed.

Convert Your Files to VRML

Instead of saving your files to the Web in DWF format, you can convert your AutoCAD files to VRML, or Virtual Reality Modeling Language. (If you're unfamiliar with VRML, see Jake Richter's excellent column on VRML and

AutoCAD, originally published in *CADALYST,* at `www.richterscale.org`.)
VRML plug-ins and browsers are much more popular than the WHIP! plug-in,
so a graphic you publish in VRML format is likely to be viewable by a much
wider range of people. (I know that Internet Explorer auto-downloads the
needed ActiveX controls, but Netscape Navigator doesn't, and it's still used
by more people.) At this writing, AutoCAD doesn't include the capability to
save a file in VRML format. Instead, you have to save your drawing as a DXF
file and then find a 3D VRML editor that imports DXF files. 3D Studio MAX
from Autodesk is one editor with this capability, but at $3,495, it's an expen-
sive option. By the time this book appears in print, a wide range of such
editors should be available.

Another option is to use third-party tools that convert DXF or even DWG
files directly to VRML. The first such tool I've heard of is VRMLout from CAD
Studio in the Czech Republic, a $150 program that converts many (but not
all) AutoCAD objects to VRML equivalents. (Thanks to Peter Sheerin of
CADENCE magazine for the pointer.) To find out more, visit CAD Studio's
Web address, given in the next section. Look for other tools from other
companies, and eventually expect Autodesk to knuckle under and build
VRML output capability into AutoCAD.

Get AutoCAD Information on the Web

The Web is a great source for information about AutoCAD, almost as good as
CompuServe and getting better every day. Here are a few URLs, in addition
to those in Chapter 16, to get you started:

- `www.vcampus.com` The Autodesk Virtual Campus, with courses,
  products, and services for different kinds of CAD users.

- `www.autodesk.com/products/acadr14/features/whiteppr.htm`
  Release 14 white papers that give a lot of details about the new
  features in Release 14.

- `www.autodesk.com/products/autocad/whip/whip.htm` Download
  the WHIP! plug-in.

- `www.autodesk.com/products/autocad/whip/whpsites.htm` (Notice that's "whpsites," not "whipsites," as you may expect.) See sites
  that use the WHIP! plug-in.

- `www.public.iastate.edu/~sbilling/ada.html` Americans with
  Disabilities Act info for architectural work.

- `www.power.org/oldstuff/home.html` The Silicon Valley AutoCAD
  Power User's Web site with AutoCAD resources, including SVAPU's
  latest newsletters.

✔ www.wit.com The Wentworth Institute of Technology is an Autodesk Training Center whose site includes an online skills test and online training courses.

✔ www.cadstudio.cz/indexuk.htm CAD Studio's Web site, with information about its VRMLout product and more.

Be forewarned that each of these links, plus the ones in Chapter 16, are additionally linked to dozens or hundreds of other relevant and not-so-relevant Web sites. Set aside a few hours for a couple of Web-surfing sessions, and find out how to create bookmarks in your browser to save pointers to your favorite sites. Your efforts will be well rewarded by quick access to information vital to your work.

Chat about AutoCAD on the Web (Autodesk's Site)

At the Autodesk Web site (www.autodesk.com), you can find pointers to Web-based online chat sessions about AutoCAD Release 14 and other topics. If you don't have CompuServe but want to chat about AutoCAD, this is the place! You may feel a touch inhibited, knowing that Autodesk not only reads the forums but runs them, but don't worry; Autodesk just uses these forums as input to help create better versions of AutoCAD, and they really won't "forget" to send you your next AutoCAD upgrade on time if you criticize them too much.

Create Your Own Web Pages

The biggest single reason for the Web's popularity is that anyone, and I do mean anyone, can put a Web page or a Web site on it. Here comes some self-serving self-promotion: As the coauthor of *Creating Web Pages For Dummies,* 2nd Edition, I've discovered many free and easy ways to get a Web site up and running on the Web. If you want to try the most popular self-publishing sites on the Web on your own, go to www.geocities.com and follow the instructions; you can probably get a simple, free Web site up and running within 24 hours. For detailed instructions and descriptions of the best Web publishing options and tools, buy the book!

Part VI
Appendixes

The 5th Wave — By Rich Tennant

"That reminds me – I installed AutoCAD Release 14 on my 386 last week."

In this part . . .

In your body, an appendix is something that's unnecessary at best and hazardous to your health at worst. The appendixes in this book, however, are meant to be more helpful — and certainly less harmful — than that other kind. Installation is one of the trickiest parts of using AutoCAD; if you install AutoCAD yourself, you're going to need a few of the tips you find in Appendix A before you get started. You find, too, as you get into the program, that AutoCAD has a vocabulary all its own; with Release 14, you'll find that the needed terminology includes World Wide Web terms. The glossary in Appendix C should help you cross the bridge from English to the language of CAD. And, of course, as you soon discover, getting your drawing to print at just the right size and scale is tricky; ah, but the tables in Appendix B make setting everything up for optimal printing . . . well, a snap.

Appendix A
AutoCAD Installation Survival Tactics

W ith Release 14, installing AutoCAD has gotten much easier. Because Release 14 only works on 32-bit versions of Windows (Windows 95 and Windows NT), which have much better memory management and device-handling capabilities than previous versions of Windows, many of the problems found in earlier releases of AutoCAD are gone.

The problems that do come up tend to be "legacy" problems involving old device drivers. For example, to get raster image support, you need an ADI 4.3 driver that supports raster images. (ADI 4.3 print drivers that don't support raster images have "NR" at the end of their names.)

Following are a few suggestions for making the AutoCAD installation process easier. They supplement the instructions in the AutoCAD Installation Guide and the information that you're likely to find from other sources. Paying attention to these suggestions before installing — or, if you're having problems, re-installing — AutoCAD can make your life easier.

If you are upgrading from an earlier release of AutoCAD and want to hear from some experts about how to avoid problems, check out the "Release 14 Upgrade Guide" by a couple of AutoCAD dealers and AutoCAD savant Mark Middlebrook, technical editor of this book. You can find the Release 14 Upgrade Guide at:

    http://www.mcneel.com/whatsnew.html

Buy a New Machine

Whoa! Did he just say *buy a new machine?* Is this some kind of joke?

Well, no. With a new machine, you avoid problems such as having old device drivers hanging around and getting loaded in place of the new ones. A new machine also gets you a new period of technical support and the latest and greatest configurations of hardware and software. Though a new machine doesn't guarantee success — far from it — it does eliminate some possible sources of grief, and it gives you someone to call on if you do have problems.

(Back Up and Then) Reformat Your Hard Disk

If you don't want to buy a whole new computer, you can still avoid problems by backing up your hard disk, reformatting it, and then reinstalling all your software. Doing so makes the system more of a "known quantity" to you, helps eliminate problems, and helps make you better able to fix any problems that do occur.

Get a Dealer to Do It

One of the main functions in the life of an AutoCAD dealer is to install the software for you. A dealer may charge you a bit, but the cost is probably less than your time is worth. If you do try doing the installation yourself and then run into problems, call a dealer before things get too bad. You can all-too-easily start deleting files to get more disk space or trying to reconfigure — and before you know it, you're in a real jam. So don't be afraid to call; the sanity you save may be your own.

Back Up Vital Files

If you're the type of person who backs up your system regularly, good for you! Do it again before you install AutoCAD. Now! If not, at least back up the key data files that you're working on. That way, if you have problems with installation, you can still take your current project to another machine and continue working until the problems are resolved.

Get It All Together

Find and install all the latest upgrades and updates to your system before you start the AutoCAD installation. That means checking to see whether new drivers are available for your hardware, as well as getting upgrades to your third-party applications and new versions of your utilities. Get all these pieces together and, if possible, get them installed and working before attempting the AutoCAD installation. The odds of quick success increase greatly if you do.

Take Your Time

Set aside a solid chunk of time to perform an AutoCAD installation or upgrade; half a day is a good starting point. Don't try to install the program if you have a deadline or are otherwise in a hurry. Install AutoCAD, run it, and make sure that it works. Then install that new Release 14-specific add-on program and try it out. If you do run into a problem, you're more likely to solve it (and less likely to compound it) if you have some time set aside to think things through, call technical support, or do whatever else is needed. Everyone depends on computers so much these days that you don't want yours to be unusable; so set aside the time to do the job correctly now and avoid problems later.

Appendix B

Paper Size and Scale

● ●

*T*he standard paper sizes are called A, B, C, D, and E. The measurements of the sizes for ANSI (American National Standards Institute) standards are described in the following list:

- ✔ *A* = 8 $\frac{1}{2}$ x 11". Standard letter size in the U.S.
- ✔ *B* = 11 x 17". Double the length of *A* paper.
- ✔ *C* = 17 x 22". Double the length and width of *A* paper.
- ✔ *D* = 22 x 34". Double the length and width of *B* paper.
- ✔ *E* = 34 x 44". Double the length and width of *C* paper.

Figure B-1 shows how the various standard paper sizes relate to one another.

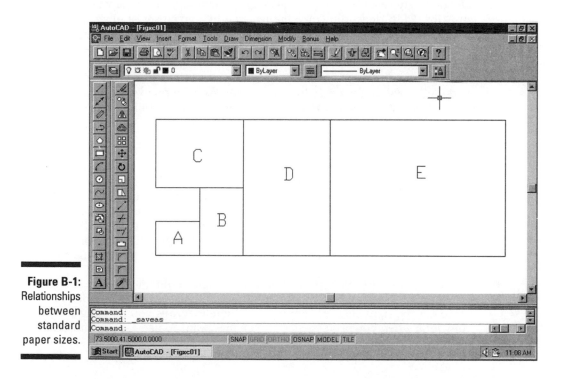

Figure B-1: Relationships between standard paper sizes.

Use the size relationships among the various paper sizes to your advantage in doing small check prints of large drawings. You can, for example, perform a check print with correct proportions and layout for either *C* or *E* paper on plain old letter-sized *A* paper on a standard laser printer. (Your check print, of course, lacks the color and detail that appears on the full-sized plot.)

For a *C* final plot, your *A* check print has measurements half the size of the final; for an *E* plot, the *A* check print has measurements a quarter the size of the final version. (But don't do a check print to take down to the bank and try to cash!)

The paper size and the real-world size of the objects you want to represent in your drawing are the determining factors in setting up the parameters for your drawing. Another limitation is the use of certain standard drawing scales. You generally can't pick an unusual drawing scale such as $^3/_{16}" = 1'$ just because it makes the drawing fit on the paper nicely; you generally must use a 1 in the drawing scale's numerator, or upper part of the fraction, and an even multiple of two in the drawing scale denominator, or lower part of the fraction. Examples of drawing scales that fit these rules are $^1/_2"$, $^1/_4"$, $^1/_8"$, $^1/_{16}"$, $^1/_{32}"$, $^1/_{64}"$, and so on to 1'. (Hope this stuff doesn't become "2" confusing.) After you know the real-world sizes of the objects, the paper size, and the drawing scale, you can choose the limits you want to use.

Of course, in real life, you may have some flexibility in the paper size and drawing scale, depending on what lets you fit a given set of objects conveniently. So knowing all the possibilities is very helpful, and that's what the tables in this chapter are for.

The tables show you most of the combinations of paper size, drawing scale, and limits that you're likely to want to use. You can review the tables and discover what works for your drawing. Table B-1 is for units in feet and inches; Table B-2 is for any unit of measurement that works by powers of ten.

In addition to columns for paper size, drawing scale, and limits, the tables include columns for grid distance, snap distance, and linetype and dimension scale. These columns can help you set up your drawing so that everything works together. The grid distance and snap distance aren't too important, because you can easily change them as your needs change during the drawing process. But linetype and dimension scale do matter. Getting these settings correct from the start can greatly ease the process of printing a usable drawing. Use the values listed in these tables as a handy guide.

The number in the Linetype and Dimension Scale column is the *drawing scale factor;* the number that you multiply the left side of the drawing scale by to get the right side. Depending on which linetypes you're using and how they look when you print them out, you may want to use a value that's half the drawing scale factor for linetypes.

Table B-1   Picking Limits — Architectural Units, Horizontal Orientation

Paper Size	Drawing Scale	Limits	Grid	Snap	Linetype & Dimension Scale
8¹/₂ x 11"	¹/₆₄" = 1'	704 x 544'	100'	10'	768
8¹/₂ x 11"	¹/₃₂" = 1'	352 x 272'	10'	10'	384
8¹/₂ x 11"	¹/₁₆" = 1'	176 x 136'	10'	10'	192
8¹/₂ x 11"	¹/₈" = 1'	88 x 68'	10'	10'	96
8¹/₂ x 11"	¹/₄" = 1'	44 x 34'	4'	1'	48
8¹/₂ x 11"	¹/₂" = 1'	22 x 17'	2'	1'	24
8¹/₂ x 11"	1" = 1'	11 x 8¹/₂'	1'	6"	12
11 x 17"	¹/₆₄" = 1'	704 x 1088'	100'	100'	768
11 x 17"	¹/₃₂" = 1'	352 x 544'	100'	10'	384
11 x 17"	¹/₁₆" = 1'	176 x 272'	10'	10'	192
11 x 17"	¹/₈" = 1'	88 x 136'	10'	10'	96
11 x 17"	¹/₄" = 1'	44 x 68'	10'	1'	48
11 x 17"	¹/₂" = 1'	22 x 34'	2'	1'	24
11 x 17"	1" = 1'	11 x 17'	1'	6"	12
17 x 22"	¹/₆₄" = 1'	1408 x 1088'	100'	100'	768
17 x 22"	¹/₃₂" = 1'	704 x 544'	100'	10'	384
17 x 22"	¹/₁₆" = 1'	352 x 272'	10'	10'	192
17 x 22"	¹/₈" = 1'	176 x 136'	10'	10'	96
17 x 22"	¹/₄" = 1'	88 x 68'	10'	1'	48
17 x 22"	¹/₂" = 1'	44 x 34'	10'	1'	24
17 x 22"	1" = 1'	22 x 17'	1'	1'	12
22 x 34"	¹/₆₄" = 1'	1408 x 2176'	100'	100'	768
22 x 34"	¹/₃₂" = 1'	704 x 1088'	100'	100'	384
22 x 34"	¹/₁₆" = 1'	352 x 544'	100'	10'	192
22 x 34"	¹/₈" = 1'	176 x 272'	10'	10'	96
22 x 34"	¹/₄" = 1'	88 x 136'	10'	1'	48
22 x 34"	¹/₂" = 1'	44 x 68'	10'	1'	24
22 x 34"	1" = 1'	22 x 34'	1'	1'	12
34 x 44"	¹/₆₄" = 1'	2816 x 2176'	100'	100'	768
34 x 44"	¹/₃₂" = 1'	1408 x 1088'	100'	100'	384
34 x 44"	¹/₁₆" = 1'	704 x 544'	100'	10'	192
34 x 44"	¹/₈" = 1'	352 x 272'	10'	10'	96
34 x 44"	¹/₄" = 1'	176 x 136'	10'	10'	48
34 x 44"	¹/₂" = 1'	88 x 68'	10'	1'	24
34 x 44"	1" = 1'	44 x 34'	10'	1'	12

Table B-2	Picking Limits — Mechanical and Other Units, Horizontal Orientation				
Paper Size	Drawing Scale	Limits	Grid	Snap	Linetype & Dimension Scale
8^1/$_2$ x 11"	^{1}/$_{1000}$ = 1	11000 x 8500	1000	100	1000
8^1/$_2$ x 11"	^{1}/$_{500}$ = 1	5500 x 4250	100	100	500
8^1/$_2$ x 11"	^{1}/$_{100}$ = 1	1100 x 850	100	100	100
8^1/$_2$ x 11"	^{1}/$_{50}$ = 1	550 x 425	10	10	50
8^1/$_2$ x 11"	^{1}/$_{10}$ = 1	110 x 85	10	10	10
8^1/$_2$ x 11"	^{1}/$_5$ = 1	55 x 42.5	10	1	5
11 x 17"	^{1}/$_{1000}$ = 1	17000 x 11000	1000	1000	1000
11 x 17"	^{1}/$_{500}$ = 1	8500 x 5500	1000	100	500
11 x 17"	^{1}/$_{100}$ = 1	1700 x 1100	100	100	100
11 x 17"	^{1}/$_{50}$ = 1	850 x 550	100	10	50
11 x 17"	^{1}/$_{10}$ = 1	170 x 110	10	10	10
11 x 17"	^{1}/$_5$ = 1	85 x 55	10	10	5
17 x 22"	^{1}/$_{1000}$ = 1	22000 x 17000	1000	100	1000
17 x 22"	^{1}/$_{500}$ = 1	11000 x 8500	1000	100	500
17 x 22"	^{1}/$_{100}$ = 1	2200 x 1700	100	100	100
17 x 22"	^{1}/$_{50}$ = 1	1100 x 850	100	10	50
17 x 22"	^{1}/$_{10}$ = 1	220 x 170	10	10	10
17 x 22"	^{1}/$_5$ = 1	110 x 85	10	1	5
22 x 34"	^{1}/$_{1000}$ = 1	34000 x 22000	1000	1000	1000
22 x 34"	^{1}/$_{500}$ = 1	17000 x 11000	1000	1000	500
22 x 34"	^{1}/$_{100}$ = 1	3400 x 2200	100	100	100
22 x 34"	^{1}/$_{50}$ = 1	1700 x 1100	100	10	50
22 x 34"	^{1}/$_{10}$ = 1	340 x 220	10	10	10
22 x 34"	^{1}/$_5$ = 1	170 x 110	10	10	5
34 x 44"	^{1}/$_{1000}$ = 1	44000 x 34000	1000	1000	1000
34 x 44"	^{1}/$_{500}$ = 1	22000 x 17000	1000	1000	500
34 x 44"	^{1}/$_{100}$ = 1	4400 x 3400	100	100	100
34 x 44"	^{1}/$_{50}$ = 1	2200 x 1700	100	100	50
34 x 44"	^{1}/$_{10}$ = 1	440 x 340	100	10	10
34 x 44"	^{1}/$_5$ = 1	220 x 170	10	10	5

Appendix C
Glossary of AutoCAD Terms

● ●

*T*he definitions that appear in this appendix are mine only; they are informal and describe the term in the way that this book uses it. For more complete and general definitions, see the AutoCAD online or printed documentation.

aerial view: A separate window that displays an aerial view of your drawing. As you pan and zoom within the Aerial View window, the main drawing area also pans and zooms.

Angle 0 Direction: Specifies the direction that AutoCAD regards as 0 degrees within a 360-degree circle. The Angle 0 Direction is measured relative to the following coordinate system: north is up, south is down, west is left, and east is right. So an Angle 0 Direction of 90 means that an angle of 0 degrees will point straight up on the sheet (north) instead of to the right (east).

ANSI: American National Standards Institute, a leading standards body.

AUGI: Autodesk User Group International, the worldwide user group for AutoCAD and other programs from Autodesk.

AutoLISP: A programming language for AutoCAD. AutoLISP is an AutoCAD-specific version of LISP, a computer language used mostly in artificial intelligence programming.

AutoSnap: A new feature in Release 14 that makes connecting objects to specific spots on other objects — such as the endpoint of a line or the center of a circle — much easier.

batch plotting: The capability, new in AutoCAD Release 14, to plot several drawings at once rather than having to send each plot to the printer or plotter separately.

blips: Little marks that show spots you've "picked" on-screen with the cursor. Turn the BLIPMODE system variable ON if you want the screen to show blips, OFF if you want to get rid of them.

bounding rectangle, bounding window: A rectangle surrounding objects. When you select objects with a bounding window, AutoCAD includes only objects that are fully enclosed within the window. ***See also*** *crossing window.*

CAD: Computer-Aided Design. Also known as CADD, or Computer-Aided Design and Drafting. The term CAD is now used to describe activities that include computer-aided design, computer-aided drafting, or both.

chamfer: A straight line that connects two other lines short of the point where they would otherwise intersect.

command line: A specific area of the AutoCAD screen, usually at the bottom, in which you enter commands and options. Many menu choices in AutoCAD also cause commands to appear on the command line.

command-first editing: Modifying the current drawing by entering a command and then selecting the objects that the command affects. The opposite of *selection-first editing.* See also *Noun/Verb Selection.*

coordinate entry: Locating a point in the drawing area by entering numbers on the command line that represent the point's cursor coordinates. ***See also*** *cursor coordinates.*

crossing window: A selection window that includes objects that are enclosed within it or that cross the window's boundaries. ***See also*** *bounding window.*

cursor coordinates: The location of the cursor as represented by its horizontal, or *X,* coordinate and its vertical, or *Y,* coordinate.

dialog box: A set of related options that are displayed on-screen in a rectangular window, or box, for you to specify or change.

digitizer: A drawing tablet. The name comes from the fact that the tablet converts lines and curves that are entered by drawing, into a series of numbers (or digits).

dimension: A set of drawn objects including lines, numbers, and additional symbols and text to indicate the distance between two points.

dimension line: The line that shows the extent of a dimension.

dimension scale factor: The number by which the size of the text and arrowheads in a dimension should be scaled in order for them to appear correctly in the final printout of a drawing.

dimension text: The text that denotes the length of a dimension.

direct manipulation: Entering or modifying data by using the mouse to move or change an on-screen representation. Dragging a file icon into a trash can icon to discard it, for example, is direct manipulation.

displacement: Fancy word for the X and Y distance between two points.

display list: A set of directions that AutoCAD uses for displaying the current open drawing and viewport on-screen.

docked: Embedded in the program's interface. A docked toolbar is a toolbar that has been dragged to any edge of the screen until its appearance changes. A docked toolbar has no title, and the area around the title has no color, so it takes up less space. *See also* toolbar.

donut: Two concentric circles with the space between them filled in so that you can enter and edit as a single object (the favorite concentric-circle pastry of police officers).

Draw toolbar: A toolbar that enables you to start commonly used drawing commands quickly. Usually found on the far left side of the drawing area.

drawing area: The part of the AutoCAD screen that you can actually draw on. It's an all-too-small area wedged between the menus, toolbars, and command line.

end point: A point at which a line or other non-closed object has only one other point on the object adjacent to it.

extension line: In dimensioning, a line connecting one end of the dimension line to one of the objects that determines the size of the dimension.

fill: The pattern used in filling (placing a pattern in the interior of an object). See also *hatch, boundary hatch, associative boundary hatch*.

floating toolbars: Floating toolbars are groups of icons that you can drag around on-screen and that always appear — or float — over the drawing. Each icon represents an AutoCAD command.

floating-point numbers: Numbers that can indicate an extremely wide range of mathematical values. Floating-point numbers take longer to process than integer numbers and may take up more storage space in the computer.

flyout: A group of icons that appears, or "flies out," after you click an icon. The flyout expands your choices from one icon to a choice among several icons.

freehand sketch: An object entered as a smooth series of pen strokes. AutoCAD converts it into a polyline made up of relatively short line segments.

geometry: The drawn objects that make up a drawing, not including additional elements such as dimensions and text.

grid interval: The distance between grid points. *See also grid, grid mode.*

grid, grid mode: A grid is a visible array of dots used to indicate distances on-screen. The grid is intended to serve as a kind of flexible graph paper in which the user can, at any time, redefine the size of the grid.

grip editing: Editing an object by dragging one of the "handles," or grips, that appear on an object after you select it. *See also grips — hot, warm, cold.*

grips — hot, warm, cold: A hot grip is the grip that you can directly manipulate; it appears on-screen in red. A warm grip is any other grip on a currently selected object. A cold grip is a grip on an unselected object.

Internet: A worldwide computer network that connects (via modem) universities, government bodies, and individuals.

ISO: International Standards Organization, a leading standards body.

hatch, boundary hatch, associative boundary hatch: A hatch is a pattern placed in the interior of an area enclosed by objects. A boundary hatch is a hatch that is begun by calculating the boundary from among the objects surrounding an empty space. An associative boundary hatch is a hatch that updates automatically if one or more of the objects that make up its boundary is modified.

layer: A group of objects that are associated for purposes of displaying and updating.

leader: A pointer that connects a dimension or note to an object.

lightweight polylines: A new way of storing polylines within AutoCAD that describes a polyline as a string of vertices rather than as a group of separate lines. Lightweight polylines take up less storage space than the previous type of polyline, reducing the size of some drawings in Release 14.

linetype: The pattern of dashes and dots used to draw a line.

menu bar: The list of menu names displayed across the top of the AutoCAD screen.

model space: The mode in which most AutoCAD work takes place; where you create and edit objects. ***See also*** *paper space.*

Modify toolbar: A toolbar that enables you to start commonly used editing commands quickly. Usually found on the left side of the drawing area, just inside the Draw toolbar.

multiline: A line that displays and prints as two or more parallel lines; you create and edit a multiline in the same way as a regular line.

Noun/Verb Selection: An option that runs most commands on an existing selection. With Noun/Verb Selection turned off, the commands that you enter ignore any existing selection, and you must select one or more objects after entering the command.

object: A single item that you can select and edit separately. In previous versions of AutoCAD, objects were called *entities.*

Object Grouping: An option that enables you to place objects into named groups. You can then use the group name for quickly selecting the objects in the group.

Object Properties toolbar: A toolbar that enables you to view and specify object properties, such as layer and linetype, with little or no keyboard entry.

object snap: Makes certain points on an object act like magnets so that clicking near a point is the same as clicking the point itself.

ortho, ortho mode: A setting that forces lines to be drawn horizontally or vertically only.

pan: Panning is moving the drawing around so that a different part of the drawing appears on-screen in the current viewport.

paper space: A different mode for working with your drawing that enables you to change the view of a drawing, but not what's in the drawing itself. Paper space is best used to create a printout that combines multiple views of the same object. ***See also*** *model space.*

polygon: What your 3-year-old says when your parrot dies. (Groan!) Seriously, any closed shape made up of three or more line segments. Triangles, rectangles, pentagons, hexagons, and other multisided shapes are examples of polygons.

polyline: A single object made up of multiple line or arc segments.

Press and Drag: Specifies that you can create a selection rectangle by pressing the right mouse button at one point, holding the button down while moving the mouse, and then releasing the button at a second point. (Moving the mouse with the button held down is called dragging.)

RAM: Random-Access Memory. The memory that your computer can access quickly and use as a "scratch pad" while working. Typical computers sold today have 16MB (MB is for *megabytes,* or million characters) of RAM. AutoCAD Release 14 requires 32MB of RAM.

raster image: An image made up of a bunch of dots, as opposed to the typical CAD *vector* image, which is made up of a bunch of lines. A scanned photograph is an example of a raster image.

real-time pan and zoom: The capability, added to the ZOOM command in Release 14, to pan and zoom smoothly by dragging the mouse.

redraw: Clears the screen and redraws the drawing by using the current display list. ***See also*** *display list.*

regeneration (REGEN): Clears the screen and uses the drawing database to create a new display list and then redraws the drawing with the new display list. A *regen,* as it is referred to, can take from several seconds on simple drawings to many minutes on complex drawings.

SCSI: Small Computer System Interface. Affectionately known as "scuzzy," a method for connecting peripheral devices, such as hard disks and tape drives, to the computer. SCSI is relatively fast and enables several devices to be connected to a single port by plugging each new device into the previously connected one.

selection set: A set, or group, of objects that you have selected.

selection settings: Options that affect how selections are made and treated, such as Press and Drag and Noun/Verb Selection.

selection window: A window used to create a selection. Bounding windows and crossing windows are the types of windows used to create a selection. ***See also*** *bounding window* and *crossing window.*

selection-first editing: Editing by first creating a selection and then entering a command that affects the selected objects. Opposite of *command-first editing.*

side-screen menu: A menu of options that appears on-screen, usually in a strip down the right side of the screen.

snap grid: If snap mode is on, the snap grid is the array of imaginary points that the cursor jumps to, based on the *snap interval.*

snap interval: The distance between snap points if snap mode is on.

snap, snap mode: A mode that causes the cursor to be attracted to points on-screen that are a specified distance apart.

solid fill: Your trustworthy friend Philip. Also, a new type of hatch pattern in Release 14 that fills an area with a color.

spline: A flexible type of curve that has a shape defined by control points.

Standard toolbar: A toolbar with icons for commonly used functions such as opening a file. Usually found near the top of the screen, between the menu bar and the Object Properties toolbar.

Start Up dialog box: The dialog box that appears when you start a new AutoCAD session by double-clicking on the AutoCAD icon, rather than by double-clicking on a drawing. The Start Up dialog box gives you several choices for creating a drawing, including using a wizard to help with setup or creating a drawing from a template.

status bar: A "toolbar," always positioned at the bottom of the screen, that displays information about the current AutoCAD session, such as the current coordinates of the cursor and whether ortho mode is in effect. You can also change some options (such as model space versus paper space) at the status bar.

system variable: A setting that controls the way that a particular aspect of AutoCAD works. You can change system variables from the command line by using the SETVAR command.

tangent: An object that approaches a circle and touches it at a single point. A tangent point on a circle is the only point at which a line at a specific angle to and direction from the circle can be tangent.

template: An AutoCAD drawing that serves as a starting point for new drawings. When a template drawing is opened, a new file is created with the contents of the template file, which prevents you from saving a changed drawing over the template drawing accidentally.

text height: The height of text, in the same units that are currently in effect for the drawing.

third-party application: A program that works with or within AutoCAD.

title bar: The strip across the top of the screen that displays the name of the currently active drawing.

title block: An area on a drawing that is set aside for descriptive information about the drawing, such as the company name, project name, drafter's name, and so on.

tool tip: A descriptive word or phrase that appears on-screen if you hold the cursor over an icon for a brief period of time.

TrueType fonts: A kind of font that is standard within Microsoft Windows. TrueType fonts first appeared in Release 13 and are also supported, with better performance, in Release 14.

UCS: User Coordinate System. The current set of coordinates used to describe the location of objects.

UCS icon: The "X-Y-Z" icon that appears in the lower-left corner of the drawing area to indicate the angle of the User Coordinate System.

Use Shift to Add: An option that determines what happens if a selection is already made when you click an object. If Use Shift to Add is turned on, you must press and hold the Shift key to add an additional item to the selection set; if this option is turned off, you must hold down the Shift key to remove a currently selected item from the selection.

viewport: A rectangle that displays part of a drawing.

Web, World Wide Web: A network of interconnected servers that support access to integrated text, graphics, and multimedia by using the HTTP (HyperText Transfer Protocol) networking standard and the HTML (HyperText Markup Language) display standard.

Wizard: A form of online help in which you are taken through a series of steps to accomplish a goal, such as setting up a new drawing.

zoom: Zooming is moving the viewpoint closer to or farther from the drawing so that more or less of the drawing appears on-screen.

zoom dynamic: An option of the zoom command that places a zoom window that you can resize on-screen, which enables zoom to be specified interactively and combined with panning.

Index